W9-CMA-623

THE DIGNITY OF MAN

Books by

RUSSELL W. DAVENPORT

回

The Dignity of Man

U.S.A. The Permanent Revolution
(*With the editors of* Fortune)

My Country

Through Traffic

THE
DIGNITY
OF MAN

by

RUSSELL W. DAVENPORT

HARPER & BROTHERS

New York

THE DIGNITY OF MAN

FIRST EDITION

C-E

Library of Congress catalog card number: 55-6574

My country will be generous to the bold:
To those who do not fear the dangerous thrust
Of progress toward the far and unforetold,
But know that like a promise freedom must
Lie forward of the darkness, not behind,
And know the Brother in their hearts, and trust
This light at last to liberate mankind.

My Country by Russell W. Davenport

Contents

THE DIGNITY OF MAN

RUSSELL W. DAVENPORT

A Sketch

Shortly before he died Russell Davenport wrote a friend: "I have worked out my 'philosophy,' have developed a coherent approach to the whole problem of freedom, and rough-drafted about three-quarters of a first book." This volume is that three-quarters, carried as far toward a conclusion as his notes would permit. Even in its unfinished form, it is the best thing Davenport ever wrote. How good that is, and how relevant to current American thinking, can be better appreciated with some knowledge of his life and previous work.

Russell Wheeler Davenport was born July 12, 1899 in South Bethlehem, Pa., and died in New York City April 19, 1954 (the anniversary of "the shot heard round the world"). His mature life, brief as it was, spanned a period of nearly unprecedented change in the patterns of American life and the direction of American national policy. In these changes Davenport participated as an intensely committed citizen, and some of them he directly influenced as a publicist. While America was groping reluctantly for the role of successful world leadership, Davenport was groping for the ideas and policies that would support this role.

The qualities he brought to his search were among the best qualities that America was at the same time bringing to her ordeal. They were qualities that George Santayana

1

once touched on in a classic description of the Yale man. "Nothing could be more American," wrote Santayana. "Here is sound, healthy principle but no overscrupulousness, love of life, trust in success, a ready jocoseness, a democratic amiability, and a radiant conviction that there is nothing better than one's self. It is a boyish type of character. . . . But the boyish ideal is a healthy one, and in a young man, as in a young nation, it is perfection to have only the faults of youth." And in an aging and threatened civilization, it may also be salvation to recapture some of the virtues of youth, such as the large-minded courage and puzzled idealism that characterized Davenport all his life. There was in any case a peculiar fitness in his own chief preoccupations, which were freedom and the fulfillment of "The American dream" on the world stage. Far more than with most American intellectuals of his time, Davenport's own conflicts, aspirations, and even personality were those of his nation.

He came from a nonconformist New England family with strong ties to Yale. His original American ancestor was the John Davenport who founded (with Theophilus Eaton) the New Haven colony in 1637 and who gave refuge in his home to the regicide judges of Charles I. His first Yale ancestor was Colonel Abraham Davenport of Stamford (class of 1732), who was sitting in the Connecticut assembly on that sinister May 19 of 1780 when the sun scarcely appeared at all. Thousands took it for the end of the world, including many members of the assembly, who proposed to adjourn. Said Abraham: "The Day of

Judgment is either approaching, or it is not. If it is not, there is no cause for adjournment; if it is, I choose to be found doing my duty. I wish therefore that candles may be brought." (Candles-in-the-dark became one of Russell Davenport's favorite metaphors for creative thought.)

Russell's father, for whom he was named, was a distinguished metallurgist, one of those early graduates of the Sheffield Scientific School who helped introduce the latest European scientific methods into American industry. As general manager, first of the Midvale and then of the Bethlehem Iron Co., he did more than any single man to give the U.S. Navy a domestic source of armor plate and heavy gun forgings, thus enabling it to take a front rank among the world's navies before the Spanish-American War. Honorary degrees from Harvard and Yale attest his achievements as a practical scholar of steel.

Russell's mother, *née* Cornelia Whipple Farnum, was a Philadelphia beauty whose grandfather was the Anglican missionary Bishop Whipple of Minnesota. She was also a woman of intelligence and character, the founder and headmistress of a girls' school and later a businesswoman. In 1903, the year before her husband died, they took Russell on his first trip to Europe. His second was in 1912, this time to Switzerland, in quest of a climate favorable to the hearing defect (left by pneumonia) that was to trouble him all his life. The same quest then took the family (now including his younger brother, John) to California, where Russell attended the Thacher School in

Ojai from 1913 to 1917. Horses and mountain trails were part of the Thacher curriculum; from them Russell won a special feeling for the old frontier days when all a man needed, as he later wrote, were "a horse, a gun, and a rope . . . and an endlessly rolling prairie on which to seek one's fortune." It was at Thacher that he got his lifelong nickname, "Mitch," after the difficult little brother in Tarkington's *Penrod.*

Still a schoolboy when the U.S. entered World War I, Russell went to France (via the American Field Service) and enlisted as a private in the U.S. Army, driving an ambulance on the Western front for seventeen months. He took part in five major engagements, was repeatedly exposed to gas as well as shrapnel, and won two Croix de Guerre. The first came when, having evacuated three *blessés* from a battery under heavy shellfire near Mount Kemmel, he volunteered for the next trip to the same battery. "Knowing the road, I thought it was my duty . . . nothing very heroic," he wrote his mother. His was a crack unit (attached to the Forty-first "Granite" Division) and as the citations piled up young Davenport began to get boy-hero writeups in the Philadelphia papers. "Please stop them!" he ordered his mother. His war letters began as a boy's but ended as a man's. He came back with a special feeling for France that lasted his life, an ability to take a Ford apart and put it together again, and a sense of battlefield realities that gave him a better grasp of history than many more learned men.

When he entered Yale in 1919, his war-forced maturity

set him somewhat apart from most of his classmates; and although he eventually achieved eminence (and Skull and Bones) on the ruthlessly competitive Yale campus, it was by a lonely and circuitous route, chiefly literary. He read and wrote a great deal of poetry. He did hard honors work in philosophy under Professor C. A. A. Bennett. He took up fencing, then an exceedingly minor sport, and became captain of the team and intercollegiate champion. He and his fellow editors of the Yale *Literary Magazine*, in the mood of the mid-twenties, upheld the cause of romance and individualism against the philistines; in his friend Phelps Putnam's poem, *"Les Enfants Pendus,"* Russell is described as challenging the enemy with a nonexistent *épée* and the cry, *"Pour la Reine!"* As a senior he wrote a vigorous column of campus news in the Yale *Alumni Weekly*, reporting such things as Norman Thomas' remarks to the Liberal Club (of which Davenport was president). One unusually crusty old grad protested against "this man Davenport," who "seems to be something of an agitator."

After graduation Davenport worked briefly in New York for the new magazine *Time* and then in Spokane for the *Spokesman Review*. He went West partly in pursuit of a long love affair, dating from Ojai days, which ended in a broken engagement but was distilled into his most sensitive poem, "The California Spring" (published in *American Caravan IV* of 1931). Richly descriptive of the West, it also contains this passage:

> And ever since then we have been
> Lovers with this sword between,

Like the one Isolde kept
Along her body as she slept:
The sword, I mean, of love so great
That down its other edge gleams hate;
Whose sharpening is so profound
That it can pierce without a sound;
The sword some men have labelled 'Truth,'
Some 'Love,' some 'Beauty,' and some 'Youth'—
Its hilt all jeweled with romance—
Belted to flesh, and sheathed in Chance;
The sword of vision and great pain,
Which Arthur drew, which all men draw,
By some enchantment of the law,
And fling back to the gods again.

After an expatriate year in France, Davenport returned to Philadelphia and New York, where he wrote a novel (*Through Traffic*, 1929) whose chief merit is that it predicted the Wall Street crash. In 1929 he began to settle down by marrying Marcia Gluck Clarke, daughter of Alma Gluck, and went seriously to work for Henry R. Luce on his new magazine, *Fortune*, in June of the following year.

The next decade was the most practically effective of Davenport's life. The romantic poet and free-lance intellectual made himself into one of the best journalists of his time. The transformation did not take place overnight. It was pushed by his capable and ambitious wife (the well-known novelist) and slowed by the incubus of a long autobiographical manuscript, part prose and part verse, which he used to carry around in a special spring-back binder, and which was the excuse for occasional leaves of absence mostly spent on his Vermont farm. In 1937 he was about to ask for another leave of absence when he was offered, instead, the managing editorship of *Fortune,* succeeding his close friend Eric Hodgins, who had just been made publisher. He mournfully took a week end to decide between the old manuscript and the new job. On Monday he appeared at the office in a new frame of mind, eager to begin work. The decision had been made easier, he explained, by the fact that he had lost the manuscript, binder and all.

Davenport was in important ways the best managing editor *Fortune* ever had; in unimportant, the worst. As an executive, he was a fountain of anarchy, indecision, and disorder. He inherited a small staff of able and somewhat pampered writers and researchers who were used to a good deal of autonomy in fulfilling their assignments. Davenport took this machine apart and put it together again, and also doubled its size. Since *Fortune* addressed an elite and powerful audience on subjects fundamental to the changing U.S. political economy, he believed it ought to be "the most important magazine in America." He also believed that *Fortune* needed to earn, through a more explicitly pro-business attitude, the right to speak for as well as critically of American business. Accordingly he sought to give the magazine more "business sophistication" and also to sharpen the controversial point of every story that had one; especially the lead story of each issue, he argued, should "come out into a charged atmosphere." But his editorial antennae, so readily agitated by remote inscrutabilities, often led him to change signals in mid-story; and in view of his noon-to-midnight working habits, there was not always time or occasion for him to make his signals clear to the staff. In the resulting crises he sometimes rewrote whole stories himself overnight, offending the writers and researchers who considered themselves responsible. Before he had been in office a year the researchers drew up an all but unanimous protest against his methods.

He surmounted this brief uprising by a long, candid memorandum and by the personal charm with which he could solve any problem of human relations, once he was reminded that he had one. He was always ready and able to talk anything out with anybody, when there was time. But a shortage of time, whether real or manufactured, was an indispensable working condition for Davenport. No other managing editor found it necessary to maintain a permanent night shift of typists and proofreaders. None went so often on emergency trips to the printer's in Jersey City on closing nights, or made so many changes in copy at the eleventh hour. Sometimes he went there direct from the opera, in full dress, black cape and crushed black hat from his Paris days; sometimes, if time really pressed, he dictated direct to the linotypers. When the last proof was read, he and his exhausted help would roar back through the Holland Tunnel and sleeping Manhattan in his big Chrysler, and he would reach his apartment at East End Avenue at dawn.

But along with chronic crisis and disorder, Davenport brought certain qualities to *Fortune* which made it the most exciting periodical of that time. One was a readiness to back his own intuitions and gradually forming beliefs about the American political economy. He would attack any subject, however well guarded by experts or other obstacles, with the naked sword of his own layman's curiosity. Wanting to know whether a small Midwestern town was economically self-sustaining or not, he amassed all its statistics of trade with the rest of the country and produced the pioneering study called "Oskaloosa vs. the U.S."—long before economists were to develop the input-output technique for war production planning. Corporate secrecy never stopped him from getting a story he wanted; he took a special pleasure in wire-pulling and porch-climbing, as in the case of stories on Allied Chemical and Diamond Match. He felt that *Fortune's* journalistic ambitions, like his own curiosity, should know no bounds. Accordingly he turned the *Fortune* searchlight on such opaque subjects as the birth-control industry, the servant problem, air safety, the economics of a debut, the organization of the Vatican and of the State Department, and how unionization came to Big Steel. Davenport's notions of what was wrong with America were frequently in advance of his colleagues'; but the main difference was that he always thought he could do something about it, and sometimes did. His journalism was directly influential, for example, in starting adequate financing for cancer research; in improving the safety of air travel; and in making American business aware of its public relations problems, attention to which is now SOP in every self-respecting corporation. But perhaps his biggest single contribution was his alleviation, in whatever measure, of the sterile and unnecessary warfare between American business and the New Deal.

He had friends and sources inside the New Deal, such

as Corcoran and Hopkins, and also in the labor movement, such as Murray and Golden. He also knew and liked business and businessmen. He felt that the American political economy was far roomier than any single interest group realized and that there was little justification for all the angry pushing and shoving. To prove this, he had first to resolve their conflicts in his own mind, which led him to write a series of editorials (the first editorials in any Luce magazine) with such themes as "Government spending is no substitute for capitalistic imagination"; "To carry on the revolution the U.S. must develop its own libertarian economics"; "American business can avoid committing suicide only by practicing some sound public relations"; and "To win back prosperity without losing reform it has now become necessary for government to consult business." The approach of war was making a business-government rapprochement of some kind inevitable. Davenport's *Fortune* editorials and round tables, in which (with the late Raymond Leslie Buell as moderator) the areas of rational agreement were hammered out, helped make this rapprochement easier when it came. The sum of Davenport's hopes and concerns, and his unlimited confidence in the American future, were expressed in a special issue of *Fortune* in February, 1940, a single-subject issue on the U.S.A. This issue was a kind of culmination of his three-year aim: to sort out the raw material of the American political-economic system so that statesmen and philosophers could derive from it a true American policy and doctrine.

In pleading for a new acceptance of reformed and

liberated capitalism, Davenport was not preaching to an imaginary audience. This was proven by the phenomenon of Wendell Willkie. Willkie and Davenport met at a *Fortune* round table in 1939. When he came home, Davenport's first words were, "I've just met the man who ought to be President of the United States." The Willkies then went to the Davenports' in Saugatuck for a week end, where the two men talked continuously, locked in each other's ideas, the tennis court and the other guests ignored. Willkie was exactly the hero Davenport had been looking for: the American businessman at his candid, articulate best, large-minded, earthy, brave, wholly committed to a bigger and better America and to a bolder and more confident foreign policy. Willkie was already a public figure and had been mentioned as a possible Presidential candidate as early as February, 1939. But when Davenport helped him write the manifesto called *We the People,* and published it in *Fortune* in April, 1940, Willkie's political career began in earnest. Within two weeks of its appearance, he received two thousand invitations to speak. Oren Root, Jr., launched his Willkie Clubs, and John Orr Young his public money-raising advertisements, uncovering a national groundswell of Willkie sentiment. On May 5, 1940, Davenport quit *Fortune* to devote full time to the nascent crusade.

Willkie's capture of the Philadelphia convention and his Presidential campaign are of course an exciting chapter in U.S. political history and have been described elsewhere. The campaign train in which strategy and speeches were improvised was twice as chaotic as the *Fortune* office had

ever been, since Willkie's working habits were as impulsive
and informal as Davenport's own. As his "personal representative," Davenport controlled not only Willkie's prepared speeches but practically all outside access to the
candidate. It was Davenport, more than anyone save the
candidate himself, who sought to keep the campaign a
crusade, more ideological than partisan and more amateur
than professional. The consequent neglect of Republican
party machinery was blamed in some quarters for Willkie's
defeat, though it seems clear that the war, which made
Roosevelt's third-term candidacy possible, also made his
election inevitable. Two things about the campaign are
beyond debate. By winning more votes than any Republican
candidate before Eisenhower, Willkie disclosed the strength
and responsiveness of the independent vote that has dominated American politics ever since. And by refusing to
exploit the isolationist sentiment of 1940, which he did not
share, Willkie saved the Republican party from a suicidal
position and kept it eligible for the liberal, internationalist
program on which its ultimate return to power was based.
Henry Cabot Lodge, who managed Eisenhower's pre-
convention campaign in 1952, has said that without the
groundwork of the Willkie crusade, the Eisenhower victory
might not have been possible.

Even after Willkie's defeat, Davenport continued to lay
this groundwork. He was and remained a belligerent liberal
and a maverick Republican, going so far as to prefer
Roosevelt to Dewey in 1944 (on foreign policy grounds).
But he continued to agitate for his principles within the

Republican party. In 1950 he and a few other liberal-minded Republicans started a movement called Republican Advance, for which Davenport wrote a manifesto and did research into what he called the "libertarian" (non-statist) solution of various current political issues, such as farm subsidies, health insurance, pensions, and labor policy. Late in 1950 Davenport, Senator Duff, and others had breakfast with Eisenhower at Columbia University and satisfied themselves that he could be persuaded to run for President in 1952. In this conviction they more or less dropped Republican Advance and went to work as individuals to secure Eisenhower's nomination. Davenport spent many telephone hours on the tricky simultaneous tasks of creating an Eisenhower following among Republicans with the assurance that he would run, and using the following to overcome the candidate's reluctance. When the movement was safely under way and in Lodge's hands, Davenport stepped aside. His subsequent connection with Eisenhower was that of an occasional ideaman, notably contributing a formulation (a more precise one than Eisenhower has used) of the "Middle Way."

Davenport's career as a journalist never regained the focus it had had before the Willkie campaign. He nevertheless did a good deal of first-class intermittent work. After a few months back at *Fortune* and a brief stretch of patriotic duty with the Citizens for Victory, he started the editorial page of *Life* (1942), setting a style of topical essay which has been more or less followed ever since. Early in 1944, with the approach of a political campaign

for which he had no taste, he quit *Life* to complete a poem
which had been welling through his feelings about the war.

The poem was *My Country*, Davenport's most ambitious
effort in verse, both metrically (large parts of it are in
terza rima) and in emotional range. Its theme is patriotic
and its style rhetorical, facts which repelled the contemporary guardians of poetic taste; it was nevertheless a
popular success, and a copy was long seen on Eisenhower's
desk both at Columbia and at SHAPE. It contains lines
which will bear quotation as long as there is an "American
dream":

> The vision that the world is waiting is
> The same that traced its way in wagon-tracks
> Across empurpled plain and precipice,
> And whispered in the starlit tamaracks
> Where travelers told of freedom in the West
> Around the fires of hopeful bivouacs:
> The vision of a mighty purpose, pressed
> By all the peoples of the earth, to make
> The hidden truth within them manifest:
> And as this continent was free to take,
> And thus awoke the hope of all mankind,
> So now, in hope, we hear the future break
> On the unsovereigned beaches of the mind.

For Davenport, poetry was an instinctive way to communicate, perhaps his real *métier*. It undoubtedly contributed to his flair as a journalist; indeed the diversion
of his energies from poetry to journalism and politics was
justified by the example of the poet he most admired,
Goethe himself. He admired not only Goethe's poetry, but

his career as a statesman-administrator in Weimar and as a philosopher-scientist, perhaps the last great exemplar of human "wholeness" before the modern atomization of society set in. (See his note on Goethe, p. 334.) If Davenport failed to reach his own age in poetry, it was partly because he wrote too little and partly because the language of wholeness was out of fashion. He reverted to prose for his final statements, but the poetic impulse was with him until he died.

After *My Country*, he made his way to the European front as a correspondent in the last months of World War II. On his return, he took a house in New Haven with his daughter Cornelia, resolved to do some "hard thinking" about America and the shape of things to come. That at least was all he promised to do, when raising money for the project from a few New Yorkers to whom he described the need for a new American political-economic doctrine and his own desire to formulate it. As one of his backers remarked, "He's confused, but less so than I am." This year of withdrawal yielded no immediate fruit. During it Russell and Marcia Davenport were divorced. He also took a semisecret job at the Columbia Broadcasting System experimenting with a plan (never tried) for an "editorial page" of the air. In 1947 he returned to the Time, Inc., payroll to direct another abortive experiment, a proposed highbrow monthly; and still another that proved initially very successful, a series of round tables for *Life*.

The first of these round tables, which were elaborately

researched, was on the subject of the Pursuit of Happiness,
and his preparation for it took him deep into the historical
reasons why Jefferson put the phrase in the Declaration
of Independence. He planned others on similarly big
themes—American women, child-rearing, religious beliefs,
etc.—and hoped to distill from all this talking and listen-
ing to intelligent laymen the outlines of a genuinely American philosophy. "America today is a country without a
philosophy, without a real doctrine," he wrote a friend in
1949. "The challenge of our time is to formulate a doctrine,
coherent with the past, yet outspread toward the future,
which will be for our time what the doctrine of the
founders was for theirs." Davenport's practical problem
was to find the right medium and vocabulary for this
philosophical quest. After a few round tables, he returned
to *Fortune* as a "special projects" editor. There he wrote a
series of studies on the same subjects (health insurance,
farm policy, labor relations, etc.) that were engaging his
attention as research director of Republican Advance. The
most notable of these was an article called "The Greatest
Opportunity on Earth" (October, 1949), which developed,
from its seeds in the Declaration of Independence, the main
lines of "a realistic alternative to the 'welfare state,' " and
reasoned "that American business now has a chance to
lead the way" in updating the rights of man for an industrial society. As the capstone of this series, Davenport
edited a single-subject issue of *Fortune* called *U.S.A.: The
Permanent Revolution* (1951) which elaborated the
Greatest Opportunity theme.

The Permanent Revolution expanded the same vision of America that had been suggested eleven years earlier in the special issue of February, 1940. That issue would have prepared any reader for the "miracle" of U.S. war production, whose latency Davenport clearly discerned behind the business-government bickering of the New Deal. In 1951 he similarly saw that America since the war had become a new kind of society, bypassing the stereotypes of contemporary political controversy and rendering Marxian economics wholly irrelevant. This new view of American democratic capitalism was soon to become a commonplace; Frederick Lewis Allen's *The Big Change* gave the new society its clinical description, and A. A. Berle's recent *The 20th Century Capitalist Revolution* has X-rayed its bone structure. But it was Davenport's intuitional journalism that prepared the way for the new view. When he broke ground it was usually located where others could quickly follow.

Davenport's influence on his time was only partly through his writing. He left a deep impress on hundreds of individuals, both prominent and obscure, who knew and loved him. He was a large, gaunt and shaggy man, green-eyed, strong and gentle. He inspired much affection and responded to it, especially in children. He was also moody, irascible and self-indulgent. His mind seemed to run in two parallel lanes, one in a bumping jalopy with complicated breakdowns and boyish self-justifications, the other in a swift, smooth Jaguar. A *Fortune* colleague has called him a "dolorous activist" whose "ups and downs seemed to coexist. His enormous urge to make things better by his own bare-handed efforts sprang from a frame of mind that seemed also to insist that everything was hopeless. But he never quit. He never thought he won, either; he was a reverse Walter Mitty, defeated to the end."

Davenport seldom took thought for his personal advancement; his mind and his impulses were genuinely disinterested and aristocratic. Even his practical jokes had a certain grandeur, as when he gave Marcia, a cat lover, a smallish lion for her birthday. He spent a large part of his life at the telephone, chair a-tilt, feet on the desk, surrounded with empty tea or coffee cups and cigarette ashes. The pockets of his high-priced suits were always bulging shapelessly with oversize notebooks and miscellaneous papers. He used his hearing aid not only for defensive purposes, like Mr. Baruch, but also for offensive: if a meeting or conversation grew listless, Davenport would adjust his headphones to his ears like a pilot climbing into the cockpit, point his receiver at the company, and thus give notice that it was time to tune up and get to work. He was a quick and skillful amateur of many arts, from war and business to sailing and music. He had an obsession for astrology, and cast horoscopes for virtually everyone he tied up with, from Willkie to a new secretary. He scattered his great natural empathy among many causes, many cities and many different groups of friends. He never lost his taste for luxury, acquired on Philadelphia's Main Line, and lived expensively. He did not believe that the garret was a suitable place to germinate ideas that might save American civilization. He inherited a little money, earned a good deal, and made some in speculation. For his later work he enlisted the support of wealthy friends, creating a foundation, the Institute of Creative Research, into which their donations could be placed.

Davenport was haunted by the conviction that he had a special mission on this earth. This mission was to precipitate in words, from the limitless flux of American life, the special meaning and mission of his country. After World War II this conviction took on urgency from the rise of communism; and his inner conflicts and even occasional despair, which were serious during this period, arose from his fear of having been faithless to his assignment. About 1951 his purpose began to clarify and his energies to align themselves again toward his goal. On the strength of Paul Hoffman's and Robert M. Hutchins' knowledge of his abilities, he secured a Ford Foundation grant in 1952. His declared purpose was to develop some "practical applications" of his "Greatest Opportunity" and "Permanent Revolution" themes. Although this grant was terminated at the end of 1953, no finished product having been forthcoming, it made possible his last two years of work, the most fruitful of his life. They were also in all probability the happiest, especially after his marriage to Natalie Potter Ladd.

As his Ford Foundation project took shape, it moved further and further from "practical applications" as commonly understood. The reason for this was not the perversity of Davenport's mind (perverse though it often seemed), but the logic of his subject, which was human freedom. In his earlier role as a lover and psalmist of America and a philosopher of free enterprise, he could take the desirability of freedom for granted. But in the *Permanent Revolution,* he came to grips with its elusive and unfinished nature. "The individual," he wrote then, "lives surrounded by darkness. He is a mere candle. The task of the permanent revolution is to increase the light of that candle, the light of every candle, so that one light may reach to another and the darkness may thus be dispelled. Here in this land, by learning to apply the [American] Proposition, we have gained some elementary steps. . . . Yet in pursuit of real freedom we have yet to gain much more than we have won. . . . We have not begun to gain freedom from error, the freedom that comes from right reason. We have not begun to gain freedom from hate, the freedom that is born of love."

In pursuit of this unfinished business of freedom, as he wrote a friend, he found himself "driven back—and back —and back," from political and economic theory to the nature of the universe and finally to the first problems of epistemology and "ways of thinking." He completely re-wrote the present volume at least twice in order to get the epistemological problem nearer its center. By 1953 he envisioned a whole series of other volumes, the series to be called "Studies in Freedom." He thought of his task as answering Karl Marx at all levels—economic, political, and spiritual; and the spiritual level came first because, he said, "Only if we can give the word 'spiritual' a real and

self-evident content can we hope, in turn, to give meaning
to the political principles on which our system is based."

As he wrote in *My Country*:

> Let us not fear Man: let us fear
> Only what he believes in. . . .
> It is Nothing that we must fear: the thought of Nothing:
> The sound of Nothing in our hearts . . .
> The belief in Nothing.

Freedom's final foe, in short, and therefore Davenport's,
was not Communist power, but the philosophical materialism on which that power is based.

With intellectuals deserting materialism in increasing
numbers, Davenport's discovery has ceased to be unfashion-
able, but his route to it was a special one. During the war
he encountered (at the home of a friend in Louisville) the
work of the Austrian philosopher and editor of Goethe,
Rudolf Steiner, who became a strong influence on his
thought (see p. 335). From closer acquaintance with Steiner
he drew badly needed confidence in the reliability of his
own divinations about the nature of things, particularly as
to the dual nature of human consciousness and the equal
validity of its internal and external observations. This
double path to truth was the theme of an address he gave
at Aspen, Colorado, in July, 1952 (called "Law, Liberty
and License") and is further developed in the present
volume. On this path, Davenport believed, the individual
could develop his spiritual resources in a strictly rational
way, and he himself could describe the path without
moralizing and without sounding a retreat to inherited

religious orthodoxy. Perhaps one of the ways he envisaged his task, the present volume being an introduction, was to transmute Steiner's European philosophy into a form appropriate to American problems and American modes of thinking.

However that may be, Davenport's application to his task became intense, even heroic, as his life drew to a close. He knew his heart was failing; he suffered violent and painful attacks in his last few months; he had long since dropped all other work ("I have removed myself from circulation," he wrote) and given up many cherished amenities. He had a fresh source of strength in the love and understanding of his wife. He feared not death, but that death might prevent him from passing along his discoveries, whose reality became the more vivid to him the closer death came.

Davenport sometimes likened his task to Paul Revere's; he pointed out that Paul's only equipment was that "he could ride a horse pretty well (as I can write pretty well) and he knew that the Redcoats were marching"—as Davenport knew that the Communist challenge is most dangerous on the spiritual plane. But Davenport had something more than his horse and his information, something that makes this book particularly relevant to the crisis of Western man. This was his conviction that Truth exists—not just quantitative truths, but qualitative Truth; that it matters; and that it is accessible, with effort, to every man's mind.

This volume exhibits all Davenport's great powers of lucid exposition and sober eloquence. It ruthlessly explores the plight of the modern Western mind in its struggle with communism, and traces this plight to its roots, including the root of excessive optimism about human nature in the eighteenth-century American concept of freedom. Its examination of the new Communist or "Dimat" mind conspicuously avoids the common Western mistake of underestimating this enemy and his intellectual appeal to the unconscious materialism of the West. In isolating the Western ailment which he calls "metascience," Davenport throws a brilliant light into a whole pitful of vulgar errors about the nature of the universe and of man. In addition he has assembled the materials for another and greater American revolution, a revolution in the way Americans think. Although he left his message unfinished, Davenport was already completing this revolution in his own way of thinking. If in this, as in his earlier intuitions, Davenport was merely anticipating the intelligent American layman, his confidence in his countrymen will be vindicated and his mission fulfilled.

JOHN KNOX JESSUP

A NOTE

The heart attack which took my husband's life came while he was at his desk working on the third chapter of Part III of this book. Three weeks earlier he had written: "Work in this field cannot be planned in accordance with a strict schedule because one gives to it not merely one's time but one's life."

At his death Parts I and II and the beginning of Part III were ready to show the publishers. The subsequent chapters of Part III and Part IV had not been finally revised by Mr. Davenport. We, who knew where the author was heading, have compiled Parts V and VI from earlier drafts. Though this book was in many ways only a beginning of a long-range project, the work appeared so important, original and urgent that the decision was made to proceed with its publication. With the exception of certain brief transitional passages all of the writing is the author's own. Had he lived, he would undoubtedly have reorganized large sections of the manuscript, and brought to its final revision that severe and painstaking craftsmanship which characterized him both as an editor and as a writer.

In the section at the end of the book marked "Fragments," the reader will find notes for a future book as well as passages from earlier writings and speeches indicating ways in which Russell Davenport's ideas embody practical solu-

24

tions. There are, in addition, some notes he intended for an appendix plus unrevised excerpts and thoughts which did not seem sufficiently developed to warrant inclusion in the main body of the work.

It is perhaps significant that he, who spent so much of his life in the cause of freedom, should have died without formulating too rigidly the answers he had in mind. He has opened many new doors and left it to the individual, in whom he so strongly believed, to cross those thresholds. It is my hope, as it was his, that among the readers some will emerge who can go on from where he left off and help others find a way to dispel the darkness of our time.

In the author's own words, "Our idea of freedom does not seem to fit either the needs or the ideals of most of the people of the globe. There is something lacking in it that people want, something that they need, something that must sound in our words if our doctrine of freedom is to ring true. And we had now better find out what that 'something' is. For unless we can produce it communism will wholly capture, and will absorb, the cause of all mankind."

"This book is a search for that something. It would be more accurate to say, perhaps, that it is a search for the search; for the real nature of the something, its content, its vital meaning, must arise from the people themselves and find its true expression through them. No single book can provide this. But a very great gain would be accomplished if Americans could learn *how* to search; the true believers of freedom are lost in intellectual mazes, so baffling that they cannot look clearly even into their own hearts. It is essential, as a first step toward an understanding of the foundations of freedom, to learn how to cut through these mazes to reality itself.

"It is indeed the thesis of this book, that reality, however limited a portion of it, is not beyond the reach of the human being. But this is the case only if a certain attitude of mind is brought to the search of it. This gives a somewhat more specific description of our task: it is a search for an attitude. Our aim is to try to open up a path for others to follow who are more skilled than we, or better equipped, to carry on the search."

There is one other point which the author considered of prime importance and which he had included in the original introduction. He wrote "There are 'experts' in the theory of freedom, as there are today experts in everything; but they are inclined to speak a highly specialized language of their own, a step removed from the ken of ordinary mortals. It is to the ordinary mortal, not the expert, that this book is addressed—the men and women to whom we refer in the text as intelligent laymen. We have in mind those millions of persons who do not pretend to any special learning outside of their own professions, but who are nevertheless forced by the exigencies of democratic life, not only to think for themselves, but to provide a certain leadership for others.

"Wherever democratic institutions flourish, such persons are to be found, though the patterns of their lives naturally differ very greatly in different countries. In America we find them in every community, and in every walk of life, sometimes in humble, sometimes in important stations. These intellectually unspecialized but generally intelligent people are the custodians of our moral values, and in the last analysis, of our policies of state; they constitute the backbone of the society which could less afford to dispense with them than with the whole machinery of government itself. If the U.S. is to understand freedom, it is in their minds and hearts that the understanding must live. It is *they* who must become philosophers, in a lay sense of the term, if the hope of freedom is to survive.

"A science of man will humbly and gratefully profit by the achievements of technicians and will draw on their conclusions. But if it is really to be concerned with *man*, it cannot, by definition, live at an intellectual level where man himself does not exist. It cannot content itself solely with the abstract. On the contrary, it must listen to the heart and live in the concrete. There is no place for a science of man to go except to man. The key to all its inquiries is the ancient injunction, 'O Man, know thyself!' If such a science is ever to be developed, the educated common man, the intelligent layman, must play an active role. He cannot leave it to technicians, because the injunction, 'Know thyself!' includes *him*. We, like the lay reader himself, have had to struggle, and on the same basis, and in the same terms; and this is all we ask of anyone who joins us in the search for freedom."

The publication of this book should not take place without an expression of deep gratitude and appreciation to Dr. Franz E. Winkler (President of the Myrin Institute) who, from the very beginning, worked closely with Mr. Davenport in the development of many of these original ideas; to the Board of the Institute for Creative Research for the trust and help they have given me; to Arthur Tourtellot for the encouragement and understanding he gave the author when he most needed it and for all that he has done since his death; to John Knox Jessup whose biographical sketch shows his deep understanding of the man, and whose kindness and generous interest have been enormous; to my brother-in-law John Davenport and to Duncan Norton-Taylor for their skillful final editing; and to other friends, too numerous to mention by name for their interest and helpful suggestions; finally, but by no means least, to Adelaide Walker who has done intensive research for the author during the past twelve years in varying fields, including this book. Without her editing and putting together of Parts V and VI and her correlation of former writings, this book might never have reached publication. In addition to the above I would like to express much appreciation to the Ford Foundation for their generous assistance in the form of a grant to The Institute for Creative Research.

In bringing out this volume, I assume in the words of its author that "Every human undertaking is at some point an act of faith. In this book, our faith is placed in the ability and willingness of free individuals to face any question, and master any problem, that challenges their freedom."

NATALIE POTTER DAVENPORT

I

THE CAUSE OF
ALL MANKIND

1

SVOBODA

At the close of World War II, when the American and Russian armies were drawn up face to face, there were a few social gatherings at which officers of the two great allies came together in a friendly way. An American correspondent attended a luncheon of this kind and found himself seated at a long table with a Russian on either side of him. The Russian on his right was an interpreter, and the one on his left, a junior officer who had been wounded at Stalingrad and had then become a military photographer. A pleasant conversation was carried on through the interpreter, with very warm admiration being expressed on both sides.

This particular American had interested himself for some years in the rising strength of communism. During the Depression he had taken to wandering down to Union Square, in New York, to listen to the orators. He got the feeling that a terrible conflict was in the making and was spellbound by the spectacle of people choosing sides. But just what was the nature of the conflict? It was not then an easy question to answer, nor is it even yet; but it took no extraordinary power of insight to see that the U.S.R.R. and the U.S.A. were going to end up on different sides of it. While he could not guess the future, he had a vague pre-

monition that the free world would someday pay heavily
for the Russian alliance.

Accordingly, as his new Russian friend expatiated on
the glories of the Red Army and the heroism of the troops,
the American turned to the interpreter and said, "Ask him
what he thinks this war was all about."

The interpreter leaned over and asked the question. The
answer was immediate, like the shot from a rifle.
"*Svoboda!*" said the Russian officer—"Freedom!" And he
looked at the American with a kind of dismay, as if to say,
"Where have you been all these years? Didn't you know?"

"What *is* freedom?" the American asked.

"Freedom?" said the Russian. He hesitated for a moment, but without taking his eyes off the American. "Freedom," he said, "is knowing how to help the other fellow.
It is brotherhood."

The American said nothing more, for the spirit of the
occasion did not invite argument. Nevertheless, he went
away from the gathering with a question burning inside of
him. Freedom and Brotherhood! How was it possible for
this Russian officer, not only with sincerity but with enthusiasm, to claim these goals for the Red Army? The
question took many years to answer in full. In the process
of trying to answer it, however, the correspondent discovered that the incident summarized, more succinctly than
any other in his experience, the predicament of the free
world in the middle of the twentieth century.

2

IN FREEDOM'S NAME

It can be said of any age that it is critical in some sense: the task of the philosopher-historian is to seek out and to define the real nature of its crisis. And concerning our own age there can scarcely be any doubt: the crisis that it embodies is the crisis of freedom. Were we to ask the Egyptian revolutionary what he is struggling for, he would reply, "Freedom." We would get this answer, in wholly different terms, in Palestine. We would get it in Indonesia and Iran. In South Africa there is a struggle going on around the issue of freedom. The South Koreans fought bitterly and bravely to be free. Pakistan and India, eying each other like boxers, are both dedicated to freedom. The thought of freedom runs through our time as blood through the body. It is everywhere. As Wendell Willkie wrote in *One World* more than a decade ago, the peoples of the earth are "on the march"; they are marching to become free. If one surveys the round globe, with more than two billion people living on it, most of whom have the thought of freedom, or some version of it, one cannot escape the conclusion that the long struggle for freedom is coming to a head in our time; that historians of the future, looking back on the mid-twentieth century, will be able to say with some conviction that this was the turning point; that here men won freedom as a universal institution, or—if it turns out that way—here they lost the hope of it.

Now, deeply embedded in the American tradition there is an old and majestic thesis. This runs to the effect that the U.S. is a kind of enormous experiment in freedom, a kind of pilot plant operation, in which the free institutions that we inherited from Europe could be assembled, tested, developed—and finally, given to humanity as a whole. For the first hundred and fifty years of our history this thesis was no more than a distant ideal. The Atlantic world then had—to use a somewhat cynical phrase—a "working control" of the cause of freedom, and it governed most of the earth by parceling it out to Asiatic and African peoples according to what seemed best for them and for the Atlantic world. But it is just that state of affairs, that *status quo* of the nineteenth and early twentieth centuries, which has now come to an end. The peoples of the earth are rising in their own behalf. The cause of freedom has got out of hand, so to speak; nobody controls it any more. It has become, as Tom Paine and others always predicted it would, "the cause of all mankind."

In the light of the American tradition this can be a very inspiring thought. Now at last the U.S. has the opportunity to transmit the lessons of freedom to other peoples, who, without our experience, would have to spend decades in bloody struggle to learn those lessons for themselves. Now at last we can sponsor the cause of freedom for all mankind, and Tom Paine's prediction can come true. Just because the peoples of the earth are really "on the march," the U.S. has the opportunity to show the way to a new world society based upon principles and institutions that have been thoroughly tested. Adapted to meet the needs of different peoples, transformed by customs and cultures, these principles would guard the sanctity of the individual everywhere and provide for the erection of democratic states in place of obsolete dependencies and colonies. A genuine world society would arise, governed by a common, representative body. The arduous political lessons of the past, purchased with the blood of martyrs and patriots, would be turned to account. Man would become a graduate of the great school of politics, able to maintain the institutions of freedom by peaceful means, and hence, to turn his attention to other and more advanced human relationships.

All this is integral to the American dream—so much so, that millions of Americans almost take it for granted. And yet this noble tradition, which has had such a profound influence upon our national politics and our foreign policies, is directly contradicted by the facts of our time. There are many such facts, but three stare us in the face with a kind of leer. The first is that the U.S.S.R., as the sponsor of world communism, lays claim to the cause of freedom. This fact emerges almost daily from the utterances of the U.S.R.R. The second fact is that a third of the population of the globe lives under the dominance of those who thus identify communism and freedom. The third fact is that the Communists have succeeded in creating grave doubts in the minds of our own half of the world that the United States has any real claim to the cause of freedom at all. This fact emerges from a simple perusal of the intellectual debates in any country of the free world, from Britain to Bolivia.

These are enormous facts. In a few brief decades they

have completely altered the American role. The U.S. once stood before the world as the unconquered champion of freedom's cause. We found our free way of life threatened in 1939 by the Nazis and Fascists. Eventually, we went to war, and perforce joined with Soviet Russia. But the victory is now claimed by Russia—and not only the victory, but the cause of freedom itself. Meanwhile our former ally heaps vituperation on us, and for some reason that we have never explained, has gained more adherents than we have. At enormous cost in dollars and nervous strain we have managed to hold our world together in the name of freedom; but also in the name of freedom, the Soviets have done much more: they have engineered a world-wide expansion, the end of which is not in sight.

There are other facts. Western civilization has grown up around certain political institutions, which vary somewhat among Western peoples, but which are known and generally recognized as free institutions. The list is familiar to every American schoolboy: freedom of speech and thought, freedom of worship, freedom of assembly, the ownership and disposal of private property, *habeas corpus,* the jury system, the secret ballot, the rule of the people by majority, the protection of minorities, and so forth. The free world cannot boast that these institutions are always fully realized: yet in a rough and practical way they define what we mean by political freedom. They are, accordingly, accepted throughout the West as practical ideals toward which society is working and intends to work.

Yet the facts show that these free institutions are everywhere flouted, everywhere violated by the Soviet system.

Wherever the Soviet system has succeeded in gaining power, no single one of them has been able to survive. The record is by now familiar. The Soviet citizen is forbidden to speak against his regime. He cannot publish scientific findings if these conflict with the official line. The mere suspicion that even his thinking deviates from that line can lead to his arrest; and when he is arrested he has no recourse to *habeas corpus* or a jury of his peers, but is forced to accuse himself. To this end he may be subjected to torture, both physical and psychological. These advocates of "freedom" repeatedly condemn millions to imprisonment, starvation, and forced labor, and they murder whom they will. The concept of the dignity of the individual, which is the keystone of the Western doctrine, is unknown to the Soviets. Individuals and minorities are deprived of rights of any kind—indeed, the very idea of giving rights to a minority, other than to the Communist party, which is the ruling minority, is treated as treason. That system survives, not through the support of free institutions, but through the very reverse—through power that bends every individual member of the society to the will of the few.

These facts are not secret. They have been reported to the remotest corners of the earth, by radio, by newspapers, by movies, by word of mouth, so that masses of people in every nation are aware of them. But here is the most stupendous fact of all: the known facts have made no difference! Communism has kept marching on just the same. It has had some reverses and has been forced into some withdrawals, but on the whole its victories, whether diplomatic or military, have far outnumbered its defeats. It continues to undermine governments, seize states, massacre patriots, and bleed people of their livelihood, all in the name of freedom. And all this, in the name of freedom, millions of people accept.

These almost unbelievable facts have shed a very different light on the world struggle for freedom. It is all very true that freedom has become a universal cause. But this is not inspiring. On the contrary, it is frightening. For the world-wide urge for freedom, we suddenly discover, does not necessarily open the way to the fulfillment of the Western tradition of freedom. It may open the way, and in our time has opened the way, to the fulfillment of Karl Marx. It makes no difference how ably we argue or how eloquently we denounce the Soviet system; it makes no difference how logical or how penetrating our criticism is— communism marches on. It is easy enough to show that the Soviet system destroys freedom as we know it and practice it. But this does not seem to be what the world wants to know. It is just as clear to the Malayan revolutionary as it is to the citizen of Des Moines, Iowa, that the Soviet system and our system are in conflict. But the Malayan revolutionary is far from convinced that our system really leads to freedom; on the contrary, thus far, the Communist appeal makes more sense to him. From his point of view, Moscow offers a better chance for freedom than Washington. And his point of view is shared by millions in many different lands around the earth.

Such were the considerations that faced the American correspondent when he undertook to inquire into the question raised by the Russian officer's astounding statement. And they pointed to a sort of preliminary conclusion. The loosely held American assumption was that the Communist propaganda was a kind of sham, that its only purpose was to fool people, that it did not really mean what it said. In reaching this assumption we had been guided very largely by our experience with Adolf Hitler. Doubtless, any propaganda has a sort of hypnotic power, so that those who live with it and in it come to believe it; and in this sense it might be said that Hitler, Goering, Goebbels, and company, very likely believed their own. But almost nobody else did. There was, in fact, very little in the Nazi propaganda to believe, because it did not speak of humanity and could therefore appeal to very few outside the Reich. It was a naked instrument of power, like a tank division or a battle fleet. Without giving the matter much real thought, we had assumed that Russian propaganda was just about the same. And this attitude was not confined to the ordinary citizen, it was the attitude of the American government, and consequently played a part in the shaping of American policies.

But as the history of the mid-twentieth century unfolded it became increasingly apparent that this casual estimate of the Communist propaganda must be wrong. Strictly speaking, the Communist propaganda was not really propaganda at all, but the expression of some sort of human reality, which we Americans had perhaps intuitively sensed, but the true nature of which had thus far escaped us. Loose analogies between Nazism and Communism had led us astray. The techniques employed by those two volcanic movements show many similarities, but the Com-

munist version conceals something far more profound. The
Communist propaganda speaks, not just to the U.S.S.R.,
but to humanity generally. It lays claim to human uni-
versals; it represents something to which, in certain places,
at certain times, millions are drawn. Maybe after choosing
it those millions regret their choice—there is evidence of
this everywhere. But in the right place at the right time it
comes into being in their political life in an irresistible
way, and there seems nothing they can do about it. At those
places and times people come to believe in something that
appears to be the direct antithesis of what the free world
believes in—to which, however, they give the magic name
of Freedom. That is the supreme and baffling political fact
of our time.

And it is by the exploitation of that political fact that the
U.S.S.R. has seized the world initiative. Throughout vast
areas of the earth she has become the champion of the people's rights and the people's hopes; the prophet of the
future, of a new day, of a New Faith. It does not matter that
our system obviously works better, is more bountiful, be-
stows on its citizens rights and immunities of which communism deprives all men. The world grants that we are
better off, that we are powerful and prosperous—maybe
even happy. But this is not the point. The point is that we
are no longer the *champion* of people's hopes. To many
millions of persons, it appears that what we have to con-
tribute belongs to the past, not to the future; our cause
seems to them to be no more than the cause of the U.S.A.
In their eyes the U.S.S.R. has taken over the "cause of all
mankind."

3

ARGUMENT BY VIOLENCE

Now there is, of course, another side of this picture which would seem to contradict every statement just made. It is an outrage, many Americans feel, to have to take seriously communism's claim to a universal cause. Even to entertain the possibility that this claim might have weight is to concede the Communists too much. No people have chosen this so-called cause of their own free will. They have been tricked into it, as in Czechoslovakia, or it has been forced upon them, as in the Baltics and the satellite countries. Rebellions in East Germany for example showed that people do not willingly accept this cause. They do not concede that it gives them freedom: on the very contrary, all the news we can manage to extract from behind the Iron Curtain shows that the satellite peoples bitterly resent the Communist tyranny.

At every step the Communists have to resort to the use or threat of force. John J. McCloy, former U. S. High Commissioner for Germany, reported in his book, *The Challenge to American Foreign Policy:*

Behind the façade of Stalinalee in East Berlin are the grim faces of people badly clothed, living in danger and in fear. The hand and the spirit of the secret police are everywhere reflected in a grey and silent mood. Likewise, if one moves along the eastern boundaries of the German Federal Republic all the paraphernalia of the police state is painfully apparent—the barbed wire, the police dogs, the machine gun posts, the evacuated areas, the plowed-up strips, the nervousness and fears of thousands of refugees.

Communist power is exercised in the name of humanity; but no one subjected to it can live as a human being. It cannot possibly be said that people have *chosen* communism. It cannot be said that they have joined a cause. They are, rather, the helpless victims of a tyranny founded upon the unscrupulous use of military and civil power. And in the light of this, the temptation is to dismiss the ideological attack of communism as nothing but vicious oratory. The temptation is to look on the struggle in which we are engaged as a power struggle, nothing more than that. We cannot believe that it is a conflict of ideas, since the Communist ideas are patently absurd. It is a contest in military power, and civilization has become the prey of a group of gangsters and can extricate itself from its predicament only insofar as it is able to speak the only language that gangsters understand, the language of guns.

And when viewed in this way the Communist threat does not seem quite so formidable. There is, of course, a constant danger of atomic attack. Yet this danger can be exaggerated. If the free world is strong enough to retaliate in a decisive way, the gangsters will not dare to drop the bomb. Analysis of events during the last decade shows clearly enough that the U.S.S.R. has done a great deal of bluffing; that she has on the whole been leading from weakness; that when she has been challenged—as by the Berlin airlift—she has not dared to go to war. This situation has not materially changed. Even though the U.S.S.R. might gain a temporary advantage through a surprise atomic attack, she can surely have no illusions as to the long-run outcome of a major war against the resources of the U.S. and the free world. Our proper course, therefore, would seem to be to dismiss the ideology as nothing but a kind of smoke screen around the gangsters, and to concentrate all our efforts upon building up the military might of the free world and molding it into a formidable fighting force. Are we not entitled to assume that if we can maintain military supremacy the ideology will shrivel and die?

Unhappily, however, this view of things is not as realistic as it purports to be. It may be emotionally satisfying to denounce the Soviet leaders as "gangsters," but the epithet, while accurate enough so far as it goes, fails entirely to come to grips with what communism really is.

Before jumping to conclusions about the Communist use of force, we must ask ourselves toward what end the force is directed. And when we do so, we find that the question cannot be answered in any terms that are historically familiar. The Communists are not seeking to maintain order in the world, as the British once did with their fleet. They are not much concerned with the traditional idea of the balance of power. They are not looking for *Lebensraum*, like Hitler, nor even for colonial expansion, like Mussolini. They cannot be described as empire-builders, in the tradition of Julius Caesar, nor as military conquerors, in the tradition of Napoleon. Their use of force may resemble these classical examples in various ways; indeed, in one respect or another, it resembles all of them.

It is quite plausible to accuse the U.S.S.R. of being the most land-hungry, power-thirsty empire that the world has ever known. Yet neither the facts of history, nor the known policies of the Soviet government, nor the writings and assertions of Soviet leaders support the classical resemblances. The student who examines the evidence is left with the overwhelming impression that the purpose animating the Communist use of force has a very different and far more sinister origin.

Indeed, the entire thesis of those who place their primary faith in military power collapses as soon as one turns to the pronouncements of the great prophets of the Communist doctrine. From Marx to Stalin, those prophets have been unanimous in their affirmation that communism can, and will, *capture men's minds.* In the eyes of its leadership, at any rate, the real power and hope of the Communist movement lies in the very thing that Americans tend to discount—that is to say, in the ideology. Many will reply that that leadership is intellectually and morally corrupt, and hence, not to be believed. This may possibly be so; but before proceeding to shape policies on which the fate of civilization itself may rest, it is well to examine assumptions. The tremendous accent placed by the Communists upon the use of force may produce the impression in our minds that they are really concerned with nothing else. No good Communist will hesitate to use force when the occasion requires; but neither will he ever take action without reference to the official ideology. There is, indeed, a closer tie between ideas and action in the Communist world than there is in the free world. And in view of that fact it is merely foolhardy to dismiss the ideology as something of no importance.

The Communist ideology is derived from a philosophy which was pieced together a century ago by Karl Marx and Frederick Engels, to which they gave the name of Dialectical Materialism. This philosophy is abstruse, dogmatic, and apparently remote from the thinking of the average man. Americans tend to dismiss it as just another element of the absurd Communist line of talk, of a piece with the lies and errors. The truth is, however, that Dialectical Materialism—sometimes called "Dimat" for short —has become one of the great intellectual-moral forces of history. It is not just a dry philosophical system stored away in dusty tomes, but a way of thinking which has had enormous impact upon twentieth-century minds, and wields, consequently, enormous power over their concepts and judgments. "Dimat" is an intellectual organism, international in scope, clever, aggressive, and appalling in its implications. No one who has come under its spell in a thoroughgoing way can ever be the same again.

It will be necessary in this study of our time to return to Dialectical Materialism and have a closer look at it—a task that will be undertaken in Part III. For our immediate purposes, however, at some risk of oversimplification, we may take a brief and dramatic view. Among Western peoples, and especially in America, certain stereotypes are used to characterize this Idea of Man. We see Dialectical Man as a

kind of robot of the state, a human being reduced to an
animal status, an ant living in a highly disciplined anthill.
These stereotypes, we shall find, are not entirely adequate
to the task of portraying what Dialectical Man really stands
for; yet they are not actually inaccurate, and we may accept them for working purposes. Dialectical Man, we may
say, represents the human being in terms that can only
seem to us inhuman; man's welfare in terms that can only
seem to us his undoing; freedom in terms that we can only
recognize as tyranny. He is a sort of ideal turned upside
down, a transmutation of Western ideas about man into a
conglomerate opposite. He stands, accordingly, for the
destruction of our world: if he comes to dominate the earth,
our own ideas about man cannot survive.

There are two characteristics of Dialectical Man we need
to understand. Wherever it flourishes, Dialectical Materialism is accepted as a *total* philosophy, in the sense that it
demands of its adherents, not only the attention of their
minds, but the possession of their lives. For this reason, it is often supposed that if the zealots and inner
groups could be isolated, the progress of Dialectical
Materialism would be checked. But this is not the case.
For the fact is that the ideas behind Dialectical Materialism—to anticipate our theme somewhat—are not
wholly confined to communism. They are, rather, endemic
to the twentieth century. They permeate the intellectual
life of millions who are otherwise quite opposed to communism. Even in America, we shall find, where the opposition to this doctrine is so emotionally intense, the way

of thinking that gave birth to Dialectical Materialism exercises profound influences upon our society and our judgments. The Western world often finds itself unable to answer Dialectical Materialism in an effective way, because its thinking is already implicated in many of the premises upon which Dialectical Materialism rests. Moreover, the Communists have often been able to gain the co-operation of political groups who are opposed to communism, but whose way of thinking about man and his life on earth has led them into a position where they cannot fight it.

The second characteristic of Dialectical Man brings us directly back to the question of the Communist use of force. Dialectical Man, we must note, *is an Idea that has not yet been realized.* He does not yet altogether exist; he is coming into being. There are relatively few men on earth who can yet boast of having achieved a genuinely dialectical status. The few are the Communist élite, who, openly or covertly, provide the real leadership for the Communist movement. The Communist world, we may say, is engaged in a far-flung processing of mankind to transform flesh-and-blood man into the likeness of the image of Dialectical Man. And it is for this purpose, primarily, that Communist force is applied. Communist doctrine calls for the use of force, not for the purpose of achieving any of the classical goals of force, but for the actual, flesh-and-blood realization of an Idea. Eventually, if force is used intelligently enough, and relentlessly enough, men will all be changed; they will become the conscious and loyal representatives of the Idea of Dialectical Man.

Even that, however, is not the whole story. To understand
this whole theory of force we must take one step into a
darkness where the Western mind finds itself lost. For the
Communists have undertaken the processing of mankind,
not merely for the sake of realizing an ideal, but in order
to prove that the doctrine of Dialectical Materialism is correct. It is perhaps little wonder that this inner meaning of
the use of Soviet force has not been fully grasped in the
West. Philosophical systems have played a large role in
molding Western societies; it can be said, if one uses the
words loosely, that philosophies have often been the cause
of violence and even of conquest—and in that sense, of the
use of force. But it is scarcely conceivable to the Westerner
that force should be used as a kind of extension of philosophy, a part of the argument itself. In the West, ideas certainly affect actions; but we do not countenance the use
of violent action, in place of argument, to indoctrinate
people in ideas. Yet it is only in those terms that we can
understand Soviet force. The terror is an argument. So are
the spying, the trials, the abject confessions, the correction
of "deviations," the eradication of the past, the purging of
repugnant ideologies. These instruments of force all have
the same purpose: to cause history to take place in the way
that the theory of Dialectical Materialism says that it must
take place; to argue the thesis of Dialectical Materialism
in terms of force, and in those terms to demonstrate its
validity.

The question, then, of the purpose of the Communist use
or threat of force, opens up a deeper inquiry. We find our-

selves faced, not merely with military considerations, but
with a revolutionary drive to transform all men into one
image. To miscalculate this drive is to mistake the very
nature of our enemy.

For our enemy is not any particular nation. It is not any
particular army. It is not even any particular form of
government. It is this Idea of Man. It is perfectly true
that the collapse of the Soviet state would constitute a
tremendous blow to the revolution, and yet, we must not
count too much upon this hope. Such a collapse might put
an end, temporarily, to the further processing of mankind.
But it would not put an end to the Idea. Dialectical Man,
we must remember, was not even born in Russia. He has
grown to power there, but he does not recognize any river
or range of mountains as a boundary; he does not belong
to the Kremlin but to humanity. His home is in the minds
of men. He has inhabited this planetary home for nearly a
hundred years. He has penetrated every society on earth,
crossed every border, affected the thinking of millions. And
he is surrounded everywhere he goes with close ideological
relatives, who resemble him in everything but name. It is
possible, of course, that at any moment we may be faced
with a tremendous army trained in the Idea of Dialectical
Man, and animated by it. But it is certain that at *every*
moment, as far ahead as we can see, we have to face the
Idea itself, and in every part of the world.

The internal politics of the U.S.S.R. are characterized
by various power struggles, and it often seems to Western
observers that these are no more than the struggles of
desperate and ambitious men. Since the death of Stalin,

especially, these conflicts have resulted in various shifts of policy, some of which have been reassuring to the free world. Possibly they may be so construed. And yet, when we take the Idea of Dialectical Man into account, we must ask ourselves, "Reassuring as to what?" There is not the slightest sign of the weakening of Dialectical Man. It may seem to us that the Kremlin purges are purely personal in character, and that this fact must surely undermine the ideology for which the U.S.S.R. stands. But this is a very "nondialectical" view of the matter. Whoever holds the reins of power in the Soviet imperium represents Dialectical Man, as oriental potentates of old represented God. There is for that leader virtually no such thing as a purely personal act. He defines, by his every deed, the dialectical course of history, no matter whether this involves the condemnation of a work of art as "bourgeois" or the liquidation by treachery of a vulnerable rival.

In the Idea of Dialectical Man, in short, we find the key to the puzzle of our time. Without this key it is impossible for us to make policy of a long-term and enduring kind. Military power, as such, cannot come to grips with Dialectical Man. Ideas can only be met and overcome by ideas. If, then, the Idea of Dialectical Man is to be overcome, another Idea of Man must arise capable of overcoming it. The real issue, in other words, is not military at all. It is philosophical.

4

THE RAPE OF FREEDOM

We can begin to see, then, how the challenge that Americans have to meet is not simply the challenge of clever lies and ingenious stratagems; but the challenge of a whole concept of life, which can be met and overcome only in terms of another concept. And it is just here that Americans have failed.

How great their failure has been is illustrated by the Soviet propaganda itself. A leading characteristic of that propaganda is that, rather than inventing new ideals, it has captured Western ideals and subverted them for Communist purposes. For instance, one of the great ideals of Western civilization is "truth": we believe in telling the truth and we believe in the search for truth—indeed, without respect for truth our whole concept of freedom would fall. This, we know, is not the case with communism. The Communist is willing to lie in order to gain his ends, and his propaganda lies all the time. Yet something is going on here which we must be careful to observe. Communist lies are nicely calculated and are almost always related, however deviously, to something true. The eventual distortion of the truth may be so great as to obscure the connection: still, search will almost always show that a connection exists. But if the propaganda is willing to deal in falsehood at all, why should it not go all the way? Why should it pay any regard to truth? The answer can only be that some regard for truth makes for better propaganda. The cleverest propagandists in the world, we must observe, defer to something in human nature that even propaganda cannot ignore; they defer, that is, to a fundamental respect and yearning for truth that dwells in every human heart. Propaganda techniques are calculated, not to frustrate this yearning, but to take possession of it and to use it for the multiplication of lies. Truth is thus subverted and delivered over to falsehood.

This transformation of something into its opposite is brought about in other ways. For example, take the word "democracy." Many Western thinkers have had doubts about the desirability of democracy, and some still do; but there has never been any substantial doubt about the meaning of the word, namely (as Webster puts it), "a form of government in which supreme power is retained and directly exercised by the people." The Communists, however, have set up an endless chain of "People's Democracies" and informal "democratic" groups, which are actually the most extreme form of authoritarian dictatorship. A word of crucial importance to the West has thus been transformed into its opposite. The same is true of a long list of terms, such as "liberal," "justice," "peace," and "brotherhood." These are the very terms of freedom, converted dialectically to serve the aims of the enemies of freedom. The cause of Dialectical Materialism thus advances by the appropriation of basic concepts that have played major roles in the long struggle of Western man for political emancipation. They are concepts, like that of truth itself, to which men respond, because they are derived from fundamental needs and aspirations of the human being. He who would rule the modern world must appropriate them.

The propaganda subverts Western ideals in still another way. In every situation where there is a conflict with the Western world, it turns back on itself, so to speak, and frankly appeals to Western values and principles. The Soviet system suppresses free speech, the propaganda brazenly denounces the West for its failure to achieve this ideal. At the very time when the Soviet system decides to purge a number of Jews, the propaganda shouts louder than ever that the West is riddled with anti-Semitism. The system murders minorities, the propaganda makes it the champion of civil rights. The system travesties judicial procedures, but if Communists are indicted for subversive activities in foreign lands the propaganda screams for justice. All this is just another manifestation of the same phenomenon: the Soviet system recognizes that it cannot win its way to power without the use of Western ideals. Shorn of them, its propaganda would no more be accepted outside the Soviet system than the propaganda of Adolf Hitler was accepted outside the German Reich. Western ideals are the indispensable ingredients of Soviet expansion, by means of which it lays hold of the minds of men.

That which the free world has been witnessing is a kind of philosophic rape. What we face in the Communist threat is not an aggressor in a recognizable sense. This aggressor does not attack, he betrays. He does not do physical violence to the temples: he enters them in priestly garb and performs his acts of rape upon the altars. Only after the temples have been corrupted from within does he attack and destroy them from the outside. The harrowing process is known to every nation that has fallen within the Communist power. All such nations have been the victims of a kind of treason—treason against man. They have experienced the total corruption of their governments and their hopes, their cultures and their institutions, by a power which acts upon them in the name of humanity. The Communist ability to invert Western ideals and Western principles, and to harness them to ends which are the very opposite of those that engendered them, cannot be without meaning. If we learned how to meet and overcome this process, the achievement would perhaps be more important to the survival of the cause of freedom than the military defeat of the Soviet Union itself.

The purpose of the present study may be defined as a search for that hidden but all-important key. The search will lead us into many questions that do not seem at first glance to have much bearing upon our immediate problems; yet the record is clear, that so long as we define our struggle only in terms of those problems, we cannot resolve them. If we are to reanimate the cause of freedom we must be willing to go behind them, to come to grips with forces that have been driving us in a direction contrary to our will.

5

THE AMERICAN FRUSTRATION

But how is it that the Communists are able to subvert our ideals and concepts to their own ends? It is we of the West who gave birth to those concepts and ideals, it is we who nourished them, fought for them, developed them to maturity, and it is we, therefore, who should be recognized as their champion. Since in about half the world this is not the case, since it has become possible for the Communists to appropriate our ideals as theirs, it is difficult to escape the conclusion that we ourselves have failed to make the meaning of those concepts clear, failed to explain them, failed to stand behind them in a vital and convincing way. In short, the phenomenal success of the Soviet propaganda in making tyranny look like democracy, slavery look like freedom, evil look like good, error look like truth—this extraordinary success cannot be due entirely to the cleverness of the Soviet propagandists. It must also and equally be due to a failure on our part to give meaning to those concepts, to breathe life into what we ourselves believe.

That we have failed is, perhaps, more obvious to the European than to the American. For we Americans live in a state of confidence with regard to the self-evident quality of our political beliefs. We may not be too clear as to what the principles of freedom are, but we know that there are such things and that our way of life is founded upon them. And what is true of freedom is true also of

numerous familiar concepts having to do with the nature
of man, such as the dignity of the individual, the pursuit
of happiness, the desirability of education, the natural
virtues and ethical behavior. We have confidence in these
ideas about man, which, in our view, our system is designed
to serve. Outside of the U.S., however, this confidence is
not always to be found. In the eyes of the rest of the world,
we Americans are very rich and very lucky; but our so-
called principles of freedom are not self-evident, and if
we really believe in them it behooves us to explain them.

Yet this is just where the trouble starts. For some reason,
at just this point, we become inarticulate. We have a deep
belief in our way of life but we seem unable to transmit
this belief to the rest of the world. This is not to say that
we have not tried. Books and magazine articles attempting
to expound American doctrine pour off the presses; societies are founded; long and eloquent speeches are delivered on every patriotic holiday. Toward the end of the
Truman administration even the State Department had a
project to frame a "ringing declaration" of American
principles capable of rallying the world to the cause of
freedom, as we have known it.

Yet the net gain from all this earnest search and oratory
has been illusory, like the gain of a man rowing a boat
against the tide. We have strengthened our own convictions;
but the great tide of world opinion is flowing toward
Moscow. The best evidence of the futility of our present
efforts has come from our own friends and allies. "It is
not what separates the United States and the Soviet Union

that should frighten us," wrote François Mauriac in the anti-Communist *Le Figaro*, "but what they have in common. . . . Those two technocracies that think themselves antagonists are dragging humanity in the same direction." The American knows this to be shockingly untrue. But he cannot say what he thinks in a way to convince anybody. His magnificent experiment has been successful beyond the dreams of those who conceived it; but now that the rest of the world is ready to take advantage of it, he finds that he cannot tell anybody what it really is. Tom Paine's prophecy has come true—that freedom would become the cause of all mankind—but Tom Paine's progeny cannot deliver.

This inarticulateness in the face of a great crisis, this inability to explain to others our most cherished goals, is the more baffling to us because, from childhood, we have been taught to believe that we are in possession of a valid and inspiring philosophy of man. For we are the inheritors, not just of the inflammatory Tom Paine, but of a whole group of distinguished men, to whom we proudly and confidently refer as "the founders." Washington, Jefferson, Ben Franklin, the Adamses, Hamilton, Madison, Mason, Sherman, Jay, Marshall—these and many others were not little men struggling for power but great and generous souls, who believed in man, and who shed the light of their belief all around the world. These men made, not just American history, but world history. One may even go so far as to say that never in the history of the world have there come together so many men of such high intelligence in political matters. In America, they gave the world an example of what freedom could mean; and in the world, they gave America her mission. They taught us what political freedom is. We were always able, thereafter, to draw upon them for our fundamental philosophy. Nevertheless, we cannot suppose that the doctrines formulated by the founders were absolutes, handed down from on high. They do not represent the last word on the subject of man and his freedom, and they do not in any way, therefore, relieve *us* of the necessity of thinking for ourselves. We cannot pass back to our forefathers the burden of our responsibilities in the realm of ideas, nor can we hope to find, in their ideas of man, the final means of overcoming the dialectical monster that we actually face.

The founders' doctrines are *built into* the American governmental structure in a permanent and somewhat inflexible way. Our Constitution, which was framed by them, is still the vital key to our processes of self-government. Legal theory has greatly changed since the Constitution was established, and the outlook of the Supreme Court reflects such change; nevertheless, all the decisions of that Court stem from principles set forth in the Constitution, and are in this sense tied to the founding doctrines. Thus the ideas of the founders are kept alive in American society, so that they live side by side with contradictory ideas. On patriotic occasions, the contradictory ideas are easily swept away, and the basic eighteenth-century doctrines treated, inferentially at least, as political absolutes.

But for those who live beyond the pale of the American Constitution, the doctrines of the founders do not have this special meaning. In European eyes the American founders were eighteenth-century *philosophes*—very great ones, no doubt, but long dead, nevertheless. Humanity faces today questions that were quite unknown to those thinkers. Vast changes have come over society since they lived, and profound revolutions, in which Americans themselves have taken the lead, have altered the outlook of mankind. When the American expounds his ideas of freedom in those somewhat archaic terms, what can a European do? If he is charitable he will shrug. If, on the other hand, he considers himself a "realist," he will doubt the sincerity of the speaker.

And since, here in the mid-twentieth century, realism is supposed to be a very desirable state of mind, the sincerity of Americans is, in fact, constantly doubted. It is indeed inconceivable to the European intellectual and his followers that a rational human being in the mid-twentieth century can seriously entertain political convictions defined for him by John Locke. Can such a person be ignorant, in the first place, of the fundamental philosophical contradictions in Locke's position? But even granting that he may not be aware of these contradictions, can he still be so ignorant of political developments in the last two centuries as to accept with any confidence, for example, the fundamental Lockeian doctrine of "natural rights"? Where does a natural right come from? Who guards it? Who can name a single such right that can stand up in the face of actual historical pressures? Take the so-called natural right to property. The great discovery of the twentieth century is that freedom cannot be defined without reference to those millions who do not own any property except their inconsequential personal effects. For such persons, property represents, not something which they own, but something which threatens to own *them*. The right to property, in short, in the eyes of the masses, is not a natural right, but a highly *un*natural one, against the misuse of which the masses insist that the state shall guard them. With regard to such a question, neither Locke's "Life, Liberty, and Property," nor Jefferson's more confusing "Life, Liberty, and the Pursuit of Happiness," has anything substantial to say. Or, if they do, Americans have certainly not revealed it to the world.

It is not necessary to conclude from all this that the eighteenth-century formulation of the fundamental rights of free men is without meaning for the twentieth century. Quite to the contrary, anyone who is willing to inquire into those concepts, and to interpret them in terms of their inner meanings, will find that they lead him out to a view of freedom of which the modern world is in search. But the point is that they have not been so interpreted by Americans. They have, rather, been taken for granted, as absolutes that relieve us of the necessity of thinking for ourselves. As a result, they have aged. They have slipped back into the eighteenth century, where they were born; events and ideas have marched on without them. And when we Americans cite them as if they were still living and true, we arouse a profound incredulity. How can a nation whose deeds and problems are so vitally of the present, live intellectually in the past—and still be counted sincere?

When, therefore, the American turns to the problem of how to check and master the Communist power, he finds himself deeply frustrated. His is a frustration that lies in the realm of ideas, where he feels defeated and helpless. If his problem were one of production he could lick it. If it were a question—as it was in 1944—of storming the beaches of some distant land with the biggest expeditionary force in history, he could do that. But it is not a question of that. The cause of freedom has not been stolen from the American with guns, it has been stolen from him with ideas. And he has found himself powerless to formulate his ideas in any way that can engage the confidence of the people of the world.

6

ESCAPE FROM IDEAS

Instead of overcoming our weakness in the realm of ideas, we have sought to escape from ideas into that which comes most naturally to us, that is to say, into action. We have sought to define the struggle of the free world in actionable terms—military terms, economic terms, political terms, geographic terms—any terms that would give us an excuse to avoid the basic philosophical challenge presented by Dialectical Man. In making this escape we have failed to get at the reality of the world situation, and consequently have failed to stem the Communist advance.

The very first action that we took after World War II was an act of withdrawal: we brought the boys home and conspicuously disarmed. While it ostensibly asserted nothing, this action was a perfect illustration of the American weakness; for it was taken without any real consideration of the ideas animating the Communist power, of what those ideas meant in terms of the aspirations of free men, or of where they would inevitably lead if unopposed. The result was that the Soviet began to make enormous gains. We were then forced to take action again, but this time in precisely the opposite direction. We began to rearm and to urge our friends to do so. But this new line of action merely got us into greater difficulties. Our allies began to demur. Was it not perhaps true after all that Americans *wanted* war, wanted—action? The Soviet propaganda easily fanned these little fires of suspicion, so that the Western world began to find itself divided in serious ways, with the U.S. scolding and prodding Europe, and Europe sullenly suspicious of the U.S.

Another form of action—a rather sly one—beguiled us. One of the breeding grounds of communism, we observed, was poverty. Let us therefore take action against poverty—economic action with dollars. Under the Truman administration we devised Point Four, the purpose of which was to help "backward" countries. There is nothing wrong with such a program except the terms in which Americans have tried to explain it. To raise the productive power of people who have not yet industrialized themselves, to increase their standards of living, to help them to provide for themselves in a world dominated by industrial forces—these are indeed strong goals worthy of the American people. Yet there has been a curious failure to explain to anyone, even to ourselves, what lies behind these goals, what our purposes really are.

For instance, the argument is advanced (especially in Congress) that our realistic, hard-boiled purpose in aiding "backward" peoples is to make things tough for the Communists. But the inference latent in this argument is that other peoples are no more than pawns in our war against the U.S.S.R., to be fed and developed only because we need their backing. This is certainly not a very inspiring philosophy of man; it is indeed deeply resented beyond our shores and has earned us some bitter ridicule. The story went the rounds of the U. N. that a minor power once asked a major power to lend it a couple of thousand Communists so that it could get some American aid! It is not true that our only motive for helping people to develop themselves economically is to fight communism. American democracy has certain responsibilities to humanity at large which it must fulfill if it would survive. But we have completely failed to make this clear. We have sought to define our policy in the realistic terms of action—with the result that we put the rest of the world in the position of mercenaries, whose energies and ideals we are trying to buy.

The most characteristic American policy of the postwar period has been "containment." This policy was the product of a school of thinking on international affairs which presents itself as realistic and whose chief spokesman has been the able career diplomat, George F. Kennan. In his words, it is a policy of "long-term, patient but firm and vigilant containment of Russian expansive tendencies . . . the Soviet pressure against the free institutions of the Western world is something that can be contained by the adroit and vigilant application of counterforce at a series of constantly shifting geographical and political points, corresponding to the shifts and maneuvers of Soviet policy."

This policy was accordingly adopted in substance by the Truman administration. Nevertheless, it was not a success; communism continued to gain ground. The reason for this was the usual one, that the policy did not address itself to the real issue between us and the Communist world. To see this one need only ask what *idea* containment embodied. What did it set up as a reality for the peoples of the world to believe in? The answer is, that it set forth no idea *save that of action*. It was a policy of acting to prevent the expansion of the Soviet Union. Nothing else. It told the world nothing about the reasons for such action. It told nothing about what the American people believe. It said, merely, that if we could act in such a way as to keep pressure on the U.S.S.R. and prevent her from expanding, then the Communist system, which, according to Mr. Kennan, "bears within it the seeds of its own decay," would begin to disintegrate from within. If only we could *act* in a "long-term, patient but firm and vigilant" way, our problem would solve itself through the collapse of our enemy.

The remarkably static view of history implied in this position should certainly give us pause. Can it really be true that the collapse of the Soviet imperium, should it be brought about by such means, would constitute a victory for the free world? Can we truly say that such a collapse, without any contribution on our part to the thinking of mankind beyond a "realistic" view of international politics, would leave behind it the kind of world we need in order to realize our institutions of freedom? These questions have to be answered in the negative. For the truth is that, although the disintegration of the Russian imperium would be a tremendous blow to Dialectical Man, it would not necessarily result in the kind of world in which men could live in that state of existence that we call free. Since Dialectical Man has indoctrinated millions in a way of thinking that is altogether hostile to the Western tradition of freedom, and unless the free world can present those millions with something more than a realistic diplomacy, they are not going to rally—they will not even know how to rally—to the banners of the free.

Mr. Kennan himself is aware of this; for in his memorable statement in *Foreign Affairs,* in which he made his proposal public and signed it "X," he summed up his case as follows: "But in actuality the possibilities for American policy are by no means limited to holding the line and hoping for the best." These possibilities can be realized in terms "of the degree to which the United States can create among the peoples of the world . . . the impression of a country which knows what it wants, which is coping successfully with the problems of its internal life and with the responsibilities of a World Power, and which has a spiritual vitality capable of holding its own among the major ideological currents of the time." Containment, in short, is not enough. Realism ends up, after all, in "a spiritual vitality capable of holding its own among the major ideological currents of the time." What does this mean? We can only guess (since Mr. Kennan does not explain) that the American people are here called upon to achieve something in the realm of ideas.

A parallel question to the question of containment and one that is being frequently asked is whether we can live peaceably with Communist Russia. It is the wrong question. Democratic peoples, acting in the name of freedom, are able to make all kinds of adjustments; and it might well be that if some way could be found, not so much to contain the U.S.S.R., as to contain Dialectical Man *within* the

U.S.S.R., we could live with Russia in a friendly way. But the real question is the reverse one: that is to say, whether Russia can live with us. The Idea of Man to which Russia is totally committed, permits of no relativism; it is based, as we shall see, upon an interpretation of history that claims absolute validity, and it is essential to the demonstration of this absolute that every other Idea of Man be destroyed. This is why, again in Mr. Kennan's words, "there can never be on Moscow's side any sincere assumption of a community of aims between the Soviet Union and the powers which are regarded as capitalism. It must invariably be assumed in Moscow that the aims of the capitalist world are antagonistic to the Soviet regime." Opposition to capitalism, to the "bourgeois world," to freedom as we know it and enjoy it, is the very stuff of which Dialectical Man is created. In the survival of our Idea of Man the Communist world sees the inescapable destruction of its own; and there can therefore be no meeting with the Communist world except in terms of an epochal struggle for Man's idea of himself.

7

A NEW SPIRIT OF INQUIRY

This brings us to the very heart of the problem facing the free world. We have now several times referred to an Idea of Man which the free world has to have if it is to combat Dialectical Man. Yet the objection will be raised that the free world, by definition, cannot have any such single Idea. The intellectual life of freedom thrives on heterogeneity and disagreement; any attempt to impose a particular philosophy upon free thinkers would constitute a denial of the very terms of their existence. Such an effort, if it were to succeed, could only result in the rise of another totalized power, just as sinister as the Communist power, whatever its definition of man. Humanity would then be torn apart, and the earth devastated, by two colossi, each having the primary aim of destroying the other—in the name of freedom.

It would seem, then,—and it has often been observed— that in their ability to marshal the minds of men the Communists have a weapon that the free world cannot meet. However, there is another way of looking at the matter. The free world, we may say, must live in disagreement. But in this fact, which constitutes a weakness, we must somehow find the source of its strength. What can be the strength of disagreement? The answer can only be, *the strength of truth.* The thinkers of the free world disagree, not because they care nothing for truth, but because they seek it. It is some-

times supposed that agreement among observers means
that truth has been ascertained. This may be so, but it is not
necessarily so; total agreement, as in the case of the Communist "party line," may mean that no one is really concerned with truth at all. It is in the conviction that there is
such a thing as truth, and in the dedicated search for it, that
the strength of the free world must be found. The Idea of a
Free Man is not the idea of a man in agreement with every
other man: it is man searching.

History has many aspects. One may view it from the
vantage point of war, diplomacy, and the struggle for
power. One may view it in terms of economics, or of technological development, or of science, or of art. One may
also view it as a search. If we take this last vantage point, a
peculiar phenomenon is observable which provides us with
a kind of clue to our present task. Certain periods emerge
from history as brilliant and memorable chapters in the
story of the human race. As we look back upon those periods
—let us say, the Italian Renaissance, or the German Reformation—we are struck by the fact that we have very little
to learn from them in terms of knowledge and information,
as such. We have at our disposal techniques of investigation
that were unknown to them, and these have resulted in a
vast accumulation of knowledge that renders the knowledge
of all previous ages largely obsolete. Yet the fact remains,
also, that familiarity with those great ages of the past is
indispensable to our own enlightenment. What then is it that
they have to give us? It is an approach to truth. Each such
age has searched for truth in its own way; each has given

expression, so to speak, to its own characteristic spirit of inquiry. The important thing about Aristotle today is not his knowledge of the physical world, a great deal of which was erroneous, but the spirit in which he inquired into the physical world. This spirit was different from that of the Middle Ages and the spirit of the twentieth century again differs from that of the Enlightenment. Viewed in this way, the story of man emerges as a series of efforts to relate himself to truth, each effort expressing a different spirit of search, and each, therefore, resulting in new insights into his own nature and that of the world.

If this view seems much too generalized, further consideration will show that it has its true being in the infinite specifics of history. Among those specifics may be counted the struggle of our own time. The spirit of inquiry that has dominated the last three hundred years or so of Western civilization likewise has its own special and unique characteristics. It will be our task to gain an understanding of these.

But meanwhile, from the ground already covered, we can scarcely avoid a certain suspicion—when conditions are ripe, as we have seen, the Idea of Dialectical Man appears to attract the people of our time with an irresistible power. May it not be, then, that the spirit in which twentieth-century man relates himself to truth leads him in the direction of Dialectical Materialism? May it not be, that in order to understand and master the bewildering forces of our time, we must face Dialectical Man as the logical outcome of our twentieth-century spirit of inquiry? Many will be shocked by this suggestion, and many will undertake to refute it. We agree that substantiation is required, and this will be provided, at least in part, in subsequent chapters. But in the light of the factors we have thus far reviewed the possibility is clear. As long as we view Dialectical Man as a concoction of the Communists, a mere invention for the purpose of waging psychological warfare, his extraordinary power over the minds of men must remain wholly incomprehensible; but if it is the case that he and the philosophy in which he is armed are the native outgrowth of the spirit of inquiry of our time, then his power can be explained. We can then begin to see why it is that the Russians have been able to usurp the "cause of all mankind"; why it is that Communist propaganda is so effective; why it is that that propaganda embodies a hidden reality, which so troubled the American correspondent at that friendly social gathering of the officers of the two armies after the war.

And when we speak in *these* terms of begetting an Idea of Man capable of meeting and overcoming the Idea of Dialectical Man, we see that our objective is not just a rival image armed in a rival philosophy. Our task, rather, is to relate ourselves to truth in a new way; to beget a new attitude of search, which will make Dialectical Materialism obsolete; to awaken a new spirit of inquiry, in which the Idea of a Free Man can become a reality for all men everywhere.

It is clear, moreover, that this new approach to man and the truths of man must make its beginning in America. It must grow from American soil and animate the minds of American citizens. The reason for this is not a chauvinistic one. The U.S. has inherited the leadership of the free world because of her vast power. It is well to remind ourselves, perhaps, that it was for no other cause. We do not possess leadership today by reason of any great clarity in our doctrine of freedom. Our contemporary poets have not opened up new vistas for man, nor have our philosophers conspicuously enlightened him. We are where we are because of our immense accomplishments in the world of "things" and the immense power growing out of such accomplishments. The question that the free world cannot help asking is whether we have enlightenment commensurate with that power—whether we are in fact fit for leadership. Until we answer this question we cannot effectively lead the free world.

The United States is thus faced with a far greater task than most Americans have hitherto visualized. This task cannot be defined in terms of action. The task cannot be achieved with dollars, however many we spend, nor with atomic bombs, however many we manufacture. Nor can it be brought about by increased zeal and cleverness in psychological warfare. These are necessary, since without them the entire free world would be exposed, as the satellite nations are at present exposed, to the threat of Soviet force, and to counter that threat we must have force at our disposal. But that is only part of our task. American leadership may be likened to a stone of many facets—military, economic, psychological, political, technological, and so forth. This stone, however, will pass into history as a thing of little value unless, like a faceted diamond, it is suffused with light. It is the light, and only the light, that can give meaning to American power.

We do not have to reach far for this light: its source is within ourselves. Something of its nature can be gleaned from an incident of the American Civil War. In that war both sides, the North and the South, were calling upon God, much as today both sides are calling upon freedom. Someone asked Abraham Lincoln how it could be that both the North and the South should expect God to be on their side. Mr. Lincoln replied, in effect, that he could not pray with much confidence for God to be on his side: his constant prayer, on the contrary, was that he should be found upon God's side. Whatever may be our religious convictions, we can find the clue to our present task in that attitude of mind. For the light which has now become indispensable to American leadership is the light that is always engendered when men seek in a dedicated spirit to relate themselves, not merely to their needs and prejudices, but to truth.

We are not engaged in a struggle to show that freedom is on *our* side, that it works for us, that we can invoke it more legitimately than the Communists. Such an effort could never win us the confidence of the freedom-seekers of the world. They want to know who is on freedom's side. Armies cannot decide this question. Neither can prejudice, self-assertion, or the waving of flags. We can arm the Western world to the teeth, and fight the biggest war in history, and win the biggest victory—and still lose freedom. Our power cannot win it for us, nor can our wealth. We can win it only insofar as we are able to awaken a new spirit of inquiry capable not merely of blocking, but of *rendering obsolete* the Idea of Dialectical Man. And we find the clue to our procedure in the dedicated humility of that clear-sighted leader who saved us, almost a hundred years ago, from what was then the greatest peril we had ever known.

II

PRELUDE TO CATASTROPHE

1

THE RISE OF INDUSTRIAL MAN

The object of this study is to achieve, if possible, a fundamental understanding of some of the great forces of the
human spirit that have led us into this desperate ideological
conflict. To this end it is necessary to gain a somewhat
better perspective on the road we have been traveling.

Probably no century in history ever started off with so
much promise as the twentieth. The Western world was for
the most part at peace and had every prospect of remain-
ing so. Many believed that war, in the life-or-death sense of
the word, was a thing of the past, a form of barbarity that
man had outgrown. The "enlightened" policies of Great
Britain dominated most of the earth. If these were tragically
slow to grant freedom to backward peoples, or to lift them
from the status of economic slavery, they were nevertheless
the indispensable instruments of law and peace, on the
basis of what was at least a recognizable moral order.

Moreover, it seemed that the reluctance of the British
to grant freedom to colonial peoples would perhaps be
rectified by the Americans, whose policies with regard to
their own recent conquests were on the whole anti-imperial-
istic, and who were about to undertake a New World experiment in the Philippines. Political freedom, in the view of
the people of those days, was something that had to be
earned. The British made the price a bit stiff, but it was a
reasonable hope that in the course of human progress they

would liberalize their policies and that the blessings of freedom would be bestowed on more and more people around the globe.

Hope, indeed—hope for free institutions, hope for education, hope for the physical sciences, hope for medicine, hope for mankind—was the dominant note in the mood of the Western world at that time. Americans felt sure that they could observe a new world springing forth from the dying and unjust remnants of the old. They could see the transformation taking place before their eyes. New industrial wonders broke upon them every year. Gas lights had replaced oil lamps; now electric lights were replacing gas. Automobiles began to appear on the highways. Something called an "aireoplane" had actually flown. Distant cities were linked by railroads, whose speed was ever increasing; already there were more than half a million telephones in the U.S. and Marconi had successfully sent messages by wireless; and new industrial shapes were rising like mushrooms in and around the bursting cities. There was talk of even greater wonders. If one took all the knowledge that had already been applied and multiplied it by a factor representing what was in the laboratory, or merely in scientists' heads, it was easy to make projections into the future of a very exciting kind. The twentieth century, it seemed certain, was about to achieve objectives that man had dreamed of for millennia, was about to breed a kind of superman whose supercivilization would reach a degree of enlightenment hitherto unheard of. Someday men would talk to each other over the air waves; new sources of energy would be discovered, from the sea,

from the sun, perhaps even from matter itself; the forces
of Nature would all be harnessed to the service of man;
the struggle for existence would be over; the pain and sorrow of human labor, inherited from Adam, would be reduced—might even be eliminated altogether by a kind of
push-button existence in which man would be made "free"
for other and better things.

On the scientific front the twentieth century has not only
fulfilled these optimistic predictions, it has in large measure
outstripped them. In *Anticipations*, published in 1900, H.
G. Wells made a series of remarkable scientific predictions, the accuracy of which seems today almost miraculous.
But he made these predictions for the year 2000! In
scientific matters we are a good fifty years ahead of his
schedule, and in addition we have the airplane (which he
did not think would be practical) and atomic fission (which
he did not predict at all). Mr. Wells and other prophets, indeed, failed to take account of an important law
which was at work in the field of science, and which Henry
Adams was the first to grasp. In a chapter of his auto-
biography, written in 1904, Adams formulated a "law of
acceleration," based on his researches into the consumption
of coal. From this law he was able to derive the general
prediction, that "the new American—the child of incalculable coal-power, chemical power, electric power, and
radiating energy, as well as of new forces as yet undeter-
mined—must be a sort of God compared with any former
creature of Nature."

This, of course, is exactly what has happened. In a half-century a transformation has been wrought; in certain parts of the earth there has arisen a new species of man. We may call it "Industrial Man," a super-animal with augmented faculties of many kinds, who has developed what may even be described as new organs. He has projected from himself mechanisms that give him the strength of hundreds, even thousands, of horses. His amazing tools, some of them bigger than the houses he lives in, endow him with power that dwarfs that of the legendary giants. Wheels extended from his body enable him to move faster than the wind and a "stick" in his hand enables him to outstrip sound. He is possessed of claws with which to burrow miles into the earth and fins with which to swim under the surface of the sea, while antennae, surpassing anything known to Nature, give him the ability to see in the dark and to communicate with other men all the way around the globe. Man of the mid-twentieth century does indeed live as the ancients might have imagined the gods living, a creature of almost limitless extensions, whose power to control the forces of Nature reaches down into the very interstices of the atom.

This genetic view of industrialization need not be pressed too far; there is an obvious difference between new organs developed out of the body itself, on the one hand, and mechanical extensions to already existing organs, on the other. Still, if only an analogy, the view is useful in that it suggests a somewhat different approach to the problems of our time from that usually taken by conventional sociology. This latter science leans heavily, in its search for causes, upon environmental factors; but the geneticist knows that, important as environment may be, it cannot in itself account for the transmutation of species. Until we are able to see that powerful forces have been at work within man himself, and are able in some degree to define them, we shall possess only a superficial knowledge of our time. Indeed, the attempt to explain what has been going on in purely environmental terms is doomed to failure, for we are faced with no mere accretion of small changes but with the most abrupt and radical transformation of recorded human history. Historically speaking, the rise of Industrial Man has been an explosion, transforming society on a planetary basis. Neither religions, nor arts, nor moral codes, nor political systems, nor ways of life have been able to resist the new species rising to dominance. In the Far East, especially in India and China, its impact has disrupted, in the course of a brief generation or so, cultures whose traditions are to be measured in millennia. If we are to account for Industrial Man, in short, it is necessary to consult internal, not merely external, forces.

The triumphal and virtually uninterrupted expansion of Industrial Man has begotten a new dream for man, which would have been meaningless to our forefathers. This is the dream of world economic security. Ever since the hopeful turn of the century, the conviction has been growing that it would become possible to provide every one of the two billion inhabitants of the globe with adequate food, clothing, and shelter—all the necessities of life, and some luxuries besides. It is an ironical but enlightening fact that the two greatest powers of our time, the U.S.A. and the U.S.S.R., have become the leading sponsors of this ambitious idea. World economic security has in fact become something more than a dream, has grown to the status of a *goal* to which statesmen are obliged to address themselves. The idea of riches for all is doubtless an illusion, but the idea of scarcity for none seems actually within our grasp. It seems really true that Industrial Man has the know-how, and either has or could develop the resources, to abolish want. Such is the far-reaching implication of the miraculous progress achieved during the first half of the twentieth century.

2

THE PHILOSOPHICAL OPTIMISTS

Now the excitement caused by the prospect thus opened up in the Era of Hope was not merely the excitement of the spectacular. It had a philosophical foundation upon which the prophets of the new age could stand. In the U.S. particularly, the prophecies of the early twentieth century were derived from certain assumptions about man, which, according to American tradition, were self-evident, and which the prophets proceeded to elaborate into the doctrine of inevitable progress.

To comprehend the doctrine of progress we must remind ourselves that the entire history of human culture is permeated with a sense of tragedy. For most of his history, man has lived under the impression that he was descended from other realms, that he was in some way divine, or born of divine parentage. His religions have linked him with those lost realms; his arts have expressed the tragedy of his loss; and his philosophies have wrestled with the insuperable problem of reconciling the sorrow and evil of his earthly life with the intimations of bliss and beauty living within him like half-forgotten memories. Religion, art, and philosophy have had different things to say about this problem in different ages in different parts of the world. Nevertheless, the burden of their teaching has generally been the pessimistic one, that life on earth can never fulfill those intimations, cannot of itself yield happiness, let alone the realization of the good. The best that can be said of life on earth, according to this fundamental view, is that it is a kind of school, where man is trained and tested for something else, where suffering, pain, fear, loneliness, and death are endured, in order that human beings may learn the mysterious lesson of rebirth into a more exalted sphere.

This view of life on earth, which is fundamental to all the recognized world religions, and specifically to Christianity, might be referred to as philosophical pessimism. This is not a narrow pessimism, such as that of Arthur Schopenhauer, for example, which rests chiefly on the observation that the cravings of the human will can never be satisfied. The doctrine to which we refer offers a far more profound view of man and of his earthly struggle. In a sense, philosophical pessimism is fundamentally *optimistic*, because it asserts that man belongs to, or has connection with, higher spheres, where his intimations of bliss and beauty may be confirmed. But with regard to life on earth the doctrine is *pessimistic* because it asserts that the goals of the earth do not lead to those spheres. Salvation, in other words, cannot be won in terms of the earth life alone: on the contrary, through his life on earth man has become hopelessly implicated in evil. It is possible for a man to will the good; but it is not possible, through his unaided efforts, for him to achieve it. To this end supernatural intervention in some form is necessary, whether this be the magic invoked by the savage medicine man, or the processes of Hindu karma, or the redemption made available to man by Christ. Man can only be saved from evil and pain by the recognition of his intimations of bliss and beauty, and by working inwardly toward them—that is to say, toward the spiritual, toward the divine. The things of the earth can offer him nothing but illusion and suffering. He must pass *through* these in order to realize his true self.

But the philosophical structure in which the American doctrine of progress is now embedded is very different from this. It may be called philosophical optimism. Here again, the reference is not to a superficial optimism having to do with merely temperamental peculiarities, but to a basic evaluation of man and his life on earth. With regard to man, his will, his works, and his destiny, this way of thinking comes to optimistic conclusions. We do not have to look to any other sphere for man's salvation—indeed, the very idea of salvation is a questionable one, because it leads over into dogmatic notions like that of original sin. It is, of course, true that the Calvinist doctrine (that man is from birth guilty and corrupt) has been one of the major currents in American culture. But it is just the characteristic of American culture that it has gradually undermined the strict Calvinist thesis, or modified it so radically, that it is now scarcely recognizable. Indeed, in the mid-twentieth century, Calvinism (as preached by its founder at any rate) is regarded as intellectually obsolete, perhaps even morally reprehensible. The indispensable principle of the doctrine of progress is the ability of the individual to carve his own salvation out of the challenges of his environment; and in his confidence in this principle the American optimist does not wait upon anything so intangible as the grace of God.

The philosophical optimist concedes, of course, that life

is full of pain and evil. But, he insists, *these can be cured.*
He does not necessarily deny the existence of God, but he
is a firm believer in the principle that "God helps him who
helps himself." There is no evidence, he would contend, of
a necessary supernatural guidance, let alone a redemption;
to talk in that way is to indulge in illusion and superstition.
Man can and must save himself—or, as the optimist would
prefer to put it, fulfill himself: and this must be done in
earthly terms, not in supernatural terms. As for the intimations of bliss and beauty, the philosophical optimist accepts
these as evidence of the soundness of optimism: these
supposed intimations are really no more than natural
cravings for a perfection that has not yet been attained.
Just like other cravings, such as hunger or sex, they have
their origin in our human nature, which is guiding us,
through them, to its own natural fulfillment. They tell us,
in effect, that the goal of happiness is a legitimate one for
us to work for; that it is, so to speak, proper to human
nature and can be achieved by human means.

The crux of the issue between the philosophical pessimist
and the philosophical optimist is the problem of evil. The
optimist sees man as inherently good. The overwhelming
majority of men and women, he points out, are persons of
good will who desire the good for their fellow men as well
as for themselves. The pain and evil of human life, he main-
tains, are the result of human errors and failings that can
be overcome. He is, therefore basically, a reformer. The
causes of evil, he believes, are external; they arise from
underlying environmental conditions such as ignorance and

poverty, which beget delusion, selfishness, fear, and hate. These conditions are, largely, the result of man-made institutions, such as the state and the church, which were created to meet legitimate needs, but which have often thwarted the march of progress by the exercise of tyranny and the encouragement of prejudice. The philosophical optimist sees the resolution of the problem of evil in terms of the reform of these environmental factors. If man could only succeed in molding his environment to serve his own "higher" impulses, nothing could prevent him from transforming life on earth into a life of happiness, in which those intimations of bliss and beauty, which have so long tugged at his heart, could at last be realized.

Now, whatever its more distant origins, philosophical optimism first emerged as a world force in the eighteenth century, at which time it molded the thinking of many of the founding fathers, notably Thomas Jefferson. There were, to be sure, pessimistic influences at work in the formation of the new nation, particularly that of John Adams; but it is historically accurate to say that philosophical optimism was built into the American system at the very beginning, and that its seeds have taken root in our soil more vigorously than in any other. The wild and expansive Jacksonian democracy, for example, was a sort of optimistic uprising, in which the Adamsian view of things was wholly routed. By the turn of the twentieth century, the "radical" tenets of the optimists had been so thoroughly assimilated that they had become bipartisan. Theodore Roosevelt gave expression to them in his person.

And his illustrious cousin, Franklin, won more popularity than has ever been accorded to an American President by reforms that were designed to improve man's lot on earth at virtually any price.

American optimism, however, cannot be understood in merely political terms. It is not really a doctrine, in the ordinary sense of that word: it is a point of view, an orientation to life as a whole, related to profound developments in the human psyche itself. The chief ingredient of modern philosophical optimism has been provided by that method of inquiry generally referred to as "science." It is true that some of the important principles of optimism—such as the inherent goodness of man—are primarily the fruit of eighteenth-century rationalist thinking and, for that matter, can even be traced much farther back. But in the achievements of science the optimists have found what seems to them to be literal confirmation of their beliefs. That man's lot is infinitely improvable, that the improvement can be brought about by the transformation of environmental factors, and that such a transformation, in turn, can have very desirable social results—these are no mere academic propositions, but propositions that have been deeply impressed upon twentieth-century American culture by the extraordinary advances of science.

It was these propositions that fired the era of hope with which the century opened. Technology, the gigantic child of the human intellect, was beginning to transform the earth so radically and so thoroughly as to render pessimism obsolete. By taking from men the burden of mere existence, technology would free them for the nobler impulses of their nature. Was it not the case that most of the sorrows of man, including wars and pestilences, could be traced back to the lack of such elementary necessities as bread, shelter, clothing, sanitation, and opportunity? If technology could provide all these, men would then be set free for the conquest of ignorance; and through that conquest the way would be opened for men to attain to a higher level of individual and social intelligence, proper to their real nature. They would at last become capable of living in accordance with the Christian ethic and the Golden Rule.

In this light, the American prophets of the first decade could even construe the bursting technological revolution as the necessary preface to a realization of Christianity. Of course, in order to do this, one had to edit the New Testament somewhat. Christianity, like all other great world religions, is fundamentally pessimistic: whatever role its various theological schools may assign to man's works, all must agree that the ultimate object of his endeavors is not the improvement of his environment, but the salvation of his soul. Moreover, according to His own oft-repeated statement, the founder of the Christian faith was not a mere man, but the actual Son of God—a divine being who did not really belong to the earth at all, but only came here in order to perform an immense sacrifice on behalf of mankind. This view of the matter, which presumed the existence of another realm, higher than that of the earth life and indispensable to it, ran directly counter to the optimistic premise that the earth life could, in itself, provide man with what he needs. Since the American optimists were steeped in this Christian tradition and were unwilling to relinquish it, they had, therefore, to resolve their dilemma by editing the Testaments that His followers left behind them.

And as a matter of fact, this was not very difficult to do. The task had already been performed in part by Thomas Jefferson, who had confidently glossed the Scriptures from time to time, in order to relieve Christianity of the embarrassment of coming into conflict with that rational view of things that so deeply animated him. Since his time, the new research facilities at the disposal of the human intellect have made it possible to show that the New Testament was not really authoritative in the historical sense of the word; most of it, if not all, had been written long after the death of Jesus by persons who had never seen Him. In their extreme admiration for Him, those ancient writers had probably attributed to Jesus a divine status which He Himself would not have claimed. The Catholic Church, of course, anchored in a body of dogma inherited from pre-scientific ages, never countenanced this apologetic attitude toward what is, after all, the most fundamental tenet of Christianity. But many of the Protestant sects, with the Unitarians and Emerson's transcendentalists in the van, had moved more and more toward a "rationalistic" view of religion and a "humanistic" view of the Christian founder. Jesus came to stand for those things in man which were self-evidently good: a man whom we could see only dimly, because he left no firsthand historical testimony behind him, but who had apparently enacted a tragedy of gentleness, love, and self-sacrifice on a heroic scale.

From this edited view of Christianity and its founder, it was possible to derive a useful religion that fitted comfortably into the requirements of Industrial Man. The good in man, which Jesus stood for (so the thesis ran) had been choked and warped by environmental conditions, of which three stood out in bold relief. These were: ignorance, poverty, and tyranny. The cure for ignorance was education. The cure for tyranny was the encouragement of democratic institutions. And the cure for poverty, which many of the optimists saw as the key to the other two, was the widespread development of industrial economics. In those three fundamental reform policies the enthusiasts of the early twentieth century saw the hope of the world.

3

INVOLVEMENT IN EVIL

Such, in general terms, was the point of view from which the great American expansion of the twentieth century was launched.

The first important sign that there might be something wrong with this thesis was the outbreak in 1914 of a world war. The picture of men of "good will" sitting in mud-soaked trenches shelling each other to bits did not jibe with either the premises or the conclusions of those—among them, Woodrow Wilson himself—who had been prophesying a reformed and more enlightened era. A certain disillusionment gripped the Western world. Was it really true that the age of science was leading us out to a new Christianity?

Now in Europe this disillusionment was real, and it changed the quality of European thought in radical and permanent ways. But in America it was histrionic and romantic. The self-appointed "Lost Generation" took over. It indulged in a kind of Nietzschean reversal of values, yet it always seemed to be looking over its own shoulder, to watch the effect upon the audience of its tragical utterances. Rereading even the best productions of that period, one finds a dramatization of the self that produced a kind of pleasure in despair: there was a lot of glamour in being "lost." And it was just this romanticism that saved American philosophical optimism for another day. People at last got tired of being tragic. A "scientific" analysis of the war and its aftermath showed nothing that could not be cured. Human nature, it seemed, was not guilty of the war, but rather the institutions which had been inherited from the nineteenth century, and to which men had become enslaved: the Hohenzollern, for example; the munitions-makers and other "merchants of death"; outworn customs and manners; yes, even the Church itself, which had attempted to bind men in dogma instead of encouraging them to guide themselves by the clear light of their intellect. The problem was merely how to free men from these pernicious influences, so that the good in them could assert itself. They would then never again tolerate war.

The result of this line of reasoning was the continuation of philosophical optimism during the twenties as the major current in American thought. And the optimism was now very greatly assisted by the fact that the war had brought about vast new technological advances. That wonderful day, when man would be the master of Nature and could use his works for the creation of an earthly paradise, seemed closer than ever. The great economic upsurge in America during the twenties made this doctrine popular, and was climaxed by the famous 1928 Republican campaign promise of "two chickens in every pot, and a car in every backyard to boot." The doctrine of progress was re-established, stronger than ever.

Nor, strangely enough, was American optimism refuted by the Great Depression of the thirties. The Depression had, to be sure, a somewhat sobering influence. A strange new doctrine began to be preached, that the U.S. had reached maturity and that the problem was no longer one of expansion but of conservation and distribution. Yet these sobering thoughts were applied, chiefly, in the economic field. So far as a philosophy of man was concerned, the Depression not only failed to dampen philosophical optimism, it actually provided an opportunity for the optimists to take over. The old institutions were again blamed. The Depression had been brought about, it seemed, by that iniquitous institution known as American business enterprise, which had exercised privileges and acquired power at the expense of the people. One heard the phrase "industrial democracy," which was never very clearly defined, but which conveyed, certainly, the connotation that if "the people" could take over industry, as they had taken over government, the industrial system would somehow be redeemed. An army of reformers went forth to modify or abolish the wicked institutional practices that had "caused" the Depression. The leading philosophical optimists of the day, whose bellwether was the venerable and benign John Dewey, took over the campuses of the universities and gave their support to the institutional reforms.

It can scarcely be said that these men squarely faced the question at issue, the question of whether man was in fact "good." This question was hardly ever examined by the reform philosophers of the thirties. An outstanding exception was Reinhold Niebuhr, the great Protestant theologian, who, while supporting the reforms of the New Deal, also and at the same time raised his voice to warn that the basic proposition of the reformers was a fallacy. But he was regarded, in most circles, as an intellectual maverick who had somehow got crossed up in theology. The inherent goodness of man, so confidently set forth by so many Americans, from Thomas Jefferson to John Dewey, had become American dogma.

It took Adolf Hitler to bring the philosophical optimists face to face with reality. As the appalling drama of World War II unrolled, their thesis ran into serious difficulties. For instance, how could one square one's faith in man with this spectacle of human beings captured by the lies and distortions of a mustached pygmy obviously bent upon evil? This and other fundamental questions became lost in bloody battles and shattered cities all over the world only, however, to re-emerge after the war, with the postwar disclosures of the brutalities in the concentration camps. Then it became evident that not only Hitler but thousands of Germans had acted as if they were the very incarnations of evil; had become, as it were, super-evolved beasts— beasts endowed with intellect. All the technological paraphernalia of the age, which was to have been the prelude to a new Christianity, was at the disposal of these beasts; nor, once they had decided to use this paraphernalia for evil, could all the good intentions in the world, or all the acts of Congress, or all the high philosophical assumptions, prevent the Nazis from bringing ruin, suffering, and degradation upon their fellow men. And as if this were not enough, suddenly, in the closing hours of the war, there burst on Hiroshima, and on horrified mankind, the atomic bomb. The long technological trail that had had its origin somewhere in prehistoric caves had led at last into the interstices of matter, so that man might now be able to blow up the earth, not just figuratively, but literally. Man had *better* be good by nature! But was he? Were the optimists sure?

The dogma was so strongly implanted, however, that the optimists continued to hold their ground. Perhaps this was the last world conflict. The United Nations was formed. It had its weaknesses, and the Russians were being difficult, but one should not despair. Were not the Russians good men? Had they not fought on our side? Did they not also believe in a new society, which, if different from ours, was based on the same optimistic premise, that men could find salvation through materialistic advance? But gradually the evidence piled up. There were the vetoes in the Security Council. There were the Russian concentration camps. There was the slave labor. There were the aggressions. Esthonia was swallowed up, as were Latvia, Lithuania, Poland, Hungary, Rumania—even Czechoslovakia. There were the mass murders, the tortures, the forced confessions —worse, apparently, than anything the Nazis had tried. The Nazis, at least, had frankly integrated their system to war: the new "men of good will" were doing these things in the name of peace.

What was worse, the observer could discern in all these events an upward curve whose projection pointed toward infinity. Within the space of a short half-century, philosophical optimism had been faced with three men—Kaiser

Wilhelm II, Adolf Hitler, and Josef Stalin—each more destructive than his predecessor. These men had all but wrecked civilization. They had devastated Europe. They had attacked and occupied their neighbors, subverted governments, committed genocide, spread terror, promulgated lies, and planted the seeds of hate—all in a crescendo, the end of which is not yet in sight. Yet the men were only symbols. They had had aides by the thousand and followers by the million, and the numbers of these were increasing. By mid-century Communist dictators were sitting upon a mountain of human suffering and broken cities, in control of one-third of the population of the world. More people had enrolled, or had been conscripted, in their cause than in any other in the history of mankind.

The American awakening to the meaning of these facts of history has been delayed by a peculiar assumption that has characterized the whole development of the U.S. As the leader of the free world, it is necessary for us to take account of the evil with which the world seems to be infested; but in our minds, sometimes only half-consciously, we make an invidious distinction between ourselves and others. It may be true that the world is evil, but this is not the case, we feel, with America. The evil deeds of the twentieth century have not originated here. We have, on the contrary, come to the rescue of the free world on bloody battlefields far from our own shores, and have at the same time carried out momentous popular reforms. Among us education is virtually universal, the standard of living is

fantastically high, and our society is dominated by democratic institutions which have constantly overthrown or
reformed the "bad" institutions of the past. As a result we
tend to feel that philosophical optimism, while it has failed
to meet the requirements of the world situation, still holds
good for America. This land can still live and flourish on
the assumptions that men are good, and that they are capable of working out their own salvation.

Among those who have commented on this fact is again
Reinhold Niebuhr. One of the fundamental characteristics
of the United States, he points out, has been the assumption
of innocence. "It is particularly remarkable," he says,
"that the two great religious-moral traditions which in-
formed our early life—New England Calvinism and Vir-
ginian Deism and Jeffersonianism—arrive at remarkably
similar conclusions about the meaning of our national
character and destiny. . . . Whether, as in the case of the
New England theocrats, our forefathers thought of our
'experiment' as primarily the creation of a new and purer
church, or, as in the case of Jefferson and his coterie, they
thought primarily of a new political community, they believed in either case that we had been called out by God to
create a new humanity. We were God's 'American Israel.' "

De Tocqueville, Dr. Niebuhr points out, found these same
"illusions of unique innocency" many years later on the
American frontier. "If I say to an American," De Tocqueville reported,

that the country he lives in is a fine one, aye he replies and there
is not its equal in the world. If I applaud the freedom its in-

habitants enjoy he answers "freedom is a fine thing but few nations are worthy of it." If I remark on the purity of morals that
distinguishes the United States he declares "I can imagine that
a stranger who has witnessed the corruption that prevails in
other nations would be astonished at the difference." At length I
leave him to a contemplation of himself. But he returns to the
charge and does not desist until he has got me to repeat all I
have been saying. It is impossible to imagine a more troublesome
and garrulous patriotism.

Now it is of course true that this American assumption
of "innocency" has had very constructive effects upon
American society. In acting *as if* men were inspired by
good will Americans have in fact nurtured and stimulated
the development of good will among those who shared the
optimistic tradition—that is to say, among themselves. The
average American is shrewd; but he is not unduly suspicious of his fellow men, and he does not waste too much
time worrying whether they will take advantage of him.
American business and industry operate in an atmosphere
of mutual confidence which is the more remarkable in
that the component units are still for the most part highly
competitive. The ever-present theme of perfectibility—has
given American society a buoyancy which has defied all
obstacles. The opinion may even be ventured that philosophical optimism is in some sense indispensable to the
successful operation of a democratic system, for in it
people find the impulse and the faith to search for new
opportunities that constantly refill and refresh the social
reservoir.

The recognition of the merits of philosophical optimism,

however, can no longer be permitted to blind us to its fatal limitation. In the eyes of the rest of the world, the American pretension to a special innocency, when not infuriating, is merely ridiculous. Yet this is not the point of the debate between philosophical pessimism and philosophical optimism. The philosophical pessimist is not concerned to show that one person is better or worse than another. His position is the more profound one, that all men, regardless of their relative merits, are implicated in evil. The fact that the Nazis were Germans, not Americans, has really no bearing on this point. The Nazis were human beings. The evil to which they gave expression was not German evil but human evil, and if Americans are to become the possessors of an Idea of Man in conformance with the realities of human nature they must take this evil into account just as much as if they themselves had committed it. To escape into some vague idea of their own innocency is to foreclose all hope of achieving an Idea of Man that can have general validity for mankind; hence, to abdicate from the leadership of the cause of freedom, in which Americans so persistently profess to believe. The assumption of our "innocency," therefore, is not merely infuriating, it is suicidal. It creates a kind of philosophical vacuum in which the American tradition itself must eventually gasp for air— and die.

And it is nothing but an illusion: Americans are just as deeply implicated in the problem of evil as anyone else. Let us leave aside the question of how much American policy during the twenties and thirties contributed to the rise of national socialism and Hitler's decision to strike the free world. The fact remains that the predicament in which we now find ourselves is a predicament of guilt. However we may have sought to escape evil, we have been unable to do so, and the prospect is only of more to come. Dr. Niebuhr's comment on this situation is unimpeachable.

Whether or not we avoid another war, we are covered with prospective guilt. We have dreamed of a purely rational adjust-ment of interests in human society; and we are involved in "total" wars. We have dreamed of a "scientific" approach to all human problems; and we find that the tensions of a world-wide conflict release individual and collective emotions not easily brought under rational control. We had hoped to make neat and sharp distinctions between justice and injustice; and we discover that even the best human actions involve some guilt. . . .

Thus an "innocent" nation finally arrives at the ironic climax of its history. It finds itself the custodian of the ultimate weapon [the atom bomb] which perfectly embodies and symbolizes the moral ambiguity of physical warfare. We . . . could not renounce the weapon because the freedom or survival of our allies de-pended upon the threat of its use. . . . Yet if we should use it, we shall cover ourselves with a terrific guilt. We might insure our survival in a world in which it might be better not to be alive. . . . In this way the perennial moral predicaments of human history have caught up with a culture which knew nothing of sin or guilt, and with a nation that seemed to be the most perfect fruit of that culture.[1]

Great evil has been visited upon our time; and the thesis that this is to be accounted for by political, economic, ecclesiastical, or cultural institutions—which are after all composed of *men*—becomes increasingly implausible. It

[1] Reinhold Niebuhr, *The Irony of American History*, New York, Scribner's, 1952, p. 18 and pp. 38-39.

is certainly true that tyranny, such as that which the Communists practice, begets evil. But how does one meet this fact? Does one go to war at the risk of destroying civilization? That, surely, could not be productive of good. On the other hand, it cannot be the course of virtue—let alone, of leadership—to do nothing. Indeed, it becomes increasingly clear that it is just when we do nothing that evil gains. The question of evil cannot be begged, as it most surely was begged by the American reformers of the nineteen-thirties. Whatever may be one's theory of evil, the *fact* of evil is evidently a reality. It is an essential ingredient of life on earth, in which man is deeply implicated.

4

THE PURSUIT OF HAPPINESS

At a group discussion held in 1948 among students of the University of Illinois, under the auspices of *Life* Magazine, the following colloquy occurred between the moderator and a married veteran student. The subject of the discussion was the "Pursuit of Happiness." The group had decided that peace was essential to happiness, but the student in question qualified this by saying that he could not accept peace at any price; under certain circumstances he would go to war.

MODERATOR: In other words, peace is not essential?

MR. ZIMMERLY: I am saying that peace *is* essential; if I am going to be happy there must be peace. But I am willing to *waive my right to happiness* in order that other people may have it.

MODERATOR: Would it be correct to say that you would be happier in going to war than in doing nothing about it?

MR. ZIMMERLY: No. I don't think there would be any happiness whatsoever in going back to a garrison state.

MODERATOR: What I am getting at is a better understanding of the word "happiness." Wouldn't you be happier in sacrificing than in pursuing just your own happiness?

MR. ZIMMERLY: I wouldn't use the word "happiness" the way you have used it. I don't think there would be any happiness whatsoever in sacrificing.

When placed in the context of the American optimistic tradition, this brief interchange leads to some rather crucial observations. If evil can be done away with by means of environmental reforms, why not also sorrow and pain?

Granting that there are some pains and sorrows that appear
to be ineradicable—such as, for instance, the fact of death
—may we not hope, through our advances in medicine, and
through education and reform, to reduce these to an absolute minimum, while at the same time assuring that most
men can enjoy themselves most of the time? The optimistic
answer to this question has invariably been in the affirmative; and the optimistic assumption that men are inherently
good helps to make that answer convincing.

All this is summed up in American life in the general
proposition that the proper aim of man is *happiness.* As
pointed out by Howard Mumford Jones in his succinct
study, *The Pursuit of Happiness,* this proposition was incorporated into American political institutions from the
very beginning. The eighteenth-century founders were wont
to define the purpose of government as the happiness of the
people, and we find the right of "pursuing *and obtaining*
happiness and safety" written into George Mason's Virginia
Declaration, which preceded by two months Mr. Jefferson's
more famous Declaration of Independence. The quest of
happiness, sometimes stated as a right, sometimes as a goal,
is implicit in the writings of all American statesmen; even
Lincoln, immersed though he was in tragedy, would scarcely
have contended against it.

When it comes to defining happiness, however, Americans have run into difficulties. Different eras have had different definitions. As Howard Mumford Jones shows, eighteenth-century writers were prone to extol happiness in
terms of the life of the landed gentlemen, the Cincinnatus,

who, having loyally served his country, was able to retire to his fruitful acres, his books, and his memoirs. Then came the westward-moving days, when the idea of the land was still dominant, but now no longer gentlemanly, but harsh and adventurous. Thereafter, during the latter third of the nineteenth century, industry and its products began to replace the land. The great slogan of the Republican party, "the full dinner pail," symbolized happiness to be achieved through hard work and high wages. We finally come down to our own time, when new governmental powers have been created to secure Mr. Mason's "happiness and safety" in concrete and detailed ways; and when, in 1948, Harry Truman won one of the most spectacular victories in American political history by promising a kind of cornucopian welfare.

If we study these mutations in the American idea of happiness, two constants emerge that shed a great deal of light on our current predicament. The first of these is that American ideas of life and of victory have always been strongly oriented to the outer world. In order to understand this better, let us make a brief reference to the familiar distinction between the extraverted and introverted types of human beings. "The extravert," said Dr. Carl G. Jung, "is distinguished by his striving toward the object, his feeling into and identification with the object, and his willed dependence upon the object. . . . The introvert, on the other hand, is distinguished by his apparent self-assertion in presence of the object. . . . All the more . . . is he dependent upon the idea."

The American people, of course, are neither all extra-
verts nor all introverts, but within this reference a valid
generalization can be made. In differentiating the types
an even more fundamental distinction is made; i.e., between the world of the subject, which we may call the
"inner" world, and the world of the object, or "outer"
world. The human consciousness makes this distinction.
When we look at a chair we are conscious of it as an object
outside of us. When we experience a twinge of conscience
we are aware of something that has its being inside of us.

The outer world with which we may be intimately connected, and into which we may channel our energies, is
nevertheless the world of the "not-I," of things and events.
The inner world is the world of the "I," the world that
pertains directly to what we call the psyche and what in
other times was called the soul. It is an active and living
world comprising many different phenomena—our
thoughts and reasonings, our principles and standards, our
beliefs and deep prejudices, our pictorial images and symbols, our dreams and hallucinations, reaching down into
the unconscious, which is apparently fathomless. There is
rarely any possibility of confusing these two aspects of our
consciousness, except in one area. This is the area of our
physical body, which stands as a kind of barrier between
them and yet is intimately linked with both.

The means of achieving happiness which are practiced
by a Buddhist monk, which involve a complete concentration upon inner judgments and evaluations, do not appeal
to Americans; indeed, they seem somehow obsolete, if not

actually perverse. We are not an inward-looking, but an outward-looking people. We seek to express ourselves primarily in terms of action; in terms of doing things, making things, changing things, owning things—to fulfill ourselves in outward, tangible, and measurable ways. The leading characteristic of American society is thus the externalization of human energies and human values—a characteristic which has exerted on the contemporary world a cultural force of immense importance.

It may be objected that this was not the case with the Pilgrim fathers, who came here primarily to assure themselves of certain inner values and judgments included under the general heading of "the right to worship God in one's own way." The objection is sound, but it leads directly to the second constant observable in the American idea of happiness, namely, a *constant increase* in the externalization of the criteria of happiness.

The ideas of happiness that characterized Jefferson's time placed a far heavier accent on external blessings than did those of William Bradford and John Winthrop.[2] If we move forward another hundred years, to the era of the trusts and the empire-builders, we find that the quiet agrarian virtues that so beguiled Messrs. Washington and

---

[2] This is not to say, however, that the ideas inspiring the Pilgrim fathers were purely religious. One does not have to be an economic determinist to acknowledge that the Pilgrims were a very practical group with strong economic motives. But despite this fact, the general observation holds that their view of happiness was much more inward-looking than that which prevailed a century later. See Winthrop's *Journal*, under the title of *The History of New England from 1630-1649*, edited by James K. Hosmer, New York, Charles Scribner's Sons, 1908.

Jefferson have been swamped by the advancing tide of
industry. Happiness is now defined in terms of outward
success, of "self-made" men possessed of the energy and
astuteness to "get ahead in the world." And that was by no
means the end of the process. Materialistic the McKinley
era certainly was, but we had not yet reached the point of
equating the good life almost completely with the products
of modern industry. That was to come in mid-twentieth
century—today when the American ideal requires that
everyone should have a home with at least one bathroom,
plenty of water, electric light, and heat; simple but attrac-
tive clothes (styled in Paris, if you like, but less expensive
than any other well-styled clothes in the world); radio-
television, an automobile, an electric washing machine,
dishwasher, vacuum cleaner, a toaster, a telephone and
plenty of filtered cigarettes. These things are no longer
considered luxuries. Together with dozens of similar items,
they have been incorporated by the Department of Labor
into its cost-of-living index, which, in turn, is used by many
corporations and unions to measure the fairness of their
wage rates. The American way of life does not "guarantee"
all these things to everybody, and could not do so even if
it wanted to. But it is driving in the direction of fulfilling
the ideal of happiness in these terms.

Moreover, woven through the warp of things, there is a
woof of intangibles, which blend with the things and bind
them together. From infancy we are taught to revere the
wonderful achievements of Industrial Man. Our realistic
toys, the remarks of our parents about the neighbor's new

automobile, the urge that animates everyone we know to acquire more and better extensions (the wheels and claws of Industrial Man)—all this profoundly orients us to a definition of happiness that can *only* be fulfilled in outer terms. Even our educational system places its final accent on the preparation of young men and women to meet the external trials and challenges of American life. A great controversy is now raging over this issue in educational circles. Those who are urging a return to the liberal arts have in mind the need for developing inner evaluations and for discovering how to achieve happiness in terms of them. But they are battling against heavy odds. Young people have been taught at home, and by all forms of communication and entertainment with which they come in contact, to externalize their values; hence, when choosing their college courses, they concentrate on that which will enable them to do this, whether it be "journalism," "home engineering," or "traffic safety." It seems to them no more than a kind of academic luxury to inquire into the inner meaning of Aeschylus—or even to know who he was.

Now Americans do not really think that the purposes of life can be defined in terms of iceboxes, washing machines, automobiles, plumbing, and television. On the contrary, it may be said that no people in the world are more willing to respond to a moral challenge, however painful, or to give their loyalty to high purposes that their environment alone cannot define. But the optimistic tradition in which we are steeped has led us deeply into a philosophical trap. The philosophical optimist does not necessarily deny the existence of an inner world, as distinct from an outer or environmental world, but he does not look to it for the real values of existence. Indeed, if he is to remain an optimist, he cannot. It is just from the inner world that his opponent, the philosophical pessimist, derives his view of human existence: that evil is a reality that cannot be eradicated by environmental reform; that the struggle against evil is not merely a struggle against poverty, ignorance, and tyranny, but fundamentally, a struggle in man's soul, in his inner being; and that this struggle is related to, and gains meaning from, the existence of a realm where man has his true home above or beyond the earth realm. If the optimist were to look inward the way the pessimist looks inward, he would come face to face with these propositions in a way that would make optimistic answers impossible. The optimist, therefore, while not denying the inner world, tends to belittle it and may even attempt to show that it is after all nothing but a subjective reflection of the environment. The real values of life, he insists, are the outer ones after all, that can be measured, weighed, handled, and compared, without reference to the uncertainties of the individual psyche.

All this was implicit in the remarks of Mr. Zimmerly at the student discussion group at the University of Illinois. In making his firm distinction between "happiness" and "sacrifice," he was not talking about nothing. For him, as for millions of Americans, happiness had to be grounded in externals. A man who had already done much for his country, he was willing to meet whatever challenges and make whatever sacrifices might be necessary for the preservation of the American way of life; but he could not identify with happiness the realization of the inner values that created such challenges and demanded such sacrifices. For this purpose he believed he had to waive his right to happiness.

It is this contradiction that characterizes the philosophical trap into which the optimistic tradition has led us. We find ourselves acting from high and noble motives, which often actually contradict the values that we declare to be "real." The result is a kind of national frustration in the realm of ideas—the very frustration of which we took note in Part I, when speaking of America's inability to explain to the world what her doctrine of freedom is. The trap arises from the simple fact that in belittling the realities of the inner world, or in trying to explain them away, the philosophical optimist does not expunge them, any more than the ostrich escapes its enemies by hiding its head in the sand. These inner values assert themselves from time to time in crises that human beings cannot avoid. In such crises we find ourselves thrown into conflict with ourselves. We discover that we cannot survive as a nation without sacrificing, but we cannot tell anyone why. The great moral issues of our time, insofar as they pertain to the inner world, cannot be grasped. And our doctrine of freedom, which can survive only insofar as it is able to meet those issues, is reduced to the status of a beggar among the conflicting claims and ambitions of mankind.

5

PARADOX OF PROGRESS

Now some months after the student discussion group in Illinois, just mentioned, *Life* Magazine held a round table on the "Pursuit of Happiness," to which various distinguished representatives of the American way of life were invited. That table did not sustain Mr. Zimmerly in his definition of happiness. In the words of Mrs. Herbert W. Hines (1948 Mother-of-the-Year), "Those people most radiate happiness who seem to forget self in an effort to do the most for others. A mother who sacrifices for her children isn't unhappy over it and certainly I do not think she has to 'waive' her right to pursue happiness." The table undertook to introduce *moral* concepts into the definition of happiness, and some of the members went very far in urging the importance of the inner life and inner evaluations. Said Miss Betsy Barton, author of *And Now to Live Again*, when asked to sum up: "Happiness is primarily an inner state, an inner achievement. In other words, I would like to close by saying that the Kingdom of Heaven is within us."

It is noteworthy, however, that only by a dialectical device did this group of Americans reach general agreement about the right to pursue happiness. The device in question was a mutual agreement "not to raise the question of the *origin* of the moral law or of the great human principles underlying democratic society." This agreement came after a stormy session in which the participants argued far into the night concerning those very origins. Once the question of origins was begged, agreement became possible. If it had not been begged the table would have remained divided—as indeed the nation is divided—to this day.

It seemed to a number of the round table participants themselves that so complex a question as the origin of the moral law could have no practical bearing on the subject in hand. But the ground we have now covered shows that it does. If the moral law originates in an inner world, then the question arises of the nature of that inner world; and if this is in some way connected with a Kingdom of Heaven —as Miss Barton asserted—the optimistic thesis, that the moral law can be fulfilled through environmental reforms, thereupon collapses. Such reforms may, indeed, help to create conditions in which inner evaluations can more easily be realized; but they cannot define what is good, or even define the purposes of life. The agreement "not to raise the question," therefore, was really an agreement not to force the issue against philosophical optimism. In other words, despite the fact that it insisted throughout upon moral evaluations for happiness, the table never really met Mr. Zimmerly's dilemma.

It is, of course, very difficult for Americans to see all this objectively. Granting that we are a nation of doers rather than a nation of thinkers, what on earth can be wrong with this? And what on earth can be wrong in desiring that everyone should participate in the wonderful fruits of industrialization? America has become great and powerful just because her people have so assiduously externalized their values. And of America's greatness and power the free world now stands very much in need.

What we Americans constantly tend to forget, however, is that other peoples of the world simply do not agree with our ideas about happiness. Granting that nothing *on earth* is wrong with those ideas, there still might be something wrong in Heaven. There might be something wrong, that is, in terms of what man really is. It is good to improve man's environment; but the attitude toward life that arises from concentration on this goal raises questions of major importance to humanity as a whole; and it is characteristic of the optimistic tradition that it has failed to answer these questions. This fact can best be clarified by two concrete examples.

Let us take the question of American culture as contrasted with that of Europe. Almost every European visitor has something to say on this subject, and his remarks almost always include such terms as "taste," "refinement," "grace," "enlightenment," etc. The thesis is that Americans are culturally backward, if not barbaric; they are so absorbed in industrialization that they have neglected the gay and graceful intangibles of life, and are incapable of responding to the great cultural achievements of Western civilization.

Stated in this way the case is very difficult to prove. American apologists can show that their country is swarming with cultural activities of all kinds, from Bach to Picasso. In *The Big Change*, for example, Frederick Lewis Allen resorts to impressive statistics: George Orwell's *1984* sold more than 750,000 copies, and a translation of the

Odyssey, more than 350,000; the total attendance at art exhibitions in 1948 was 50 million and "the Department of Commerce says that the sales of art supplies went up from four million dollars in 1939 to forty million in 1949"; and as for music, "fifteen hundred American cities and towns now support annual series of concerts," and "as many as 20,000 sets of Wanda Landowska's harpsichord recordings of the Goldberg Variations were sold during the first three months after they were issued." No doubt the Voice of America could adduce hundreds of such examples of American cultural activity, the net of which would be to show that Americans are avid for culture and pursue it on an enormous scale.

But, as Mr. Allen himself was quite aware, the appreciation of art cannot be measured in statistics. It makes no difference how many millions of people attend an exhibition: the question is whether more than an insignificant minority of them can really *see* the paintings. The kind of "sight" that is involved is not circumscribed by what the observer "sees" with his eyes; it has to do with entities and values in the world of ideas, which lie behind the external manifestations, and which are the stuff of a genuinely cultural experience. To get at the cultural reality of a painting, in short, it is necessary that the observer accept as real certain inner experiences. Only insofar as a society carries such inner experiences over into its life and its evaluations of life, would the European call that society "cultured."

It is probably true that appreciation, if not active participation, extends farther down the social scale in America than in any European country: the French peasant can scarcely be described as a patron of the arts; but the American farmer, or more likely his wife, may be an active agent in supporting a local orchestra or in bringing a famous collection of paintings to town, so that we cannot be accused of *denying* the inner realities that such works of art represent. But what we do, however, is to relegate such inner realities to second place. Since the real values by which we live are external values, and the real achievements by which we measure success are external achievements, our interest in the arts seldom actually gets translated into life. We do not care how ugly our towns are, how cluttered our highways, how uninspiring our churches, how drab our houses, how dismal our furniture, how tasteless our food; for with regard to all of these environmental factors, considerations other than the aesthetic are dominant. These considerations are not derived from the inner world, where aesthetic judgments are made, but from the outer world, where the criteria of usefulness, economy, efficiency, and time-saving prevail. An American town exists for utilitarian purposes, and these are so dominant that its aesthetic development does not even come into the question. When, indeed, Americans decide to "beautify" their towns, this can only be done in a self-conscious way, and may be even more objectionable to the European than the ugly but strictly genuine original.

It is perhaps time for the Europeans to stop calling us "cultural barbarians"; but it is also time for us to realize that in the pursuit of the goal of happiness, as our optimists have defined it, we have carried the externalization of values so far as to make us—in European eyes—culturally unrecognizable.

Let us take the second example. One of the key questions facing Americans today is the survival of our system of private enterprise, and this in turn raises the question of foreign trade and foreign economic development. It is of course true that technical considerations having to do with the tariff, the dollar, the dollar gap, and capital investment are of great importance. Yet in the long run these technical matters cannot be resolved in favor of private enterprise without regard to the philosophy of enterprise. And it is just here that the American optimistic tradition leads us into great difficulties.

In the course of the last several decades the American enterprise system has been in the throes of a bloodless revolution, which is perhaps to be counted among the most important achievements in American history. It has been referred to by some observers as the American "transformation" of the capitalist system, resulting in the emergence of what might be called a "consumer capitalism."[3] In classical capitalism (from which the Marxists originally rebelled) capital was treated as an end in itself; the system existed and was operated for the owners, the capitalists. In the American transformation, however, the capitalist is ousted from his classical position and becomes merely one of five parties—the owner, the management, the worker, the general public, and the consumer. Each of these parties

[3] See, for example, *U.S.A.: The Permanent Revolution* by the Editors of *Fortune* and Russell W. Davenport, New York, Prentice Hall, 1951. Also Frederick Lewis Allen, *The Big Change*, New York, Harper & Brothers, 1952.

has different but rightful claims upon any given business enterprise, especially where the enterprise is a substantial one. The history of the last two decades in America has been largely the history of the establishment of those claims and of their definition. The result has been a dispersal of economic power on a truly democratic scale, and the redefinition of the purpose of the capitalist system in such a way as to recognize economic rights for the common man. Main Street has overcome Wall Street.

Yet that is not quite the end of the matter. There is, of course, a constant internal struggle between the five parties concerned, and in practical economic terms this struggle is held in balance by the party who has the final word—that is to say, the consumer. The ousted capitalist has not been displaced by the worker, as might have been the case in a society with a proletarian bias. He has not been displaced by a political bureaucracy, as is inevitably the case in a society with a Socialist bias. He has not even been displaced by management—an eventuality, predicted by some, which would lead in the direction of a kind of corporative fascism. In the American transformation, the capitalist has been displaced by the consumer. Each individual consumer stands at the economic heart of a vast industrial complex, which exists to serve him. It is he who defines the purpose of the new capitalism.

All this has been highly constructive. It undermines the economic thesis of the Marxists and makes most of their arguments ridiculously obsolete in this country. In addition, because every individual in the world is a consumer, it seems to offer the hope of an economic doctrine having universal appeal. And yet it has wholly failed to rouse the peoples of the earth or to inspire their confidence in American ideals.

And when we search for the reason for this we come out inescapably to the same one that enabled us to account for the cultural misunderstandings between ourselves and Europe: that is to say, to the American tendency to externalize all human values. According to the new capitalism, the consumer gives purpose to the capitalist system, but the question that the American optimists have failed to answer is: What gives purpose to the consumer? Can it be said, for example, that the consumer exists for the purpose of developing those marvelous extensions that give him such an unprecedented command over time and space? The tendency of a high-pressure industrial system is to force an answer in the affirmative. Man may be an end in himself; but the only way he can fulfill himself *as* an end is by acquiring the extensions that his industrialized system demands or makes available. We are thus led into a vicious circle. The rightful end of the industrial system is the consuming individual, but the necessary end of the consuming individual is to consume.

As a result of this inference, which is implicit in the philosophy of enterprise as Americans now preach it, nothing but frustration has greeted American efforts to spread the doctrine of consumer capitalism to other lands. Everywhere the observer turns, he finds the impression that Americans are pure materialists exercising a powerful influence upon men's minds. And the impression is certainly not diluted by the American propaganda, which constantly emphasizes, as its major theme, the material aspects of American life and the material benefits to flow from American programs. The doctrine of consumer capitalism asks, primarily, that consumers should learn to consume; but what Americans find, to their naïve amazement, is that the consumers of the world will not accept this role. They will not consume on anything like the scale that is necessary to support a system of consumer capitalism. In casting about for a means of overcoming this obstacle, the old optimistic theme of "education" usually emerges: if only we could educate the peoples of Europe, Asia, and Africa to know and demand the products of industry, vast markets would be created and "backward" countries would quickly become industrialized. The plain fact is, however, that the peoples of the world—the peoples, even, of highly industrialized countries—are unwilling to accept that definition which is implicit in American industrialization—that the purpose of man's life is the happiness engendered by technological extensions. They are unwilling to be educated along those lines, and American efforts in that direction—often very generous ones—are resented. It may be assumed that every individual in the world desires to improve his lot on earth; but it cannot be assumed that the achievement of this goal answers the final question of human existence.

In the transformation of the capitalist system we have made a great and significant advance in political economy, which, under other circumstances, could be productive of economic and social gains for the entire world—gains which would immensely help to consolidate and stabilize our own. But because we have failed to define, or have taken for granted, our ideas about man's inner nature, our achievement in political economy has thus far inspired very few people beyond our shores. Indeed, the transformation has to some extent worked in the opposite direction. Rather than accept the definition of man that is implied in our industrial optimism, the rest of the world, with but few exceptions, has turned more and more toward socialism and the economic state. With the help of Russian propaganda, America emerges, not as a revolutionary force that has transformed an obsolete capitalist system into a true economic democracy, but as a reactionary power dedicated to the pursuit of happiness in terms of the selfish acquisition and use of private property.

This brings to a sort of climax our observations on Industrial Man, the new species that emerged in the Era of Hope at the turn of the twentieth century. For Industrial Man, we find, is not a god: indeed, his trouble is that he is not even a man. As Americans have interpreted him, through the optimistic tradition, he is a being without an inner life: a sort of highly evolved and well-intentioned animal caught in the toils of a theory of happiness that survives by means of disregarding realities of which real men are made. Industrial Man—and with him, America—has thus fallen into a cruel and perplexing paradox: the brilliance of his outer achievements, the darkness of his inner life. This, the Paradox of Progress, is as excruciating as any that has ever emerged from history, for it represents the dedication of great energies and great intelligence to ends that disappear in the sunless and starless uncertainty of our inner selves. It reveals men toiling, and even dying, for purposes which they cannot define—purposes which, for all they know, may not even exist. The doctrine of progress exacts our labors, challenges our intelligence in countless enterprises, calls us to high and heroic efforts on the beaches of distant lands. But when we turn to ask the reasons for these challenges and exactions, we find ourselves in a dim and nihilistic world, through which we can find no path, because the optimistic tradition in which we have been reared has, in effect, denied its reality.

Americans disguise this predicament from themselves in many ways. One way is not to think about it at all, to pursue the optimistic goals with stoic resignation. Another way is to elevate those goals to the status of dogma, supported by a faith as fervent—if also as blind—as that which animated medieval civilization. Another is to beg the question entirely, as the *Life* round table did; to call ourselves humanists and to preach a doctrine of human cooperation and brotherhood, without in the least explaining what those terms mean, or why those goals should be accepted by human beings at the cost of their lives. This latter course is the most characteristically American and finds expression in almost all of our official propaganda. Yet we have never been able to hide the fact from those whom we propagandize, that we are incapable of evaluating any of our great humanistic projects in truly *human* terms. To do this we should have to break a path to where the light is to be found, deep in the human soul. But the doctrine of progress requires us to leave this task to the Buddhist monk.

6

THE MAKINGS OF AMERICAN TRAGEDY

Now there is only one word to describe all this, and it is a word almost unknown to the optimist's vocabulary. It is the word "tragic." The tragedy of human life on earth, which has been known to seers since the beginning of time, is catching up with America.

The idea that their country should be involved in tragedy is repugnant to Americans—almost intolerable. We find it almost impossible to visualize the destiny of our country in any other terms outside of the optimistic tradition in which we are immersed. For that matter, we have only a rather hazy notion of what tragedy is. The word is connected in our minds with the "sad ending" that Hollywood so studiously avoids, with unhappy events and disappointments. It is not in this sense, however, that the word is here intended. He who views the world from the standpoint of philosophical pessimism, sees man as a tragic figure, not because man is necessarily sad, but because the truths of his inner life, which the pessimist recognizes, do not always conform to the frame of reference of the outer world. Man is caught in a mesh of desires and passions that demand outward expression; yet, more often than not, these conflict with his own inner evaluations of what is good, or beautiful, or just, so that their satisfaction more often than not fails to yield him the happiness that they seem to promise. He is thus a creature of conflict; and his tragedy resides in his inability to resolve this conflict in terms of his own character and endowments.

In America the human tragedy takes a specific form, which is becoming more and more apparent. It is tragedy by default. Involved in evil as we are, we have not *chosen* it, we have not deliberately committed it. In terms of deeds, of overt acts, our claim to a special "innocency" carries a certain weight, and this is not just because we are a young nation, but because our intentions have really been good. We have actually tried to better the lot of man. But for all our good intentions, and for all our extraordinary power, we beget evil, nevertheless. Things have a way of coming out just the opposite of the way we intended. The contemporary world, which we have done so much to shape, is not the kind of world we intended to shape. The postwar era is the very reverse of what we fought for in the war. It is an era of conflict, fear, and aggression, in which the U.S.S.R., who was our great friend, has become our mortal enemy, and Germany, whom we regarded as the destroyer of civilization, has become a promising ally. We dreamed of a world in which the passions of nationalism would gradually be liquidated: instead, nationalism, even among the allies of the free world, has become almost frenetic. We dreamed of peace; but in order to maintain even a vestige of it we have to keep American soldiers and armaments posted all over the earth.

The mid-century, indeed, is a mockery of the Era of Hope. Industrial Man, who was supposed to establish a new, Christian civilization, seems to represent the very antithesis of the spirit of Christ. We placed our faith in science; we find that the powerful offspring of science threaten to destroy us. The exciting technological extensions that were supposed to set man free for the higher purposes of his nature, have tended rather to plunge him into confusion and crisis. In theory, the airplane and other forms of transportation were to have made the earth "smaller"; but trade barriers, blocked currencies, dollar shortages, immigration restrictions, and other fruits of high industrialization, have multiplied the obstacles, and in effect increased the distances, between the earth's peoples. Radio was an intoxicating idea: but in the hands of private parties it has become the tool of commercial nonsense, and in the hands of governments, the purveyor of lies and hate. Far from adding to the enlightenment of humanity, television is supplanting the reading of books and competes against the schools for children's homework time. As Dr. Niebuhr suggests, it threatens to destroy our culture in much the same way as atomic weapons threaten our civilization generally. Industrial Man has indeed acquired new powers. But his ability to use them has not kept pace with his acquisitions.

It is, of course, true that America alone is not responsible for all these reversals and disillusionments. The errors of the industrial world have been committed by every nation in the West, and compounded by the passions and poverty of the East. Yet we are by all odds the leading exponent of the Idea of Industrial Man. Nowhere else in the world has this Idea produced such prosperity, and nowhere else has it evoked from its adherents such lavish promises. The responsibility is inescapably ours, to lead the way out of the errors, to resolve the doubt and fear, to show how technology by which we have set such store can really be used for the purposes for which it was originally intended —the purposes of peace and human development. This, indeed, is what we have all along *intended* to do. But our intentions have become diluted by the philosophy of happiness that has led us just as deeply as anyone else—though by a different route—into selfishness, nationalism, and fear. The tragedy-in-the-making that America represents is the tragedy of a man of good will, who is unable to carry out his good intentions because he is philosophically immature.

7

PATHOLOGY OF DOUBT

Anyone who looks back on the year 1900, and on the peaceful decades on either side of it, will find many things in that Era of Hope that were wrong and even shameful. Nevertheless, he must surely be struck by the fact that there was something rational about that world. However unjust, however restricted, however prejudiced, it had rationality— its very prejudices were supported by reasons, which gave it a confidence that is quite unknown today. It is difficult for our younger generation even to imagine the sense of order and rectitude that pervaded the closing years of Victoria's reign, the world of Rudyard Kipling and the Diamond Jubilee, which stood like a massive and indestructible background for the noisy American experiment; a world of definite moral boundaries, which were often if not easily crossed, but which left little doubt in anybody's mind as to what was "good," what "evil." When we talk about the mood of hope in which the twentieth century dawned, we must see that mood in this context of rationality, and realize that men then at least had the illusion that they could tell the true from the false.

In this respect we have come some distance from the Victorians. We have been thoroughly disillusioned: the human being, we now know, is not necessarily, nor even primarily, rational. Such has been the overwhelming lesson of the wars and political upheavals of our time, the hate,

the lies, the murders, and the destruction. And this collapse
of the illusion of rationality has destroyed confidence.
Doubtless the Victorians also lived in inner darkness, but
they were shielded from it by their illusion. We are not so
shielded; we can, so to speak, see the darkness within us.

The darkness breeds in us an attitude of doubt. Industrial
Man is the Man of Doubt. He lives in inner doubt as a fish
lives in water: it is the all-pervasive element of our time, to
which we have become so accustomed that we are often
unaware of its existence.

The corrosive effect of this inner doubt is changing
the whole outlook of human existence. In a neurotic patient
there is often a kind of hiatus between what he says he will
do and what he actually does. Even discounting the lies
and distortions of our enemies, which are largely deliberate, this same hiatus is observable between the pronouncements and the deeds of our time. In the free world there
is virtually no such thing any more as a national policy, as
the Victorians used the word. Predictable and arguable
policy has been replaced by situations, and what men *say*
about these has little connection with what they actually *do*.

To trace the evidences of this neurotic gap through the
labyrinth of our time would be a major undertaking and
would lead us very far from our theme. But by way of
illustration of how profound and far-reaching its effects
can be, let us briefly consider that extraordinary product
of Western diplomacy known as the Atlantic Charter.
Self-consciously named to suggest that it was on a par with
Magna Carta and other great human milestones, this

document is freighted with high-sounding phrases: "no territorial changes," the restoration of "sovereign rights of self-government," "access on equal terms to the trade and the raw materials of the world," "the fullest co-operation between all nations in the economic field with the object of securing, for all, improved labor standards, economic adjustment and social security," "freedom from fear and want," "freedom of the seas," and the abandonment "for realistic as well as spiritual reasons . . . of the use of force." Scarcely anybody in the Atlantic world could disagree with these lofty aspirations, but it would be interesting to know how far the authors of the document seriously examined their own ability to carry out its pledges and hopes. The framing of the Atlantic Charter was, after all, a voluntary and gratuitous act: there was nothing at that juncture that made such a wide and inclusive policy commitment necessary. Undoubtedly it was felt that a statement of "war aims" would advance the allied cause and help to justify the lend-lease program to which Mr. Roosevelt was committing the United States. Yet the historical fact is that none of these aims has been fulfilled in any substantial way. And the cynicism evoked throughout the world by our failure to fulfill them has been one of the major factors strengthening the Communist attack.

As a single example consider what happened to Poland. It is not our purpose here to fix blame, and especially not to attempt to decide, as between Great Britain and the United States, which was more at fault. The general verdict of history will be that Poland was betrayed. The characteristic of this betrayal, however, was that it was not deliberate; no one intentionally engineered it. The betrayal, we may say, was committed before the events occurred, in the announcement of guaranties so far removed from reality as to be already, in effect, lies. Of all the peoples living under Hitler's heel, or in exile from countries invaded by the Nazi armies, none had a better right than the Poles to invoke the assurances of the Atlantic Charter that the signatories "wish to see sovereign rights and self-government restored to those who have been forcibly deprived of them." For Poland was the symbol of why the war was being fought. The incredible bravery of her people under the first onslaught of the German *Blitzkrieg* had added to the popular enthusiasm for her cause. And even after the Russians, newly allied with Germany in the Molotov-Ribbentrop Pact, hit the Poles from the east, they still held out, at a terrible cost in blood and human suffering.

Both Mr. Churchill and Mr. Roosevelt were keenly aware of the justice of the Polish cause and the strength of the Polish claim. Yet already on July 31, 1941, a matter of days before the Atlantic meeting, the British had brought such pressure on the Polish government-in-exile as to force that body to sign the Sikorski-Maisky Pact, which restored diplomatic relations between Poland and the U.S.S.R., but without the clear-cut agreement on boundaries that the Poles felt to be necesary. Despite this fact, Churchill considered himself justified in signing the pledges of the Atlantic Charter, and his act reassured the Poles. Nevertheless, beneath their confidence the Poles had qualms, and these turned out to be well founded. Stalin began insisting that the new Polish boundary be fixed at the "Curzon line," which corresponded roughly to the hated Molotov-Ribbentrop line. The seizure of Polish territory up to this line in 1939 had been generally branded a clear violation of Polish territorial integrity. First Britain, then the U.S., gave in to Stalin's pressure, because of their fear that Stalin would otherwise sign a separate German peace. In December, 1943, at Teheran, an actual deal with Stalin appears to have been effected—without any consultation with the Poles—accepting the Curzon line, and even throwing in the city of Lwow, which had never, up to 1939, been in Russian hands. And finally, at Yalta, the Allies confirmed this surrender to Stalin, by withdrawing recognition from the Polish government-in-exile, which had fought so valiantly side by side with them, in favor of Stalin's puppet regime, which then took over.

Yet so deeply were the signatories caught in the neurotic gap that all during this period of betrayal they led the world, and particularly the Poles, to believe that never under any circumstances would they let Poland down. Thus in June, 1944, six months after the secret deal was made at Teheran, the Polish Premier-in-exile, Stanislaw Mikolajczyk, arrived in Washington and was warmly greeted by President Roosevelt. "Don't worry," said Roosevelt, "Stalin doesn't intend to take freedom from Poland. He wouldn't dare do that because he knows the United States Government stands solidly behind you. I will see that Poland does not come out of this war injured."[4] And even as late as the

---

[4] Stanislaw Mikolajczyk, *The Rape of Poland*, New York, Whittlesey House, 1948, p. 59.

Presidential campaign of that year, the President, sitting under a map of undivided Poland, received a delegation of prominent Polish-Americans, and assured them of his interest in Poland as the "bulwark of a permanent peace."[5] Whether or not the implication was intended, the Polish-Americans interpreted the incident to mean that Mr. Roosevelt would prevent a division of Poland. The map, however, was just "words": Poland was already divided.

Thus was the Atlantic Charter finally and flagrantly flaunted in regard to a nation whose integrity had seemed important enough in 1939 to justify the launching of a second world war. The formal recognition of Stalin's puppet regime in Warsaw by the United States was scheduled for July 4, 1945. The Polish Ambassador, Mr. Ciechanowski, mentioned to the State Department that "it would perhaps be more tactful not to withdraw recognition of a legal government on that day, if only as a mark of respect for certain, perhaps naive, susceptibilities on the part of Americans of Polish descent and of the Polish people, who attached sentimental importance to this historic date." The betrayal was therefore shifted to July 5.

"I recalled," Ciechanowski continues,

my earlier conversations with President Roosevelt: his many spontaneous expressions of tribute to and high appreciation of Poland; his written and spoken promises of American support for the cause of Poland's independence; his stirring declaration about Poland's war effort and her "unsurpassed Allied loyalty"; his public definition of Poland as "the inspiration of nations."

[5] Arthur Bliss Lane, *I Saw Poland Betrayed*, Indianapolis, Bobbs Merrill, 1948, pp. 59-61.

I recalled President Roosevelt's promises to the Polish-American Congress of Americans of Polish descent, "that he would never allow Poland to again be dominated by a foreign power."[6]

It is easy for partisan politicians to turn such duplicity against a rival administration. They can do so, however, only by using hindsight which those involved in the actual events of history did not possess. To blame Franklin Roosevelt and Winston Churchill for this and other tragic betrayals is really to miss the point. For the betrayals were not desired; they were, rather, chosen as lesser evils, in so far as the statesmen concerned could judge them. He who reads history well will understand that these betrayals were not in the nature of any particular man but in the nature of the time. We are all implicated in them. They arose from the chronic inability of mid-twentieth-century Western civilization to couple word and deed in a rational way, and from the need, therefore, to deal in situations rather than true policies. And they were enormously magnified by the incurable optimism of an American President, who could not believe that Stalin "intended to take freedom from Poland," because, being typical of his people, as Roosevelt surely was, he did not realize what the real world issues were.

The Atlantic Charter was hailed by an overwhelming majority of the American people when it appeared. And yet under no administration have we lived up to it. This is not merely a question of the betrayal of Poland, and the Baltics, and the Balkans, and Czechoslovakia, and China, and Man-

[6] Jan Ciechanowski, *Defeat in Victory*, New York, Doubleday, 1947, p. 385.

churia, and Korea (across the middle of which we drew that foolish line), but virtually everything else that the Charter stood for has been betrayed. How fervently have Western peoples pursued the goal, "access, on equal terms, to the trade and to the raw materials of the world?" Not enough to grant it even within their own spheres of influence. The most significant step in this direction, the internationalizing of European coal and steel resources remains an uncertain quantity and Europe is still a network of trade and exchange controls. And as for the United States, "economic co-operation between all nations" is so far from the economic actualities of American life that tremendous pressures have been exerted on *every* administration to maintain tariff barriers to prevent it. The pledges of the Atlantic Charter are glittering generalities which no nation in the world would dare to count on. Yet the extraordinary fact is that we take no little pride in those empty pledges. Few Americans, if given the choice, would wish to have the Atlantic Charter expunged from history. Its high, oratorical aims represent their *intentions*, and they have not felt the need to make these conform with reality, nor yet realized that hell might be paved with them.

8

THE TREMENDOUS PHRASES

The history of our time, in short, is a history of phrases, which rise to great power and then as suddenly pass away: the "merchants of death," the "malefactors of great wealth," "monopoly," "reactionaries," "liberals," the "labor power," "America first," "cash and carry," "unconditional surrender," "peace in our time," "collective security," "bring the boys home," "disarmament," "the Red menace," "the atomic potential," etc., etc. At the time of their currency, few men have had either the courage or the resources to stand up against these tremendous shibboleths. They develop unpredictable authority. Men are destroyed by them, and others are raised to power, and others are rallied to a fighting cause, and wars are declared, and peoples driven from their homes. And after all this havoc has been wreaked, suddenly the phrase disappears and is powerful no more—indeed, is lost and forgotten and replaced by something else, very likely its exact opposite. Nobody seems to understand how and why phrases live and grow in this way, but it is a terrifying thing. And it is terrifying, not just because the phrases result in so much blood and suffering, but because they raise an awful question. They raise the question of truth. Where, in all this, is truth? Or is there any such thing at all?

The modern individual is taught to look with pity on the mental powers of his ancestors, which were so unscientific

and superstitious. He is encouraged to think for himself on
the basis of known facts—that is to say, on the basis of
externalized knowledge. Yet the truth is that his vaunted
sciences, which limit themselves to this kind of knowledge,
merely lose him in mazes of facts without giving him any
guidance as to their human, their inner, meaning. These
facts, he is told, support certain opinions. But no opinion
can be based on *all* of the facts, for who in the world can
know all of the facts? On what, then, are these opinions
based? Few people come to grips with this question, but
they instinctively fear the answer. The opinions are just—
opinions. Anybody can have an opinion, and anybody can
amass facts to support it, since there are lots and lots of
facts. But the truly terrifying thing is that some of these
opinions become the foci of passions, and give birth to
symbols that rule the actions of whole areas of the earth.
The separation of word and deed has had the peculiar result, that words, in the form of popular phrases, have taken
on a strange, demonic life of their own, against which reason cannot in the least prevail.

So the mood of doubt leads into fear, which pervades
our time and colors all our decisions: the fear of economic
collapse, of depression, of want, even of starvation; the
fear of labor, the fear of capital, the fear of government;
the fear of Russia, the fear of America, the fear—which
overshadows all fears—of the West by the East and of the
East by the West. Fear has become endemic to mid-twentieth-century civilization. For what causes mid-century man
to fear is not merely the threat of some definable catastro-

phe: it is the knowledge, born of doubt, that he does not know how to resolve the problems that have in them the makings of catastrophe. His situation is generally catastrophic, because he is alone in the midst of opinions, including his own, that he cannot trust. All he knows is that at any moment somebody's opinion may take life, and grow, and become invincibly powerful. It may turn against a minority, or promote some prejudice against which no one dares to speak, or galvanize a labor union to an unnecessary strike; or it may just result in a new fashion suddenly making obsolescent all his wife's dresses. In any case, there is no controlling these mysterious, irrational forces, once they begin to grow. But what is even worse is that there is no way of telling whether any particular one of the emotionalized opinions is right or wrong, whether it is good or evil, whether it is something to be supported or something to be resisted. Men are left in darkness to decide for themselves. And in this darkness they know fear.

Such is the pass into which an optimistic thesis has led us—an optimism which was rich in promise and the lure of new adventure, but tragically deficient in the knowledge of man. And just because, in one way or another, every American was steeped in such philosophical optimism, having been educated in it at school and surrounded by it all his life, the U.S. is now in the throes of a disillusionment greater than any it has ever as a nation experienced. There is nothing romantic about *this* disillusionment, as there was after World War I. We are not looking over our shoulders as we write about it. In fact, we don't even write about it much, we would not know what to say. We carry it around in our hearts as a kind of dread—a question that we cannot answer—a feeling of doom that we cannot altogether explain. It seeps into our political oratory, into our press, and pervades our thinking. The mood of hope is gone. The high expectations have collapsed. We rake over the rubbish of the past, the phrases and rallying cries that had once seemed so lustrous—the "dignity of man," "human brotherhood," the "sanctity of the person," the "consent of the governed," "liberty or death," "the four freedoms." These old torches do indeed flare up again when we wave them, but we can always see the darkness, now, beyond the circle of light. We know there is always the imminent danger that the re-used torches will suddenly die out, to leave as our only light the irreversible explosion of a hydrogen bomb.

III

THE ADVANCE OF
MATERIALISM

1

SCIENCE AND METASCIENCE

We have tried to show how truth has been corrupted and how America may be losing the world to the corrupters. We have also tried to show how Americans became lost in the pursuit of the doctrine of optimism, and now stand frustrated in a world quite different from that which they, as men of good will, intended. The time has arrived in our study to deal at length with the enemy, whom we have identified as Dialectical Man.

The student of our time who reads Frederick Engels' Introduction to the *Dialectics of Nature* will find himself on familiar terrain. Here, ensconced in handsome prose, and supported by a preface from the pen of the eminent British scientist, J. B. S. Haldane, is a concise and lucid statement of that scientific view of Nature that dominates virtually all of twentieth-century thinking. This essay (which exists largely in the form of notes) includes, of course, a great number of scientific anachronisms, because it was written in the eighteen-seventies, before what we would call contemporary science was born. But the striking thing about it is that it expresses so clearly certain beliefs regarding man and the universe, which, with some variations, are accepted as "what every schoolboy knows."

To begin with, the idea of a supernatural Creator is swept to one side as altogether unworthy of scientific consideration. It is true, of course, that many Western thinkers, who are otherwise in agreement with the scientific view, do not dismiss the Almighty quite so summarily. Some still adhere to the Christian faith; others, who do not actively profess the faith, still agree that the idea of a supernatural Creator is a philosophical necessity. Outside of the churches, however, and even inside of many of them, the idea of a Creator is not usually permitted to interfere with the story that science has to tell. The great majority of laymen, philosophers, and scientists would concur with Engels in asserting, not only that our world has "come into being in the course of time," but that this coming into being can be accounted for by purely natural causes—or, to use the preferred Engelian term, *materialistic* causes.

Engels begins, for example, with Kant, Laplace, and Herschel, who taught that the sun and planets had condensed out of a rotating nebula through the action of forces inherent in matter. This theory, of course, has now been discredited, but the modern versions of the same event proceed from the same general hypothesis, *viz.*, that the origin of the earth was naturalistic. Thence it is but a few steps, as Engels shows, via geology, paleontology, and allied sciences, to the idea that the earth itself has come into being through the action of other materialistic or naturalistic forces working through time. Organic chemistry then steps in to assert that that state of existence that we call life was the result of still other such forces evoked by the proper conditions of moisture and temperature. Thus life arose from the bosom of matter, and the story proceeds:

"If, finally, the temperature became so far equalized

that over a considerable portion of the surface [of the earth] at least it does not exceed the limits within which protein is capable of life, then, if other chemical conditions are favorable, living protoplasm is formed." But this is not the end of the materialistic process. "Thousands of years may have passed before the conditions arose in which the next advance could take place and this formless protein produce the first cell by formation of nucleus and cell membrane. But this first cell also provided the foundation for the morphological development of the whole organic world." Thereafter, unicellular organisms "were gradually differentiated into the first plants and others into the first animals; and finally mammals, the form in which the nervous system attains its fullest development; and among these again finally that mammal in which nature attains consciousness of itself—man."[1]

Now it is not our task at present to examine the validity of the various hypotheses from which Engels derives this familiar thesis; we are concerned only with the point of view, the "scientific" way of thinking, out of which the thesis grows. And yet the term is very ambiguous. What is the "scientific" point of view? What does it represent? What is the difference between scientific thinking and any other kind of thinking? To a limited extent we shall attempt to meet these and other questions in the next Part, when we come to inquire into some of the thought processes that

[1] Frederick Engels, *Dialectics of Nature*, New York, International Publishers, pp. 8-17.

make the modern world what it is. But there is one question that cannot be deferred, which has to do with the basic distinction between those two great forms of inquiry, science and philosophy.

The very first thing we must note about science in this connection is that it is not primarily philosophical but primarily technical. Scientific knowledge is derived from the application to any given problem of certain methods of inquiry, based upon objective observation, analysis, measurement, controlled experiment, etc. These techniques do not necessarily lead to philosophical conclusions, or even raise philosophical questions. Using our words in a rather strict sense, we can say that science has no philosophical view whatever of man or Nature. The investigation of the atomic nucleus does not require the atomic physicist to enter into a debate regarding the nature of being. He may, of course, enter that debate, and he may use his scientific knowledge for that purpose; but the scientific knowledge is not in itself philosophical knowledge, and a scientist entering the field of philosophy without adequate preparation can be just as much of a duffer as a philosopher entering (similarly unprepared) the field of science.

Nevertheless, directly and indirectly, the natural sciences have had profound influences upon philosophy. Thinkers like Arthur Eddington and Bertrand Russell have freely coursed back and forth between philosophy and science to reach their conclusions about man. Other philosophers have conscientiously studied the sciences and their methods. Between the philosophers on the one hand and the scientists on the other, lay thinkers have been busy borrowing from both, passing on to the public their versions of the meaning of various scientific hypotheses, some of which (as, for example, the descent of man from the apes) have become so firmly fixed that their hypothetical character has been virtually forgotten. The result is a body of thought which rests upon scientific hypotheses and discoveries, but which extends far beyond the limits of science into a field of speculation that involves all the major questions of metaphysics.

Now, strangely enough, speculations in this field have no name: they are neither philosophy nor science, but a kind of hybrid between the two. And yet a suitable term for them is really not very far to seek. Metaphysics itself has been defined as the study of the fundamental problems relating to the ultimate nature of reality (ontology) and of human knowledge (epistemology). And this definition virtually thrusts upon us the suitable term for the kind of speculation in question. The term is *metascience*. It is the characteristic of this speculative field that it involves us inescapably in either ontology or epistemology, or both, as the works of such giants as Eddington and Whitehead have shown. Metascience in our definition, therefore, is a philosophical superstructure erected upon a foundation of scientific discovery and hypothesis—a form of inquiry having its roots in the experimental findings of science and its topmost branches in the high speculations of metaphysics.

There are, of course, various schools of metascience, just as there are various schools of metaphysics, and some are better grounded than others, or more influential, or more popular, etc. These distinctions need not concern us here. The important thing is to grasp the difference between a genuinely scientific speculation, and a metascientific one. That the sun and planetary system are not located at the center of our galaxy, but far toward its edge, in one of its huge spiral arms, is a scientific hypothesis for which much evidence has been adduced. But the inference so frequently drawn from this and allied hypotheses, that the existence of man is as accidental and eccentric as the apparent position of the solar system, pertains, not to science, but to metascience. The fact that the planet is to be found near the edge of the universe is taken by the metascientists as evidence that man is not, and never has been, the center of God's attention, as the ancients supposed. The fact that both planet and man are immeasurably small in relation to the universe as a whole, is taken as further evidence to the same effect.

Or, in another field, the fact that certain genetic characteristics can definitely be traced to certain genes, which in turn occupy certain known positions in the chromosomes, is taken to indicate that it is unnecessary to consult any supernatural source for the explanation of man's character, which can, on the contrary, be entirely accounted for by hereditary factors that are ultimately chemical in nature. And so forth. Metascience, in short, projects scientific hypotheses beyond the field of their own data into a metaphysical field. It extends the findings of experiment into questions pertaining to the origin, nature, and meaning of things, and particularly, of man.

In an age in which the chief advances in knowledge have come from experimentation and scientific analysis, this is certainly a legitimate and necessary area of speculation. Unhappily, however, the metascientist has not, on the whole, been as scrupulous as the scientist in the collection and examination of his data. The result is that many important conclusions are reached (always in the name of science) that have no adequate scientific foundation. Science has never shown, for example, that the universe—or earth, or man—came into being without supernatural attention. This may be a fair assumption, but it is nothing more than an assumption, and he who is willing to look can find a great deal of evidence to support the idea of supernatural origin.[2] Such is the power of science over the human imagination in our time, however, that the metascientist is permitted great license. Untrammeled by experimentation, which strictly disciplines the sciences themselves, the metascientist all too often borrows whatever he may need from science and philosophy alike, and leaves out whatever may be inconvenient. He thus builds a towering edifice, which is founded upon science, but which soars upward into realms of speculation beyond the reach of the instruments and techniques of scientific knowledge. Whether true or false, these cathedral-like structures of the intellect stir the imagination and exercise enormous influence over the souls of men. Metascience is to our day what poetic myth and legend were to the ancients—the most powerful intellectual and cultural

[2] See, for example, LeComte du Noüy, *Human Destiny;* also Gustav Strömberg, *The Soul of the Universe;* Ernst Lehrs, *Man or Matter.*

factor of the time. It has overturned religions, changed morals, revolutionized economics, perverted politics, altered the whole approach to education, and led us out to a view of man different from any that has ever before been held.

Now Marx and Engels claimed a scientific status for all their work, without reservation. This claim, it is important to note, was made before Engels undertook to write the *Dialectics of Nature* or any other work in the field of natural science. Indeed, neither Marx nor Engels occupied himself with the natural sciences in more than a cursory way until long after he had reached his basic conclusions from other sources and by other methods. In his preface to the tract generally referred to as *Anti-Dühring*, Engels admits this. He and Marx, he says, had so much to occupy their attention that they could not keep up with the natural sciences, interested though they were. It was not until he (Engels) gave up his business and retired to London that he really had a chance to inquire into the natural sciences; at which point he was able "to convince myself in detail—of what in general I was not in doubt—that amid the welter of innumerable changes taking place in nature, the same dialectical laws of motion are in operation as those which in history govern the apparent fortuitousness of events."

On what, then, was the Marxian claim to science based? The point is a rather subtle one that cannot be resolved by saying that it was based on nothing at all. It is perfectly true that Marx's claim that he was the first to approach

social, economic, and political problems in the same way
as the natural scientist approaches problems in physics,
chemistry, etc., cannot stand critical scrutiny. His work was
not based upon experimentation, or an experimental *attitude*—it even falls far short of a strictly objective analysis
of social phenomena. Its hopelessly *un*scientific character
has been the subject of complaint by those who, in many
other respects, have looked favorably upon Marxian views.
As Sidney Hook puts it, "the conclusions of science were
celebrated but its methods hardly studied." Nevertheless,
Marx's claim is not wholly without meaning. There *is* a
connection between Marxism and the natural sciences, but
it is not to be found where most persons have looked for it
—that is to say, in the realm of logic or the realm of
science. It is to be found only in the realm of metascience.
Marx's Dialectical Materialism had its true origin in metaphysics; but it also incorporated an idea of man identical
with that which was embodied in the prevailing metascientific doctrines of his day. That is why, when Engels
finally got around to the natural sciences, everything they
had to say about man and his origins corroborated everything that Marx and Engels had already said. This did not
prove that Dialectical Materialism was scientific, as their
followers have claimed. It proved only that Marx's metascience had all along been in conformance with his time.

We have approached Dialectical Materialism from this
scientific side, rather than the more conventional philosophic or social sides, in order to gain some comprehension

of its real power. Philosophically, few important doctrines have ever been more vulnerable: Western philosophers have riddled it full of holes and broken it on its own inconsistencies. Socially, few doctrines have ever been more repulsive: many of its own adherents view Dialectical Materialism with cynicism. *But as a metascience* it has thus far been unshakable. It represents a view of man that has become increasingly popular and increasingly authoritative during the past century. It managed to represent this view even before Engels got around to writing his "scientific" works; but those works, in which the metaphysical principles that Marx had espoused were apparently confirmed by the natural sciences themselves, gave the doctrine a metascientific standing which has been virtually unassailable ever since. From then on, it could not be mistaken for any mere economic or social theory, but stood out boldly as a whole Idea of Man, his origin and his destiny—an Idea which, purportedly, could draw upon the sciences themselves for its verification.

In the war of ideas, this fact is of great significance. During the past century or so, the thinkers of the free world have also indulged in metascience, giving expression to various "scientific" views of man and nature. If we ask ourselves what view has had the widest acceptance, we are forced to something very similar to Engels' materialism. It is of course true that most thinkers of the free world shun the term "materialism," as such. They prefer the word "naturalism"; they speak, not of material causes but of natural causes. But at bottom their thesis is the same as

Engels'. The universe was created out of matter by the operation of the laws of matter; and these laws in turn led eventually to the creation of life, animals, and man. The idea that any "supernatural" force or intelligence was at work in the long process of creation, is dismissed as primitive, unscientific, and naïve. Everything can and must be accounted for in material-naturalistic terms. This principle, indeed, together with its elaborations, has become a sort of dogma: one cannot question it seriously without being counted irrational or uneducated, or in some manner blindly prejudiced, as by the teachings of the Church. In other words, except for the dialectic (which we shall examine presently), the metascientific view of Marx and Engels is to a great extent the same as that of the rest of the Western world.

Generally speaking, this virtual identity between the metascience of the free world and that of communism, is not viewed with much alarm by anti-Communist thinkers. If these materialistic or naturalistic propositions are correct, they deserve universal recognition. No one, surely, would assert that because the Communists believe them we of the free world should reject them! That would be far from a scientific attitude. But the fact that the free world must face—which by and large it has not faced—is that *if* the materialistic-naturalistic thesis is correct, *then the case for communism is stronger than the case for the free way of life*. Matter is not free, in any meaningful sense of the word; the concept of man as a materially created being is, therefore, incapable of giving freedom any meaning. If man is the product of a combination of law and accident, his freedom can only be an illusion; and communism spares man the dreadful and futile struggle for this illusion by defining freedom in terms of the very opposite of freedom—in terms of human conformance to the laws of matter, as these may be interpreted by the masters of the society.

There are many in the free world who will disagree with this statement of the case—in particular (and perhaps most vehemently) those philosophical optimists who, as we have seen, have played such a dominant role in the development of American thought. These people have, in general, accepted a materialistic-naturalistic metascience, and yet they have believed that they could lead the free world to victory over the Communist world. It is our view that they are profoundly mistaken. If the Engelian metascience is correct, we would contend, then the Engelian-Marxian political economy is approximately correct. Their doctrine is bound together in a living way that defies both logic and science. It is like a strange and disagreeable poem based upon images that belong together, inherently. In the end, after all the elaborate argument and technicalities, it rests upon the simple proposition that if man is the product of matter and its inexorable laws, then communism is a much better solution for him than individual freedom —a much *wiser* solution. And that, as contemporary history has shown, is a very powerful proposition indeed.

Now let us acquaint ourselves in somewhat more detail with the doctrine of Dialectical Materialism itself, and with that image of man arising from it which we have called Dialectical Man. To the layman who has never attempted this before the next two or three chapters may seem somewhat abstruse. The truth is, however, that Dialectical Materialism really is abstruse, and there is no way for the honest investigator to avoid this fact. It is only by wrestling with its strange and perverse ratiocinations (at least in lay terms) that we can hope to gain a better understanding of our enemy, and of ourselves.

2

THE ABSOLUTIST REVOLUTION

The founder and father of Dialectical Materialism was surely one of the most ambiguous figures in history. His life was compounded of irreconcilable extremes, and these are reflected in the doctrine that he created. The dominant motif of his life was bitterness. The son of a Jew turned Christian, he was against everything and almost everybody—against religion, against his preceptors at the universities he attended, against the various governments under which he lived, against the Socialist leaders whom he aspired to lead: Karl Marx against the world.

He was a man of great pretensions; an intellectual whose vast learning barred him, because of the peculiar way he insisted upon twisting it, from an understanding of many important areas of human culture; a champion of the proletariat who was in no sense a proletarian; an idealist in the complete reversal of idealism; a metaphysician by temperament who sought his solution in the study of economics in the British Museum; a hater of the capitalist system, who nevertheless derived most of his living expenses from the "exploitation" of the workers in a British textile business. Two aspects only of his life shed a warm glow over the pages of his bleak biography. One was his love of Jenny von Westphalen, the daughter of a high government official, whom he married and who stood with him in loyal devotion throughout all his trials. The other was his extraordinary friendship with Engels, who was much more like a brother than a friend, and on whom he was almost completely dependent for his livelihood. The rest is poverty, pride, frustration, disillusionment—and hate.

The works of this "mover and shaker" of history are unashamedly dull. His chief work, *Das Kapital,* is an enormous tract that he never finished, compounded of closely reasoned economic argument based upon premises that he never really substantiated. And yet a peculiar magic pervades this and his other works. It is not a magic to which Americans can easily respond, for the American development, both economic and philosophical, has in large part taken place outside of the forces that gave birth to the writings of Marx. But we shall utterly fail to come to grips with Marxism unless we recognize that the magic is there, reflecting forces that have played a critical role in shaping the outlook of modern man. The close ratiocination, wholly divorced at times from reality; the peculiar mixture of prejudice and science, of will and fact, of extreme idealism and extreme disenchantment—all this is somehow representative of Industrial Man, his hopes and disillusionments, as he has developed beyond the parochial limits of the American Constitution. The greatest error that free peoples can make is to try to deal with Marxism on the basis of reason. For Marxism is above all an elaborate rationalization of subconscious forces that industrialization has brought into being. But in that fact lies its magic. And in its magic lies the secret of its power.

The fact is not as well recognized as it should be, that the great political upheaval of the eighteenth century incorporated, not one revolution, but two, one libertarian, the other absolutist. Both of these revolutions are still going on, both are still pressing toward their goals. But they stand today in mortal conflict. This conflict arises from a profound disagreement regarding the individual human being—what he is, what he ought to be, what he might become—his relationship to other human beings, and most pointedly of all, his relationship to the state.

The libertarian revolution with which Americans are familiar treated the ideal of liberty in a literal and practical way. Men were to be left free to work out their own destinies with a minimum of interference from their political institutions. The libertarian revolution recognized a limitless diversity in individual desires and interests; its great political goal was the development of a system in which diversity would be not only recognized but encouraged. Almost all of the American founders gave explicit support to this principle, but none more so than James Madison, who referred to it under the heading of "faction." Nothing, says Madison, is more dangerous to the public peace than faction, which if uncontrolled, can tear the society apart. What then shall we do about it? In the *Tenth Federalist Paper* (1788) he proceeds to answer this question by a line of argument fundamental to the libertarian thesis.

Two methods of controlling faction suggested themselves to Madison—removing its causes, or controlling its effects. "There are again two methods of removing the causes . . . : the one by destroying the liberty which is essential to its existence: the other, by giving to every citizen the same opinions, the same passions, and the same interests." Of the first of these, he says, "It is worse than the disease." The second is as impracticable as the first would be unwise, for the "latent causes of faction are sown in the nature of man." As long as there are "diversities in the faculties of men," or a connection between "reason and self-love," or "a zeal for different opinions concerning religions, concerning government, and many other points," so long will there be factions. The cure, in short, cannot be applied to the causes of faction without indulgence in outright tyranny. So we can deal with this inherent problem, Madison asserted, only by learning how to control its effects. To this end, the Constitution and federal structure of government, with their checks and balances, their protection of minorities and of the individual, provided the most promising answer.

But while the libertarian revolution was thus building a groundwork for freedom in terms of individual differences, the other revolution was firing the European Continent, and especially France, to goals of quite another sort. This was the intoxicating movement Carl Becker called "The Heavenly City of the Eighteenth Century Philosophers." Its early prophets were such theorists as Morelly, Mably, Helvétius, Baron d'Holbach, Condorcet, and Rousseau; and the men who first sought to realize their prophecies in practice were Robespierre, Saint-Just, Babeuf, and Buonarroti. Like Madison these revolutionaries claimed as their point of departure the "nature of man," and like him also they claimed individual freedom as their goal. But these similarities concealed very different concepts. The hero of this other revolution was not man-as-he-is but man-as-he-ought-to-be. Its leaders were dominated by an ideal of perfectibility and by a determination so to reform society as to achieve that ideal. In an age infatuated with the orderly mechanics of Newton's laws, the revolutionaries bent their energies to discover a unitary principle that would provide the solution to all social ills. In harmony with Madison again, they found this principle in self-interest; but their quest for perfection led them in a direction quite opposite to his. Man, they insisted, was inherently good. Hence, if the contemporary order of inequality were replaced by the "natural" order of equality, self-interest would unite men rather than divide them. Once the ideal order was established, and pursued without deviation, the natural goodness of man would assert itself to produce a society that would be perfectly democratic.

These perfectionist ideas had profound effects upon the libertarian revolution. Thomas Jefferson, for example, was deeply influenced by them. Especially at the beginning, the conflict between the two movements was often obscured. One had its being primarily in England and America, the other in France and the Continent, yet their ideas jumped back and forth across the Channel and the Atlantic. Voltaire and Montesquieu, although French thinkers, belong more properly to the libertarian tradition; their masters were such Englishmen as Locke and Hume. And Montesquieu, in turn, greatly influenced the men who framed the

American Constitution. On the other hand, the tradition of American philosophical optimism, which we have examined, draws deeply on the French *philosophes*.

The antagonisms of the two revolutions become at once apparent, however, when we turn to the problem that constantly faced the perfectionists, of how man-as-he-is can be converted into man-as-he-ought-to-be. Obviously, a period of education was needed, in order to eliminate the bad habits of the past and to establish the habits and patterns of true freedom. It was essential to bring every individual into agreement with the harmonious whole, even though it were necessary, as Rousseau put it, to "compel him to be free." Never in history, perhaps, has there been invented so perfect a formula for tyranny. What the absolutist revolutionaries devised was a rationale and justification, in the very terms of freedom, for the imposition of the will of the few upon the will of the many. We are thus led out to the exact antithesis of the Madisonian approach.

In his book on this movement, J. L. Talmon has applied to it the term "totalitarian democracy." The phrase is descriptive and useful; however, it has the disadvantage that the word "totalitarian" has acquired certain meanings that were quite unknown to those eighteenth-century visionaries. That is why we prefer, as more accurate, the term "absolutist." The single most characteristic trait of all the thinkers named, and of all the actions that flowed directly from their thoughts, was their willingness and ability to accept political absolutes, to which, in order to be "free" all men must conform. The French Revolutionists were animated, to use Talmon's words, by "the faith in a single and final cause of and answer to all evils the world over; the belief that the secret has at last been found, that humanity is heading in an irresistible march for some denouement, a violent break-through to a pre-ordained, perfect and ultimate scheme of things." Under the spell of such ideas, the Madisonian tolerance of faction was a kind of heresy. "*Il faut une volonté une* (There must be one will, one only)," wrote Robespierre. "Factions," the division of wills, is "the most terrible poison of the body politic," forcing the citizen to "choose between crime and crime." There could be no true republic until all factions were rooted out: precisely the opposite of Madison's libertarian proposition that a successful republic can be created only if faction is permitted to exist.

But this very absolutist quality made the Continental revolution an intoxicating affair. The painful and bloody period of education was worth the cost because of the magnificent result to be attained. This was to be nothing less than a perfect society, a heaven on earth, in which men would live with their fellow men in virtue and harmony; an order of society that could not conflict with individual liberty, since it would guarantee to every individual the fullest satisfaction of his wants, both physical and spiritual. This absolute and heavenly denouement shimmers in the fiery oratory of the time, reverberating through the bloody streets of Paris. "We want an order of things," cried Robespierre, "where all base and cruel passions would be chained, all the benevolent and generous passions awakened by the laws, where one's ambition would be to merit glory and serve his country; where distinctions would have no other source than equality itself . . . where all souls grow greater through the continuous interchange of republican sentiments. . . . We want to substitute in our country morality for egotism, probity for honor, principles for habits, duties for good manners, the empire of reason for the tyranny of fashion, the contempt of vice for the contempt of misfortune . . . a people magnanimous, powerful, happy, for a people amiable, frivolous and miserable, that is to say all the virtues and all the miracles of the Republic for all the vices and absurdities of the Monarchy."

What we have here is not sheer demagoguery—as the twentieth-century libertarian might be tempted to suspect—but a messianic movement with religious overtones, whose followers displayed the zeal of religious fanatics. And the fact is that although many of the prophets of this movement professed to be Christian, and many of their ideals appear to coincide with Christian precepts, they were really engaged in creating a new, secular religion that could not fail to bring them into complete opposition to Christianity itself. With Robespierre and Babeuf, the "civil religion" became a kind of parody of church worship and festivals. Carl Becker writes of the "half admirable, half pathetic spectacle of June 8, 1794, when Citizen Robespierre, with a bouquet in one hand and a torch in the other, inaugurated the new religion of humanity by lighting the conflagration that was to purge the world of ignorance, vice and folly." Man was to be saved, not in individual terms, but in social terms; not in a spiritual sense, or in an after life, but spatio-temporally, here and now, on this earth. The ideal was not the *unique* individual but the *social* individual—the socially perfect man, whose personal aims were social aims and whose personal judgments were social judgments. This ideal is embedded in all the pronouncements of the early absolutists, from Rousseau's "General Will" to Babeuf's "*terrible mystère*," the pursuit of which would tomorrow regenerate the world.

Robespierre and Saint-Just came to a bloody end on the ninth of Thermidor, 1794, when the guillotine claimed them in their turn. But their messianic dream had been born, and although it was swept from power, it lived on in the background of European political life, sometimes as a memory, sometimes even as a hope. It is not easy to recognize the connection between this dream and the doctrine of Karl Marx, because the Marxists have always done everything they could to obscure it. They have heaped scorn on the "self-evident" abstractions of the eighteenth century as "non-dialectical" and naïve. In his *Critique of the Gotha Program*, for example, Marx is at pains to state that actual equality, as the eighteenth century conceived of it, cannot be accepted as a practical goal. As for the concept of the "laws of nature," upon which so much of the earlier thinking was based, a scientific view of the world does not sustain it, and it is therefore dismissed as mere eighteenth-century romanticism. The only laws having such universal validity are the dialectical laws, which are quite different.

They are the laws of matter, and they provide no foundation for vague Utopias based upon outworn metaphysics.

Nevertheless, as Talmon and others have pointed out, the connection between the absolutist revolution of the eighteenth century and the Marxist movement of the next century presses for recognition. It is nowhere better revealed than by Marxist dogma itself. The Marxist revolution, it is necessary to remember, is no one-shot affair. As expounded by Marx and his successors, it must unfold in three phases, of which the first is the familiar democratic revolution, wherein the people overthrow the feudal or monarchical forms and institute self-government. This is only the beginning. It is followed by the "proletarian" revolution in which the workers must overturn the institutions of "bourgeois" democracy, seize power, and establish the "dictatorship of the proletariat." "You will have to go through fifteen, twenty or even fifty years of civil and international war," wrote Marx to the proletariat, "not only to change the relationships but also to change your own selves, to render yourselves fit to assume the political reins." The Russian Revolution, which was brought about long after the death of Marx, is still in this intermediary phase. The outside world has come to identify this phase with the revolution as a whole; but this is because the outside world does not always pay attention to the Communist leaders. Listen, for example, to the great architect of that revolution, Lenin himself:

Under the dictatorship of the proletariat [i.e., the second phase], we will have to *re-educate* millions of peasants and petty-proprie-

tors, hundreds of thousands of office workers, officials, and bourgeois intellectuals; to subordinate all these to the proletarian state
and to proletarian leadership; to overcome their bourgeois habits
and traditions . . . to *re-educate* in a protracted struggle . . .
the proletarians themselves, for they will not be able to rid themselves of their own petty-bourgeois prejudices at the first stroke
as if by magic, or at the behest of the Virgin Mary, or by a
slogan, resolution or decree; it can be done only in the course of
a long and difficult mass struggle.

One of the objects of the proletarian revolution, in short,
is educational. People have to be changed, socialized, per-
fected. Indeed, the goal is a new kind of society—a society
dedicated to Socialist principles, governed by Socialist
practices, inhabited by Socialist man. Lenin's ruthless un-
derstudy, Josef Stalin, left us in no doubt about this. For
example, in 1927, in answer to a question by an American
labor delegation, he pointed out that "Marx and Engels
regarded the period of the dictatorship of the proletariat
as a more or less prolonged period replete with revolutionary conflicts and civil wars in the course of which the
proletariat in power would take the economic, political
and cultural organizational measures necessary for the
purpose of establishing a new *Socialist society*, a society
without classes and without a state, in place of the old
capitalist society." The Marxists' third phase is the absolutists' classless, stateless heaven-on-earth.

Thus the dream is there, the dream of a new man—of
a new *kind* of man—which it is the business of the leaders
of the proletariat to produce, by processes however violent. And this dream is the direct offspring and heir of the

heady eighteenth-century doctrine, whose cardinal article of faith was the perfectibility of man as a social being. It is, essentially, morally, the dream of begetting a kind of man which does not yet exist, but which dwells as if potentially, so the dreamers insist, in every human being. Marxism is the same dream, dressed in modern clothes— a messianic vision, the essence of which cannot be reduced to rational terms, the purpose of which is to change mankind from top to bottom. This purpose is in fact a religious purpose. It is evident to the world, as it was not to the eighteenth century, that this secular, social religion is of necessity and with violence opposed to the Christian religion, out of which so many of its ideals originally sprang. For Marxist salvation is not of the soul but of the body— one might even say, of the body politic. It is a material salvation in social terms. The vision of earthly perfection which, in Tom Paine's day, drove its adherents to the brink of atheism, has given birth in our time to a *religion* of atheism, which is the mainspring of Communist power.

Of the reality of the link between modern communism and the eighteenth-century absolutist revolution, history has left us one bit of evidence. After the fall of Robespierre a final attempt was made in France to realize the perfect society in flesh and blood upon the earth. It was the Babouvist movement. To François-Noël Babeuf, and to his co-conspirators, "The French Revolution [was] but the forerunner of another revolution far more grand, far more solemn, and which shall be the last." The purpose of this

higher revolution, said Babeuf, was the happiness of mankind, and to insure this happiness, the most "rigorous
equality" was essential. Equality meant economic equality,
first of all—for "has any man more than one stomach?"

The detailed plan put forward by the Conspiracy of
Equals, as the Babouvist movement was called, strikes some
notes that are all too familiar to twentieth-century ears.
Thrusting aside the idea of economic liberty that had
beguiled most of their predecessors, the Babouvists became
the pioneers of modern communism. They rejected the demand for a *loi agraire* partitioning the land, which until
then had been the most popular war cry of the left revolutionists. "We aim at something more sublime, and more
equitable: we look to *common property. . . . The earth
belongs to no one*. We claim—we demand—we *will* the
communal enjoyment of the fruits of the earth." Moreover,
to live at the expense of others' work was not permissible:
all must work, and the necessities of life would be rationed
in such a way that no one could accumulate or hoard
wealth. All foreign trade would be forbidden to individuals;
it would be conducted by the state. And to insure that these
fundamentals could never be changed, the strictest kind of
educational and political regime was to be established.
Said the Manifesto of the Equals: "The country takes possession of every individual at birth, and never quits him
till death."[3]

The Conspiracy of the Equals was discovered, and

[3] *Manifesto of the Equals,* Buonarroti's History of Babeuf's Conspiracy for
Equality. Trans. by Bronterre (J. O'Brien), London, H. Hetherington, 1836.

Babeuf and many of his closest associates were executed. But the Babouvist movement has historical value, because it illustrates so perfectly the essential weakness of the eighteenth-century absolutist revolution. The view of man espoused by the absolutists was so visionary, so uncompromisingly idealistic, that their revolution was never able to hold political power. Unlike the libertarian revolution, it never outgrew the status of an opposition movement led by political dreamers, whose views were accepted in part by various minorities, but never as a whole. These views profoundly influenced the politics of Europe, and gave rise to a bewildering array of socialistic theories and parties. But outside of Russia and her satellites the absolutist revolution itself has never been realized in Europe where the forces of conservatism and libertarianism, separately or in combination, have always been just strong enough to hold the ground.

While Marx was studying economics in the British Museum, the absolutist revolution was at one of its lowest ebbs. The Socialists were warring among themselves, completely divided as to both theory and procedure. Industrialization had made a shambles of eighteenth-century rationalism, upon which the revolution had hitherto been based. The great eighteenth-century concepts that had inspired such revolutionary efforts—Liberty, Equality, Fraternity—seemed peculiarly devoid of meaning when confronted by the juggernaut of mass production. Immense wealth was accumulating in the hands of a few, but the system that was so productive of wealth made almost no provision for its equitable distribution. The basic ideal of the revolution, the ideal of a "new" man, a social man, whose institutions would serve the good of all, seemed more remote than ever. Where was the power to erect such institutions? And who would know how to frame them even if they could be erected?

The extraordinary feat of Karl Marx was the discovery of how to fill this dark vacuum between the ideals of the eighteenth-century dreamers and the actual social facts of the mid-nineteenth century. What his doctrines did, in effect, was to knock out the old "enlightened" rationalism, from which the absolutist revolution had been born, and put in its place an entirely different set of ideas about man—a set of ideas making claim to scientific validity. That the claim was spurious does not matter. The metascience that Marx developed was founded, one might say, in the deepest instincts of the age, and could not be overturned by logical and methodological criticism. As a view of man, it was as characteristic of the time as industrialization itself. All the new body of knowledge that had been derived from the sciences, which Engels so lucidly expounded in the *Dialectics of Nature* and elsewhere, was now appropriated by the revolutionaries. The social and economic doctrines of the revolution were brought down out of the clouds of Liberty, Equality, Fraternity, Justice, and Reason, to the hard-pan of "science," to whose hypotheses regarding man and the universe every individual in the industrial world seemed to be driven as if by an inner compulsion. Marx achieved a tremendous synthesis between two forces: the urge in modern man to pursue science, wherever it might lead; and a revolutionary tradition with a messianic goal dedicated to the fulfillment on earth of man-as-he-ought-to-be.

Such, in general terms, is the nature and stature of that force that rears itself today as the enemy of the free world. We have gone into these things so as to guard against the danger of underrating Marxism, which is not some kind of accident. It is not an excrescence, nor—as some have contended—a mere heresy. It has deep roots in Western civilization, and its ancestry includes some of the most illustrious names of European history. What is more, it is impregnated with the very ideas that have contributed most to the greatness of the West. Correctly or incorrectly, logically or illogically, Marxism has succeeded in coupling scientific ideas with the greatest political hopes that man has ever entertained: the absolute hopes that animated a revolution, which, at one time, shared its convictions with our own.

Marxism, then, is no minor, no accidental enemy, but one which grows out of the very errors of our civilization, to challenge us in terms of our foundations. It is an enemy that exacts of us, not merely military and economic efforts, but efforts of an intellectual and cultural kind, directed toward a true understanding of man. Let us now try to gain a somewhat more detailed view of the actual doctrine, in terms of which this tremendous challenge has been framed.

3

DIALECTICAL MATERIALISM

Marxism abounds in weird and unpleasant terms, some of which are difficult to take seriously. Among these, one of the strangest (to lay ears, at any rate), and probably the most important, is the term "dialectic." Marx obtained the term from one of the greatest philosophers of all time, Georg Wilhelm Friedrich Hegel. Central to Hegel's thinking was the concept of development. All human experience, Hegel points out, begins with a *thesis*, which will always have the important characteristic that, although it may at first seem to be the whole truth, the whole reality, it is really only a partial truth or reality. Pursuit of the thesis, therefore, leads to the creation and upbuilding of its opposite, the *antithesis*. Let us suppose our thesis to be the proposition that freedom consists in doing anything you want. We shall very soon discover that if everybody does only what he wants, then everybody's freedom will be impaired. Therefore, the contrary proposition, or *antithesis*, arises, that freedom can be achieved only by restraining everyone from doing what he wants. These two propositions, each representing part of the truth, work against each other and set up a contradiction. And Hegel called the contradiction "dialectical," from the Greek word *"dialego,"* meaning to discourse, to debate.

That is not the end of the process, however. The opposition between thesis and antithesis leads to the formula-

170

tion of a third proposition, called a *synthesis,* which includes them both but represents something new and different from either. As V. Adoratsky puts it, "In ancient
Greece . . . it was considered that in the course of an argument . . . the opinions of the disputing parties underwent a
change and that something new and of a higher nature
resulted." In the example cited the synthesis is familiar to
all Americans: freedom consists neither in complete lack
of restraint, nor in complete restraint, but in the absence
of restraint within mutual and agreed-upon limits. The
fact to note is that the synthesis really does bring about a
transformation or development. What we call the free way
of life does not consist merely in subtracting from the
things you want to do the things you are not permitted to
do. It is a wholly different kind of life, a genuinely creative solution to a conflict. The solution, or synthesis, we
may say, embraces more of reality than either thesis or
antithesis, yet this does not mean, of course, that it is in
any sense a final reality. As history unfolds it will become
obvious that the synthesis itself represents only a partial
truth, so that it in turn must give rise to its opposite: a new
conflict is created and a new and even more complete
synthesis is required. Such is the pattern and meaning of
development.

One does not have to be a rabid Hegelian to acknowledge
that all this represents a truly great insight into the structure of reality as grasped by the human mind. Thesis, antithesis, and synthesis emerge from the flux and change of
history, to provide a kind of assurance that the flux and

change are not wholly purposeless, but lead always to solutions. Temporarily such a solution represents some kind of an advance over the conflict at a higher level, and so on, indefinitely. History is thus not static; through the dialectical process it works always toward higher and more advanced experience.

Now in Hegel's view the real essence of the universe is spirit. By this he did not mean anything remote and otherworldly, but actual experience. For Hegel, as A. K. Rogers puts it, "the system of experience itself is reality, is God; and God thus is the most certain thing in the world, implicated in the existence of any reality whatsoever. . . . Spirit . . . and the laws of Spirit, are the real essence of the universe, in terms of which everything whatsoever is to be understood."[4] Rationality is an inherent characteristic of Spirit, and the dialectical process is a manifestation of that rationality. The Hegelian system is thus fundamentally Idealistic, in the technical sense of the word.

But Karl Marx swept all that aside. He abandoned Hegel's concept of Spirit as altogether "unscientific" and in its place put a concept which represented the opposite of Spirit, which he called "matter." Reality, he insisted, is only, and can only be, material. Consequently, the only doctrine that can adequately represent reality is not philosophic Idealism but philosophic Materialism.

Just what did Marx and Engels have in mind in using the word "material"? From the point of view of mid-

---

[4] A. K. Rogers, *A Student's History of Philosophy*, New York, The Macmillan Co., 1920, pp. 448-49.

twentieth-century science their concept must have been
naïve—e.g., something hard and substantial, composed
of submicroscopic particles in perpetual motion. "The
Marxist material philosophy," wrote Josef Stalin, "holds
that matter, nature, being, is an objective reality existing
outside and independent of our mind; that matter is
primary, since it is the source of sensations, ideas, mind,
and that mind is secondary, derivative, since it is a reflection of matter, a reflection of being; that thought is a
product of matter which in its development has reached
a high degree of perfection, namely, of the brain, and the
brain is the organ of thought."

Many Marxists will object to our quoting Stalin as a
spokesman for Marxism. In intellectual affairs, he is not
taken seriously. Great numbers of Marxists, moreover,
deplore "Stalinism" and believe that Stalin (and Lenin,
too) wrecked the "true" Marxist movement. Such dissidents
have included the Fabians in England and democratic
socialists in various parts of the world who have watered
Marxism down to a polite, democratic reformism. They
also include whatever remains of revolutionary anti-Stalin-
ists, such as Trotskyists and other left-wingers. Stalin was
certainly no intellectual. But communism, as we are faced
with it today, is to a very great extent his handiwork, and
from the point of view of our present predicament, it is far
more important to know what he said than to quibble over
what the founder actually said. Besides, in this instance, he
quotes one of the many passages in which Engels, speaking
for himself and Marx, stated the same thing somewhat less

clearly: "The material, sensuously perceptible world to which we ourselves belong, is the only reality. . . . Our consciousness and thinking, however supra-sensuous they may seem, are the product of a material, bodily organ, the brain. Matter is not the product of mind, but mind itself is merely the highest product of matter."[5]

Indeed, it is not possible for any Marxist to escape the fundamental tenet which was laid down at the beginning and has been carried on ever since, that this doctrine constitutes a total reversal of the Hegelian view; that reality is to be conceived, not as spirit, but as matter. This reversal does not do away with the Hegelian method for arriving at reality. But since matter, in the Marxist doctrine, now represents being, the meaning of the dialectic becomes very different. It is matter itself which is dialectical— indeed, the dialectical process becomes virtually a definition of what matter (being) is. Neither Marx, nor Engels, nor any of their successors has explained *why* matter is thus dialectical. The dialectical process is merely accepted as a characteristic of matter and virtually synonymous with it.

Such, in the briefest possible terms, is the metaphysical, or metascientific, foundation of the modern world's most aggressive doctrine of man. Before inquiring into those human and social truths which it claims to substantiate, it will be well to make note of one aspect of this metascience

[5] Frederick Engels, *Ludwig Feuerbach,* New York, International Publishers, p. 35.

itself, the significance of which will become increasingly apparent as we proceed.

The Marxian dialectical process works in accordance with certain laws, only one of which, however, need concern us here. This is that *qualitative* changes (e.g., the transformation of a liquid into a solid) are brought about by quantitative changes. But, says Engels, it is in the sphere of chemistry that this law is most dramatically illustrated: "In the case of oxygen, if three atoms unite into a molecule, instead of the usual two, we get ozone, a body which is very considerably different from ordinary oxygen in its odour and reactions." Proceeding downward from the molecule to the atoms, the principle becomes even more familiar. The human being perceives enormous qualitative differences between elements—for example, between oxygen and sulfur. These differences, however, are wholly accounted for in chemistry, and in physics, by the quantitative differences in their atomic weights, which arise in turn from purely quantitative differences in the nuclei of the atoms, and are reflected in the number of electrons that each nucleus supports. From the point of view of theoretical science, the nuclei and electrons of oxygen are qualitatively identical with those of sulfur. The difference between these two elements is essentially a question of number.

This "law" is of the greatest importance to the materialistic thesis, because it supports a concept of reality accessible to the exact sciences. Those sciences are concerned primarily with measurement, that is to say, with quantitative phenomena. If it is generally true that all the qualitative experiences of life—for example, the experience of color—can be accounted for in quantitative terms, then the search for truth reduces itself to analysis and measurement, and the exact sciences are the sole custodians of it. Life itself, we thus see, though qualitatively different from inorganic phenomena, can be accounted for by the hypothesis that living substance is nothing more than a quantitative elaboration of inorganic substance. The nature and origin of life can thus be completely explored and explained by those sciences which are engaged in the analysis of matter. All spiritual, esthetic, and even moral considerations are relegated to a secondary role. "Matter," writes Lenin, "is that which, acting upon our sense organs, produces sensation. . . . Matter, nature, being, the physical —is primary, and spirit, consciousness, sensation, the psychical—is secondary." Thus the whole human struggle changes its meaning. The great ideals for which humanity has fought and suffered—the Good, the Beautiful, and the True—honor, love, and sacrifice—the eightfold path of Buddha, the Christian vision of redemption, the Moslem communion with God—all these inspired revelations and ideals are just illusions on the surface of reality, eruptive phenomena thrown up from the depths of matter. They have played an important role in the shaping of history, not because they were real, but because men erroneously believed them. The realities of history are quite different, in the Marxist view of things.

4

THE SOCIAL ABSOLUTE

In his exposition of the dialectical process Hegel gave special attention to history. Karl Marx also observed the dialectical process in history. But since he equated reality to matter, rather than to spirit, his observation led to a view of history very different from that which Hegel had entertained. If reality is matter, then the realities of history can only be stated in material terms. One could list a good many of these. Geographical and climatic conditions, for example, are material phenomena that have definite effects on history. So are such factors as population, natural resources, hereditary characteristics, etc. But Marxists, while acknowledging the importance of these, do not give them a primary position. There is, according to them, only one material factor that can be considered primary, namely, the *mode of production*. This factor is central to Marxism and modern communism.

In the first place, the Marxist proposition is advanced that all human production is of necessity social in character. Not only does it have social effects, it is a uniquely social activity—indeed, *the* activity without which a society cannot exist. It follows that the mode of production determines the nature of any given society. In general, primitive modes of production give rise to primitive societies; it is the elaboration of the mode of production that causes a society to "advance." All history, therefore, can be understood by reference to modes of production, and to their development. "It is not the consciousness of men that determines their existence," wrote Marx, "but, on the contrary, their social existence that determines their consciousness."

This view of history enables us to see more concretely how the dialectic operates. At a certain stage of their development the methods of production come in conflict with existing relations, for the most part property relations which have developed out of the preceding mode of production. A period of social revolution then ensues. With a change in the economic foundations there comes a change in the "entire immense superstructure."

In our own time we see this principle at work in the famous Marxian "contradictions of capitalism." In *Das Kapital* Marx contends that the form of production that we use in our industrial system is, in fact, a socialist form, but that the social relations (that is to say, chiefly, private ownership) have been inherited from a previous age, and therefore frustrate our own productive system. The division of labor, the bringing together of large aggregates of physical capital and large numbers of workers, has already progressed on the technical side to what it will be, and must be, under socialism. The great step that it is now necessary for socialists to make, in order to realize their goal, is simply to put an end to private ownership of the means of production ("expropriate the expropriators") and thus bring social relations up to date with the mode of production. And as to that, these bourgeois relationships constitute the last barrier on the way to the fulfillment of socialism.

All this may loosely be summarized in the proposition that economics is made the key science, essential to an understanding of history, and even of man himself. The economic struggle, being a material struggle, embodies, so to speak, the realities of history; the dialectical process manifests itself in forces that are inseparably related to that struggle—to the formation, for example, of social "classes" engaged in it. Thesis and antithesis give rise to owner and slave, employer and worker, perennially in conflict. The advancing mode of production constantly tends to render obsolete the existing social relationships and to pen up revolutionary possibilities for the achievement of a new, and higher, synthesis; but since all wealth (except untouched natural resources) is the fruit of labor, and since no social relationship has ever actually reflected this fact, no final synthesis has ever been reached, nor can it ever be, until the owners and employers have been liquidated and the proletariat takes over the earth. Then, and only then, can the dialectical process reach a final consummation, in the establishment of a truly Socialist society from which classes—and with them, states—have been eliminated.

Now among the far-reaching results of this line of reasoning there is one which is extremely baffling to the non-Marxist bourgeois mind. It is the emergence at the end of the line of a kind of absolute by which all history—and for that matter, truth itself—is measured. We may call it the *social absolute*. And in an understanding of it we shall find an important clue both to the strength in our time of the Marxist thesis, and to the relative weakness and uncertainty of the free world.

According to the non-Marxist way of looking at things which prevails in the West, the search for truth involves a certain relativity of view. It is both permissible and necessary to distinguish between various lines of discovery and activities of the mind. A philosopher may show, by a chain of reasoning, that man is a moral being. At the very same time, a biologist may show, by a series of empirical experiments, that human characteristics are the result of certain activities of the genes, and are thus (or so the scientist may infer) basically chemical in their origin. Simultaneously, a social scientist may conclude, from a controlled study, that men would be more efficient, happier, and even more moral, if certain changes could be brought about in the ownership and management of the production line. For Western thinkers, these three conclusions represent three different aspects of the truth about man. Within their limitations, they may all three be right. They are the results of different angles of observation, and they must accordingly differ, just as one's picture of a mountain changes depending upon the direction from which one views it.

Dialectical Materialism, however, recognizes no such relativity between different aspects of truth. It is not possible, according to this doctrine, to separate morality from biology, or biology from social science. The truth of the one must be the truth of the others. At first glance this posi-

tion might seem familiar, for the idea of the *unity* of truth
has animated most of the great philosophies, and all of the
great religions, of the world. But the Dialectical Materialist takes two steps that bring him into conflict with all
other schools of thinking. First, as we have seen, he finds
the unity of truth, not in God, nor in Spirit, nor in Reason,
nor in the world of Ideas, nor in Nature, nor in Will, but
only in Matter—and specifically, in the dialectical process
which characterizes Matter. Secondly, this dialectical process manifests itself in history, where, owing to the materialistic nature of reality, it can have only one real meaning, namely, the struggle of the working class to emerge
from poverty and establish throughout the world a classless
society. This conclusion is forced upon the Dialectical
Materialist as a logical deduction from his premises. It
follows, therefore, that there is no such thing as a truth
which does not support and further the goal of a classless
society. That social goal is absolute. Not only does the
moral philosopher fall into error if he defines good and evil
in any other terms, but so does the physical scientist if his
findings conflict with the social needs and aspirations of
the proletariat. There is, indeed, a kind of hierarchical
pattern that runs throughout the doctrine. The moral philosopher has to defer to the biologist, because Dialectical
Materialism is materialistic; and the biologist has to defer
to the social scientist, because the materialism is dialectical, i.e., it seeks to manifest itself in the supremacy
of the working class. If scientific findings in any field conflict with these proletarian social implications of history,

they must be wrong. The social absolute controls all human inquiry.

This position is not reached, of course, without a great deal more argument than is presented here. No attempt has been made to give a comprehensive summary of the whole body of Marxist theory, or even touch such well-known landmarks as surplus value or the theory of the state. The discussion in these pages is a brief examination of certain philosophical aspects of Marxism which have a fundamental bearing on our inquiry into the position of the free world in the war of ideas. The reader can find any number of statements in orthodox Marxist literature to support this condensed interpretation. Take for example the statement of George Plekhanov that "men do not make several distinct histories—the history of law, the history of morals, the history of philosophy, etc.—but only one history, the history of their own social relations, which are determined by the state of the productive forces in each particular period. What is known as ideologies is nothing but a multiform reflection in the minds of men of this single and indivisible history."

Thus the social absolute, which emerges from a literal application of this materialist philosophy to all the affairs of men, results in the liquidation of the search for truth entirely. For nothing, according to this view, *can* be true which does not conform with the dialectical forces of matter working in the direction of this absolute. This view leads to a line of action that is even more confusing to the West than the absolute itself. In Part I we pointed out the peculiar relationship between communism and the use of force. The doctrine, we said, uses force, not for the achievement of any of the classical goals of history, but as an extension of its argument. We can now see somewhat more clearly how this can be. Babeuf and the early absolutists advocated force "if necessary" in order to convert man-as-he-is into man-as-he-ought-to-be; as Talmon put it, the Babouvists approved of force "only to quicken the pace of man's progress." Communism accepts this traditional absolutist use of force, but carries it much further. In order to satisfy its claim to a scientific status, it must find positive proof in the actual events of history. The Dialectical Materialist, therefore, *uses force to make those events happen the way their theory tells them they must happen.* While to us this seems the most irrational and unscientific of procedures, to them it is a logical—although unacknowledged—conse-quence of the theory. Force is the dialectical opposite of what the "bourgeois" world knows as the search for truth. If it is used, therefore, to confound the free world's search, the result will be a dialectical synthesis: further progress toward communism's social absolute. Because force is thus used by the Communists on behalf of the dialectical proc-ess, it has to be considered as an integral part of the process. Whether things would have turned out differently if force had not been used, is an academic question. The dialectical principle of history itself evokes the force, which, in turn, overcomes the "bourgeois" state for the purpose of reaching an ultimate synthesis, the classless society.

Such were the ideas by means of which Karl Marx redefined and reanimated the absolutist revolution. For the obsolete rationalism of the eighteenth century he substituted a thoroughgoing and literal materialism, based squarely on the metascience of his time; and he wedded this materialism to the aspirations of the revolution through the logical derivation from his premises of a social absolute. The marriage between those two great forces—the absolutist revolution and the scientific impulse—was certainly one of the most important events of human history. Marxian materialism was just what the revolution needed to bring it down out of the heady generalities of idealistic egalitarianism to the hard realities of the economic and social struggle of the nineteenth and twentieth centuries. At the same time, the revolutionary impulse raised Marxian materialism to a special status, which the ponderous and labyrinthine works of its cofounders could never have achieved. It became something more than a mere philosophy; it was metamorphosed into a secular religion. Thus metamorphosed, it has projected itself into history as an Idea of Man, which we have called Dialectical Man: a great image rising out of the dullest literature that ever inspired revolutionary goals. It is the image of a messiah, who, to be sure, has never incarnated, but around whom the hopes of the elect are centered. This messiah is man-as-he-ought-to-be, as defined, not by rationalists and idealists, but by the hypotheses and criteria of "science." All truth concerning him is the monopoly of those who can speak for the materialistic dialectic. Beyond the pale of those chosen prophets, the search for truth vanishes into the night of nihilism.

From the point of view of the free world, Dialectical Man is a frightening, if not a revolting, creature. In the first place, he can be no more than a *material* man, because only matter is real, and because, therefore, any other kind of man (e.g., spiritual man, moral man) can be no more than an illusion. Secondly, he cannot be primarily an individual (since this concept would provide him with an escape from the dialectical process of history), but is primarily *social*—a biochemical unit of the dialectical process, whose welfare, happiness, and life purpose reside in the society in which he lives. Thirdly, since the needs of that society define his proper criteria of good and evil, he is wholly dependent for such criteria upon the judgment of his leaders as to what those needs may be. He thus emerges as a kind of social puppet, deprived of individual dignity, exiled from the search for truth, and incompetent to choose between good and evil. All the great insights that men have won in thousands of years of struggle, all the majestic approaches to truth, the shy and sensitive approaches to beauty, the deep inner satisfactions of free and independent decision—all are liquidated in Dialectical Man, the absolutists' definition of the social good.

5

THE OPTIMISTIC ABSOLUTE

It is just this singleness of purpose that gives Dialectical Man such impetus and such power, especially when he confronts the West. At the beginning of Part II we defined philosophical optimism as that view of human life which comes out to optimistic conclusions regarding life on earth, its purposes and its fulfillment. We also said, the optimist does not look to any "other realm" for man's fulfillment, does not acknowledge the need for supernatural intervention for his salvation; and as a consequence, he does not consider evil to be inherent in human existence, but something external that can be reformed. Our analysis of Dialectical Materialism reveals an explosive fact—that of all philosophies propounded by man, Dialectical Materialism is the most inordinately optimistic. For not only does it proclaim salvation in wholly earthly terms, it is even willing to stand on the position that the dialectical process which now grinds men against each other in conflict will vanish away when that earthly goal is attained. Moreover, Dialectical Materialism has had the courage and the acumen to apply this optimism in a thoroughgoing way, to make it a total optimism from which there is no appeal. Any interpretation of facts which does not support the optimistic absolute is, by definition, an expression of falsehood. And any use of force which does, is justified.

From the vantage point of this superoptimism, the Dialectical Materialist asks the people of the world some pointed questions. He asks what the supposedly great insights arising from the "bourgeois" search for truth have brought to the people of the world. He asks what those majestic approaches to truth, or beauty, or the arts, or freedom itself as the "bourgeois" world has interpreted it, have opened up for them. He asks what can be loftier than the aim to emancipate the working man—by force, if necessary—from a system of thinking that subordinates his welfare to goals other than his welfare. He points to the inconsistencies of the "bourgeois" world, the disagreements between its scientists and its philosophers, its moralists and its politicians, its words and its deeds. These, he maintans, cannot be the evidences of a sincere search for truth. They are the evidences, rather, of error and self-interest, of the workings of a system that contains within itself the seeds of its own destruction: evidences of corruption, selfishness, instability, greed, and doubt.

It is almost impossible for the average American, reared in the tradition of his own brand of optimism, to remain dispassionate when confronted with these questions and assertions. He cannot outbid the absolute optimism of the Marxist. But on the other hand, when he seeks to validate his own brand of optimism against the Marxist attack, he finds himself at a loss. The Marxian contention is that all the present evils of the world will be liquidated in his society. The American optimist, rooted in the libertarian tradition, and dedicated therefore to the principle of individual liberty, can make no such claim. For him, individual liberty is self-evidently good. But he is led into a difficulty which he cannot get around in purely optimistic terms, be-

cause individual liberty does not and cannot promise the
liquidation of all those evils of which the Marxists accuse
the free world. At this point the Marxist argument becomes
by all odds the stronger. The Marxists denounce individual liberty as nothing more than a political franchise for
those who have power and economic means to indulge their
self-interest at the expense of society, and especially, at
the expense of the "working class." Liberty, according to
them, is a political device of the "bourgeois" world to
prevent the liquidation of evil. Why, then, does the American optimist insist upon retaining it? Why does he continue to support the principle of individual liberty even
though that principle assures the survival of recognized
social evils?

These questions, then, force the American optimist into
a position which is untenable within the limits of his assumptions. He is called upon to defend and justify the principle of individual liberty as a good in itself. This, however, he is unable to do, for he himself is wedded to the
same kind of naturalistic and materialistic assumptions
as is the Marxist. He too is wedded to modern science.
Such science in our day has traveled a long way from the
times of Marx, but it has not yet come up with a view of
man which can support the moral truths to which the West
still clings. On the contrary, science is currently in a profound struggle with its older materialistic tenets. And to
this struggle we must now turn. It may develop that Marxism is not quite as invulnerable as it seems. It will also
develop that a new approach is needed if the West is to
recover the initiative in the great war of ideas.

IV

THE SCIENTIFIC
SPIRIT OF INQUIRY

1

THE SCIENTIFIC METHOD

The American optimist, then, is on treacherous ground, precisely because, taken alone, the scientific view of man cannot support a doctrine of freedom. If it embodies the whole truth about man and his origins the great war of ideas cannot be won by free men. If, however, freedom is a reality, then the scientific view of man cannot be wholly correct.

Surely there can be no fundamental conflict between science and freedom! Scientists (so the argument runs) are engaged in the search for truth. Unless men know the truth—about the universe, about Nature, about society, about themselves—they cannot be free. The deluded man will be led into errors which he did not intend to make and did not, therefore, freely choose. Since science is dedicated to the overcoming of delusion and error, it is not in conflict with freedom, but is indispensable to it. The trouble in the world today is just that Marxism is wholly *un*scientific and, whatever Marx and Engels may have claimed, the doctrine that they founded owes its success to the cynical exploitation of the delusions and passions of mankind.

As we shall see, each of these views of science (that it is antagonistic to freedom and that it is indispensable to freedom) contains an element of truth. But first, just what do we mean by the scientific view of man—or, indeed, by the word "science"?

The question, "What is science?" is usually answered: "Science is a *method* of search." The most obvious characteristic of this method is that it eliminates all merely personal or accidental judgments and deductions, in favor of objective judgments based on positive proof. For the purpose of achieving such judgments the observed facts are carefully controlled, and so are judgments, since they are referred back to the controlled facts. Since everything is thus checked against everything else, a conclusion is reached that has proven validity over and above what any individual might assert from his own personal convictions. A scientific conclusion, in other words, is one that is valid for *all* observers.

For a long time the scientific method was considered to be a method based largely upon inductive logic. The characteristic of inductive logic is that it starts with particular observations and draws conclusions therefrom—a method of procedure precisely opposite to that of deductive logic, which consists in starting with general principles from which particular conclusions are drawn (deduced). In order to work inductively, the scientific method leans heavily on the human faculty of *analysis*. According to this methodological view, when a scientist is confronted with an unexplained phenomenon, he may not proceed directly to an intuitive conclusion about it, but must first analyze it into its component parts. On the basis of this analysis, he may then proceed inductively to draw conclusions about the phenomenon.

In philosophical terms, this method of inquiry can be called *positivistic;* it proceeds upon the assumption that

nothing can be taken to be true unless it can be positively
proven, and it thus makes the *experiment* the ultimate test
of truth. What cannot be established by experiment is dismissed as unknown, or unknowable. In actual practice,
therefore, the scientific method has become closely linked
with the empirical (the world of experience) and the
extrinsic (the outer manifestations of reality), and many
philosophers of science have in fact defined the scientific
method in those terms. Thus John Dewey says that there
are three "outstanding characteristics" of "experimental
inquiry."

The first is the obvious one that all experimentation involves
overt doing, the making of definite changes in our environment or
in our relationship to it. The second is that experiment is not a
random activity but is directed by ideas. . . . The third . . . in
which the other two receive their full measure of meaning, is that
the outcome of the directed activity is the construction of *a new
empirical situation.*[1]

Now this methodological approach to the question of
what science is, is valid enough so far as it goes. But it
runs into a number of difficulties. We have to heed the
warning of James B. Conant, former president of Harvard,
that in scientific inquiry several methods are actually involved.[2] The field of science ranges all the way from pure
mathematics to anthropology; from astrophysics to psychology; from chemistry to the study of human behavior.
We cannot speak of a single method for all these various

[1] John Dewey, *The Quest for Certainty*, New York, Minton Balch, 1929,
p. 86.
[2] James B. Conant, *Science and Common Sense*, New Haven, Yale University Press, 1951.

inquiries without running the danger of oversimplification. Moreover, as Dr. Conant points out, it is becoming increasingly difficult to describe science or the scientific method in conventional empirical terms. The atom bomb was not the product of empirical experiment, as such, but of mathematical calculations supporting and derived from hypotheses that had never had the benefit of complete empirical proof. The methods of advanced science in our time are in this regard very different from the methodological preconceptions that we inherited from the nineteenth century.

One of the most important of those preconceptions was the idea, just noted, that the "pure" scientist was one who gained his ends solely by the use of inductive logic. The history of science itself shows that this is not the case. Almost every great scientific discovery, as Conant points out, has involved some kind of "inspired guess," "intuitive hunch," or "brilliant flash of imagination," followed by a chain of deductive reasoning *leading into* new experimentation. Often enough the flash was the result of some accident in the laboratory—as when Galvani's assistant, playing with an electrical machine, accidentally contacted the legs of a frog that Galvani had been dissecting in such a way as to cause them to twitch. The flash that this event brought to birth in Galvani's mind happened to be wrong, but that is not the point. The point is that inductive logic alone could not have led Galvani to the frog's legs and all the memorable experiments following therefrom. Indeed, it is not until the experimenter can succeed in breaking out of inductive logic that the great discoveries are made. Conant goes so far as to make deductive reasoning indispensable to scientific advance. The scientific method, he asserts, has three major elements: first, "speculative general ideas" (the "intuitive hunch"); second, deductive reasoning from these general ideas; and third, experimentation "to test the deductions." The primary role of experimentation and inductive logic, in other words, is not to discover but to demonstrate and prove what has already been guessed or deduced.

A little reflection will show that the inductive method, taken alone, is incapable of achieving anything really new. Let us turn to the proverbial man from Mars. We have taken a watch to pieces and have put the parts, mixed up, in a pile. We present the man from Mars with the pile and ask him what it is. He will say that it is a lot of curiously shaped little objects. But there is no possible way that he can induce from them the idea that they are the parts of an instrument to measure time. In order to reach this conclusion he must first have a general idea. If there are instruments on Mars for measuring time, he will come to the pile already prepared for such an idea, and if he begins fitting the pieces together he will be able to induce (rather laboriously, perhaps) that they are the parts of an instrument for measuring time. The problem would be more difficult, but still theoretically solvable on an inductive basis, if he has no idea of an instrument for measuring time but has at least the more general idea of a purposeful whole. He might then induce that the parts do fit together, that he is dealing with a purposeful whole; and after he has fitted them together he might again induce, from the observation that their movement corresponds with that of the sun, that they are intended to measure time. But without at least the idea of a purposeful whole no induction whatever could be made; he could induce nothing about the pile of parts, because he could not know that they are parts. His manipulation of the curiously shaped little objects would therefore have to be a purely random operation. "It is often said," wrote Henri Poincaré, that "experiments must be made without a preconceived idea. That is impossible. Not only would it make all experiment barren, but that would be attempted which could not be done." As Poincaré has also pointed out: "Science is built up with facts, as a house is with stones, but a collection of facts is no more a science than a heap of stones is a house."[3]

These brief observations are made in order to establish an important point. The attempt to define science in strictly methodological terms is bound to lead to unsatisfactory results. Science is analytical, but not merely analytical; inductive, but not merely inductive; experimental, but not merely experimental. For the process of analysis is potentially infinite, and the processes of observation and experiment, when taken alone, are inherently inconclusive. The difficulty confronting the man from Mars is the fact that he is faced with an analytical situation which contains, for him, no hint of a possible synthesis. For an analytical proc-

[3] Henri Poincaré, *Science and Hypothesis*, trans. by George Bruce Halstead, New York, The Science Press, pp. 129 and 127.

ess to reach a conclusion, something must come to meet it which was not derived from the analysis—an idea, which in terms of the data that are being analyzed, is wholly *preconceived*, wholly untested, and hence, in a methodological sense of the word, *un*scientific. The aphorism may be ventured that if scientists had really confined themselves to the scientific method, as it was conventionally defined, they could have discovered nothing at all. In actuality, they have taken flight from the method, in inspired moments, to achieve great ideas. They have then brought these ideas to their experiments, and in the unison of the two they have made their discoveries.

Where do the ideas come from then? It is a question of what goes on inside of the investigator—a question of his experience, his character, his intelligence, his intuitive capacities—a question, in short, of substance—which leads us back to the very question we started from. What is the nature of man and of the universe itself?

2

THE SCIENTIFIC IMPULSE

That which emerges in any age as philosophically important, as we have already suggested, is not so much the conclusions reached as the attitude of search adopted in pursuit of them—or, as we also called it, the spirit of inquiry with which that particular age was endowed. This idea can be made more concrete by reference to the critical discovery of modern psychology, that the human being is rooted in an unconscious world, which is far more important to his conduct and decisions, perhaps even to his existence, than the world of his conscious mind. To describe the relative importance of the conscious and the unconscious, some psychologists have used the metaphor of an iceberg, four-fifths of whose bulk is beneath the surface; others have even gone so far as to liken the conscious mind to a mere island in the ocean. But whatever the correct proportions, the incontestable fact is that the unconscious is responsible for basic attitudes of all sorts, which may be disconcertingly irrational, but which have demonstrable, if incalculable, effects upon the conscious mind.

That among these subconscious attitudes there must be such a thing as an attitude toward truth, an attitude of search, all history indicates. Men observe essentially the same objects, but their conclusions about them vary so greatly in different ages that it is as if they had been gifted with different powers of perception. Compare, for example, the ancient Egyptian view of animals with our own. To the Egyptian seers the animals were representations of various aspects of the human soul—indeed, of the universe itself. Whether we ourselves are able to recognize such representations as valid, or whether we dismiss them as merely naïve and superstitious, changes must have occurred in the human psyche to enable men to "see" animals, in all seriousness, in such radically different ways. This fact cannot be attributed to any change in the animals. The real "differentiation" (to use a genetic term) has occurred in the human psyche itself, which has given rise, in these two far-separated ages, to conscious representations of the same objects almost wholly incompatible with one another.

These general considerations enable us to define somewhat more satisfactorily what we referred to in Part I as the "spirit of inquiry." As used in this book, this term is intended to denote an attitude rooted in the unconscious depths of the human being and manifesting itself as a reflection of them. It thus underlies the conscious intellect and determines in a general way what direction its development will take. Indeed, we may even say that this attitude of search predetermines the knowledge or, at any rate, the *kind* of knowledge that men acquire. It is doubtful whether the Greek spirit of inquiry, for example, could ever have broken through to the knowledge that is embodied in modern physics. But the spirit of inquiry that animates the modern physicist cannot yield the body of knowledge that was at the fingertips of the ancient alchemist—the serious alchemist, that is, not the quack. For let us make this point.

C. G. Jung has argued convincingly that, in addition to the discoveries which led the way to modern chemistry, alchemical knowledge was not insubstantial in the field of psychological investigation. Such knowledge had meaning in terms of human existence, and can provide us with important clues to an understanding of the human psyche. The assumption that the scientific spirit of inquiry, as developed over the past several centuries, has a monopoly on the valid search for truth, does not explain how it could be that ancient thinkers, who had no inkling of the modern scientific method, attained to insights into human nature and the nature of the world that have within them a quality of self-evidence, assuring them a virtual immortality. Even despite the gulf that separates the knowledge of one age from that of another, the truths to which those thinkers gave utterance, without benefit of science, still ring in our ears and exert profound influences upon our lives. They shine on us as through the mists of time, but they still shine. The Indian Vedas and the Egyptian *Book of the Dead* can still stir us, despite the fact that the terms in which they speak are almost lost to us. The Hebrew prophets still shake our consciences; Homer still sings; and Plato still sheds light into our minds.

How could the ancients have revealed so much about man, his soul and his destiny, if our spirit of inquiry, which we call science, were the *only* valid one? We can answer this question in the true spirit of science only when we abandon our absolutist prejudices and open our minds to the realities of man's long search for truth. These realities point relentlessly to the conclusion that there have been radical and profound changes in the human psyche, which, from time to time, have given expression to different attitudes of search; that each of these attitudes engenders a different body of knowledge, valid within certain limits; and that the attitude of search which we call science is therefore not an absolute, but represents only the latest that man has thus far attained.

There are many ways by which the difference between the scientific spirit of inquiry and the spirit of other ages might be defined. Fundamentally, it represented an enormously rapid growth in the human power of abstraction— growth so rapid that it produced, not merely a difference in degree, but a difference in kind. Abstraction is a fundamental power of the mind, and ancient thinkers made use of it as far back as history can be traced; but, despite such examples as Euclidean geometry and Ptolemaic astronomy, the difference between the general use of abstraction in the ancient world and in the twentieth century is so great that it even seems as if a different kind of mental power were being evoked. The fact that the gulf between us and the ancients is so deep and so broad is additional evidence that the attitudes of search that characterize different ages have their roots in the unconscious, where it is not easy for the conscious intellect to follow.

To everyone who saturates himself in ancient literature and philosophy, the impression becomes inescapable that the men of those times saw reality generally in qualitative terms—in terms, most obviously, of colors, sounds, and sensory experience, but also in terms of nonsensory qualities, such as "virtue" or "goodness," and even of soul qualities that we today do not recognize at all. The abstractions of the ancient world represented such qualitative differences. Even numbers were thus differentiated. Thus, for Pythagoras, the significant difference between the numbers "1" and "2" was to be found in the perception that "1" was masculine, the creator, and "2" feminine, the mother. These two qualities combined to make the number "3," which was viewed as divine. Again, the Platonic "Ideas" were not mere abstract forms; they were conceived to have living contents, each qualitatively different from the other. Today the concept "lion" is viewed as an abstraction, which is empty and lifeless until, so to speak, a particular lion steps into it. But in ancient thought "lion" stood for a quality of existence. It was an abstraction that had, in effect, a soul which endowed it with life in its own right. Aristotle came closer than any ancient philosopher to anticipating our modern way of thinking, but it is doubtful whether the Aristotelian categories can be correctly grasped in the purely formal manner that characterizes the thinking, let us say, of Immanuel Kant. Aristotelianism as a whole never abandoned its fundamental orientation to the qualitative. A qualitative spirit of inquiry, in short, characterized all of human thought, up to and including the Middle Ages, to receive its most sophisticated expression in the philosophy of Thomas Aquinas.

The new attitude of search that began to emerge in the

sixteenth century can be most simply described as a radical shift in the orientation of the human mind from the idea of quality to the idea of quantity. In the seventeenth century this shift was given clear philosophical expression by two intellectual giants—Galileo, the experimentalist, and Descartes, the theoretician. These men and their followers became obsessed with the notion that all the phenomena of Nature could be accounted for in quantitative terms. For Galileo, the irreducible elements of reality were figure (i.e., shape, extension), number, and motion. Descartes acknowledged as primarily real in the physical world only extension and motion. Hobbes, meanwhile, sought to reduce everything, including human perception and intelligence, to motion. The net result of these and other efforts was the emergence of mathematics as the absolute science, from which there could be no appeal. Qualitative differences that eluded mathematical analysis were consigned to a secondary role, and the tendency was to deny their reality altogether. Only that was real which could be mathematically accounted for.

When contrasted to modern science, of course the pioneering efforts of the sixteenth and seventeenth centuries appear crude and elementary. Nevertheless, the development in the direction of a quantitative view of things has been consistent and cumulative. For ordinary observation, for example, the phenomena of electromagnetic radiation exhibit enormous qualitative differences. Electronic and radio waves can scarcely be mistaken for heat (infra-red radiation). So, too, heat differs from visible light, and

visible light of the spectrum from ultraviolet radiation, and
so on down through x-rays; to the death-dealing Gamma
rays of radioactivity. For theoretical physics, however, the
only distinction between all these radically different phenomena is quantitative. As Louis de Broglie says, they
"differ from ordinary light only by a greater or smaller
wave-length." Even matter, which for ordinary observation
is nothing if not qualitative, is reduced by the modern
physicist to purely quantitative concepts. Each of the some
hundred elements has unique qualities and characteristics,
but for science these differences are adequately described
in terms of the *number* of electrons that their atoms
possess.

It is true, of course, that mathematics does not today
occupy the monopolistic position that was given to it by
Descartes and his followers. By observation, by comparative analysis, and by various kinds of "controlled" experimentation, science has been able to enter fields where
mathematics, as such, plays a minor role. The Darwinian
theory of organic evolution is not primarily mathematical.
But even in those fields where mathematical considerations
are reduced to a minimum, modern science is fundamentally quantitative in its outlook on the problem of truth. Its
ultimate criterion is some kind of measurement, whether
this involves the statistical probabilities of quantum mechanics, or the comparison of an elephant skull to that of
a mammoth, or Kinsey's series of interviews on human
sexual behavior, which present us with the sex impulse, not
in terms of what it is, but in terms only of its measurable

effects. We know with complete certainty how many electrons an atom of oxygen has. However, we do not know what oxygen *is;* indeed, the question seems to the scientific truth-seeker rather absurd. Oxygen *is* an element possessing eight electrons, and all our knowledge of it is an elaboration of that fundamental, measurable fact. "Science," says Sir William C. Dampier, "is not concerned with the inner nature of any of the terms used, but only with their mutual relations. . . . The truth of the relations does not depend on the reality of the *relata.*"[4]

[4] Sir William C. Dampier, *A History of Science*, New York, Macmillan, 1943, pp. 467, 468.

3

"ONE-EYED AND COLOR-BLIND"

To be sure, the relinquishment of the qualitative constituted a tremendous step ahead on the path to human freedom. It liberated the mind from the tyranny of the qualitative world, which, while it was by no means so illusory as some scientists have charged, was certainly riddled with illusion. This liberation had a signal result: instead of merely absorbing Nature and communicating with her, man was now free to master her.

But if the elimination of the qualitative has resulted in a great advance in the power of man over Nature, and thence, in the concept of freedom, it has also had profound intellectual and spiritual results of another kind, the perception of which is essential to an understanding of our times. The scientific spirit of inquiry has had to pay an enormous price for the advances it has made. If we are to gain a true perspective on the great war of ideas in which we are engaged, we must bring that fact into sharper focus.

One of the keenest philosophers of science in our time, the late Sir Arthur Eddington, was much aware of the price, and illustrated it with typical clarity. "Let us ... examine," he wrote,

the kind of knowledge which is handled by exact science. If we search the examination papers in physics and natural philosophy for the more intelligible questions we may come across one beginning something like this: "An elephant slides down a grassy hillside . . ." The experienced candidate knows that he need not pay much attention to this; it is only put in to give an impression of realism. He reads on: "The mass of the elephant is two tons." Now we are getting down to business; the elephant fades out of the problem and a mass of two tons takes its place. What exactly is this two tons, the real subject-matter of the problem? It refers to some property or condition which we vaguely describe as "ponderosity" occurring in a particular region of the external world. But we shall not get much further that way; the nature of the external world is inscrutable, and we shall only plunge into a quagmire of indescribables. Never mind what two tons *refers* to; what *is* it? . . . Two tons *is* the reading of the pointer when the elephant was placed on a weighing-machine. Let us pass on. "The slope of the hill is 60°." Now the hillside fades out of the problem and an angle of 60° takes its place. What is 60°? There is no need to struggle with mystical conceptions of direction; 60° *is* the reading of a plumb-line against the divisions of a protractor. Similarly for the other data of the problem. The softly yielding turf on which the elephant slid is replaced by a coefficient of friction. . . .

And so we see that the poetry fades out of the problem, and by the time the serious application of exact science begins we are left with only pointer readings. If then only pointer readings . . . are put into the machine of scientific calculation, how can we grind out anything but pointer readings? But that is just what we do grind out. . . . The whole subject-matter of exact science consists of pointer readings and similar indications. . . . Although we seem to have very definite conceptions of objects in the external world, those conceptions do not enter into exact science and are not in any way confirmed by it. Before exact science can begin to handle the problem they must be replaced by quantities representing the results of physical measurement.[5]

Thus qualitative knowledge of the elephant and the grassy slope is eliminated and quite a different kind of

---

[5] Sir Arthur S. Eddington, *The Nature of the Physical World*, New York, Macmillan, 1929, pp. 251-53.

knowledge emerges. Concerning this knowledge Eddington has a phrase, which he used in a somewhat different connection, but which is highly descriptive. In the acquisition of such knowledge, he suggests, it is as if we had used only a single sense of sight, which is "colorless and nonstereoscopic."[6] What this means, in the words of Ernst Lehrs, is that the physicists have exercised the faculty of quantitative abstraction to the point of looking at the world as if they had only one eye (nonstereoscopic) and as if this single eye were color-blind. They have constructed a kind of imaginary world composed of the abstract shadows of what is ordinarily regarded as real—the world of molecules and atoms, which are mostly empty space; the electrons, which, as a basis for physical matter, are hypothetical and physically nonexistent. Man is thus led into an infinite and alien Emptiness, which chills his imagination and defies his experience. This Emptiness contains nothing that he knows, nothing with which, as a man, he is familiar—no color, no sound, no smell, no feeling, and no beauty. Its ultimate criteria are statistical, amoral, and purposeless. Not only is it unlike anything he experiences in a sensory way, it is unlike anything he desires or aspires to. There exist in the vast interstices of this world of abstraction not a single spark of love, or mercy, or awe, or magnanimity, or hope. The works of the artist are as much out of place in it as the judgments of the moralist. And the revelations of the religious prophet echo and re-echo through its interminable equations, and vanish into nothing.

[6] Sir Arthur S. Eddington, *The Philosophy of Physical Science*, New York, Macmillan, 1939, p. 197. Also *New Pathways to Science*, p. 13.

And indeed, once man had embarked upon a quantitative spirit of inquiry, this denouement could not be avoided. The great realities of the quantitative world were only the bloodless phenomena of matter, which could be dealt with mathematically. Each of these realities became increasingly abstract with the advance of science, until they have passed beyond the limits, not only of human experience, but of the imagination itself. The comfortable three-dimensional space in which Newton reached his epochal conclusions could at least be imagined; but physicists now deal in space-time, a four-dimensional continuum which has its principal being, not in human perception, but in the physicists' high abstractions. As for matter, the naïve view of the Newtonians that it consists of solid particles bombarding each other has likewise been abstracted away. Matter is now judged to be composed of entities, the nature of which no one can define, except to say that they are *not* material in any sense that the ordinary human being can recognize.

This is a kind of world that results from the vision of a single, color-blind eye. In a famous passage in *Mysticism and Logic*, Bertrand Russell, himself totally immersed in the scientific spirit of inquiry, thus eloquently sums up its meaning for man:

That Man is the product of causes which had no prevision of the end they were achieving; that his origin, his growth, his hopes and fears, his loves and his beliefs, are but the outcome of accidental collocations of atoms; that no fire, no heroism, no intensity of thought and feeling can preserve an individual life beyond the grave; that all the labors of all the ages, all the devotion, all the inspiration, all the noonday brightness of human genius are destined to extinction in the vast death of the solar system, and that the whole temple of Man's achievement must inevitably be buried beneath the débris of a universe in ruins— all these things, if not quite beyond dispute, are yet so nearly certain that no philosophy which rejects them can hope to stand.[7]

Few are better equipped than Bertrand Russell to tell us where the scientific spirit of inquiry inevitably leads. But we may detect in this question a certain absolutism that verges on the dogmatic. Is it really true that a philosophy that rejects these scientific conclusions cannot hope to stand? Or is it true rather that the scientific spirit of inquiry itself, as hitherto interpreted by so many scientists and metascientists, cannot hope to stand? The question is important, because, if Mr. Russell is right, then the Marxists' doctrine of causes must be conceded, and the free world must somehow adapt itself to this etiology. But if, on the contrary, the scientific spirit of inquiry falls short of the whole truth, then there opens up before the free world the possibility of discovering wherein the shortcoming lies. There opens up the possibility, in short, of developing a new spirit of inquiry, rooted in science, but transcending the merely quantitative.

Can we honestly say that the scientific spirit of inquiry, as so often construed, is concerned with the search for truth at all? What, for example, *is* the truth about color? Can we really say that color is nothing but mechanico-chemical effects upon the retina of the eye produced by certain

[7] Bertrand Russell, *Mysticism and Logic*, New York, Longmans Green & Co., 1918, p. 47. Quoted by Dampier, *op. cit.*, p. 487.

rates of vibration? But every artist knows that the color has a life of its own, *simply as color*. There is a difference between the color red and the color blue which has nothing to do with the measurements of the physicist. The fiery activity of red is universally recognizable, and is universally contrasted with the calm coolness of blue. Is there no truth in this distinction? But science has eliminated the simple qualitative distinction between red and blue because the distinction defies measurement in quantitative terms, through wave lengths. In order to measure accurately and extensively, science has to "see" color colorlessly.

The question here is whether the physicist, in eliminating the qualities of things, is looking at reality at all; whether what he calls matter, for instance, is not some shadowy image of matter, as the cinema is the shadow of three-dimensional life thrown on a flat screen. Build a bigger telescope and we shall be able to see farther and learn more. The fact remains, however, that so long as all our knowledge of the universe is gained from telescopes, we must suspect the telescopes themselves of creating the universe that we claim to know. No telescope has ever grasped the deep sense of awe and wonder that fills the heart of him who contemplates the majesty of the galaxies. But does this prove that the sense of awe and wonder is unfounded, that it has no role to play? The evidence, if we can only learn to look at it, is all the other way; and not the least item of this evidence is the fundamental conflict that the scientific spirit of inquiry has begotten in every individual of the modern world. The search for quantitative measurement permits us to eliminate the wonder and the awe from our calculations; but deep within our being we know that the search for truth does not. We live in the darkness of quantitative research, knowing all the while that we are really the children of light.

Now the conflict comes about through the presence of a stubborn fact which the rigors of science have led us to ignore. This is the fact that for the human being *all* reality is qualitative. The human being does not and cannot live in a merely quantitative world, however high his mind may soar into the realms. The perceptions of his senses are all largely qualitative, and so are all his feelings, and even to a great extent his thought. He is constantly being called upon to make qualitative decisions, as to whether one man is better than another, or this action wiser than that. He is faced, moreover, at almost every turn, with an inner need to make moral judgments, which defy merely quantitative analysis. Many philosophers have sought to reduce such judgments to quantitative terms; e.g., by measuring a "greater" happiness against a "lesser," and many persons try to follow them. Yet the history of hedonism and utilitarianism is itself the best evidence that this procedure always involves a qualitative judgment in the end. Indeed, except in special instances, the quantitative in pure form does not enter into human life. On the one hand, a man's power of perception is incapable of exact quantitative measurement; on the other, quantitative precision is of little use to him.

The moment that men become convinced, therefore, that

truth is only quantitative, the effect is to undermine the validity of all human experience. For the metascientist this human, living world must be dismissed as a barrier to truth which has to be overcome, a jungle of variables which, since they cannot be reduced to quantitative terms, cannot be real. What the human being knows, or feels, *as* a human being, is merely illusion. The greatest achievement of mankind in culture, in poetry and the arts, in faith and "revelation," have no meaning, no reality, no place in the universe, which goes its implacable way without regard to them. They have no destiny, other than to be swallowed up in a darkness that extends for billions of light-years through four-dimensional "space," ruled only by the statistical averages of chance.

The shattering effect of this conflict was foreshadowed in the seventeenth century by Descartes himself. The most famous phrase coined by that philosopher was, *"Cogito, ergo sum* (I think, therefore I am)." We can now see with terrible clarity what that phrase really means. This is no confident assertion of a philosopher whose reasoning has led him to a great enlightenment. It seems rather, to this writer, a cry of desperation—the cry of a giant obsessed with an urge to argue himself out of existence, by abstracting from everything he can touch or feel or experience a merely quantitative reality which is not, and cannot ever be himself. He has to stop and assure himself that he exists! A far more basic proposition would be, "I exist, therefore I know." But Descartes (and we after him) had gone so far in the destruction of qualitative reality that such a state-

ment, based upon the self-evidence, could carry little conviction. Ever since Descartes, though with varying accents
and increasing complexities, men have been uttering the
same desperate cry. But the hidden impulse within them,
the attitude of search, the spirit of inquiry that dominates
their lives, will give them no surcease. The universe that
this attitude of search has revealed has been successively
transmogrified, from a geometrical entity, to a gigantic
clock, to a complex mechanism, to a vast organization of
atoms and finally, according to the most advanced concept,
to a series of statistical averages. But through it all man
remains a creature of illusion who cannot even prove the
validity of experience by pinching himself. The most that
the scientific attitude of search has ever granted to man is
what Descartes so desperately claimed for him: he exists.

The inevitable philosophical reaction to this state of
affairs has been an all-pervasive dualism. Two philosophic
worlds have come into being: an outer world, which, because it can be quantitatively measured, is endowed by the
scientific spirit of inquiry with primary reality; and an
inner, qualitative world, the reality of which is frequently
in doubt, or even denied altogether. The defenders of the
inner world, the Idealists, have been pushed back and generally routed. This is because the defenders of the outer
world, the Empiricists and Materialists, have on their side
the enormous weight of science, which, even though it may
not enter the philosophical battle in its own right, provides
them with an endless supply of quantitative facts. Modern
empirical philosophy has carried out what Edwin A. Burtt

describes as the "banishing of man from the great world of nature . . . the reading of man quite out of the real and primary realm. . . . The features of the world now classed (by Galileo) as secondary, unreal, ignoble, and regarded as dependent on the deceitfulness of sense, are just those features which are most intense to man in all but his purely theoretic activity, and even in that, except where he confines himself strictly to the mathematical method." Man now appears to be "outside of the real world . . . hardly more than a bundle of secondary qualities . . . an irrelevant spectator and insignificant effect of the great mathematical system which is the substance of reality."[8]

[8] Edwin Arthur Burtt, *The Metaphysical Foundations of Modern Physical Science*, New York, The Humanities Press, 1951, pp. 78-80.

4

QUALITY AND QUANTITY

It may be observed that this analysis of the scientific spirit of inquiry places a heavy accent on the effects on human thought of the so-called exact sciences—chiefly, mathematics, physics, and chemistry—and has to some degree disregarded what has been going on in other natural sciences that are less intimately linked with mathematics—chiefly, the organic sciences of biology, physiology, etc. An organic view of reality, as contrasted with the purely mathematical view, opens up a somewhat different vista, as A. N. Whitehead has shown. And yet the accent on the mathematical sciences is inescapable: it was through these sciences that man first broke away from the medieval world, and they have ever since played the dominant role in the development of the scientific spirit of inquiry.

Indeed, one of the strange characteristics of the scientific spirit of inquiry is the almost obsessive quality of man's pursuit of it.

Ever since the first awakening of the sixteenth and seventeenth centuries, the Western world has sought for the truth in quantitative terms with a passion that nothing could divert. For modern man has persisted in pursuing a line of inquiry which has cumulatively undermined the reality of his own being. For three hundred years or more he has pursued this dehumanized idea of reality, which has now entered into all his thinking, his evaluations, his relationships with his fellow men. The modern individual proceeds upon the deep-seated assumption that his own qualitative experiences are untrustworthy, or even false. He himself knows nothing, or nearly nothing, that is true. The search for truth is the province of "experts" and technicians who have facilities for measurement with which he, as a mere human being, is not endowed.

He is left in almost total darkness: a darkness into which, as we have seen, the American philosophic tradition, among others, has led him.

But whatever may have been the causes of the urge behind this pursuit, and however dominant it may be in the affairs of our time, there are certain signs that humanity, or at least some portion of humanity, is preparing to break out of it. These signs come to light, on the one hand, in a wide-spread popular demand, that what the free world needs just now is a "spiritual awakening." People may not be very clear as to what they mean by this, but in the light of our present analysis, we can hazard the guess that the spiritual awakening they have in mind consists, basically, of a revolt against the domination of a spirit of inquiry which insists that they view reality in purely quantitative terms. On the other hand, as all students of science know, the exact sciences are themselves in the throes of a profound revolution. Where the revolution will lead we do not yet know. But in the literature of science one finds intimations everywhere of new concepts and new approaches.

It is not our task here to enter into the complexities of the scientific revolution. There is, however, a *particular* approach, which is so essential to our theme that our study of the scientific spirit of inquiry would be incomplete if we were to fail to refer to it. This approach opens up an entirely new vista for a world dedicated to the spirit of science.

In 1932 a remarkable address was delivered before the Saxon Academy of Science by one of the greatest of modern physicists. The speaker was Professor Werner Heisenberg, formulator of the famous "principle of indeterminacy," indispensable to contemporary theorizing in the difficult and highly technical field of quantum mechanics. Having ventured further than all but a few men in the direction of pure quantitative abstraction, Dr. Heisenberg turns, in the address mentioned, to evaluate the results of this manner of inquiry. For this purpose he disregards all the brilliant discoveries with which science is easily credited, and concentrates his attention upon the sacrifices in knowledge that have been made in order to achieve them. "As facts and knowledge accumulate," he says, "the claim of the scientist to an understanding of the world in a certain sense diminishes." The path of science is a path of *renunciation*. In order to view its scientific objectives it has had to renounce "the aim of bringing the phenomena of nature to our thinking in an immediate and living way."

What does Dr. Heisenberg mean by "immediate and living" knowledge? The answer to this question is disclosed in the fact that his address was given on the hundredth anniversary of the great German poet-scientist, Johann Wolfgang von Goethe. Those familiar with the history of science may recall the struggle that Goethe put up against Newtonian optics, and the strange (and in our eyes, inadmissible) theory of color which he formulated in opposition. The struggle, of course, was won by Newton, even though Newtonian optics have proved quite inadequate to explain the phenomena of light; and the Goethian theory has ever since been dismissed as a kind of scientific curiosity. But that is really a minor matter. What we can now see, from the perspective of nearly a century and a half, is that an issue was at stake between Goethe and Newton, much more fundamental and far-reaching than any mere theory of light. This issue was precisely the one that we have been attempting to define, and it will serve us well at this point to take brief cognizance of Goethe's view of it.

Sir Isaac Newton, of course, was profoundly instrumental in the development of the scientific spirit of inquiry in quantitative terms. It was the essence of Goethe's argument against Newton that this quantitative approach to Nature could not lead to truth. Goethe insisted upon observing nature *in terms of her content.* For him the idea that the color red could be defined only as a quantitative vibration was intolerable. For Goethe, sensory knowledge, while it may involve illusion, is not *merely* illusion. It is susceptible of many distortions and contains many subjective variables, but it is not a knowledge of nothing. It is, on the contrary, the "immediate and living" perception of a qualitative reality, a quality of Nature, which exists and is true. And it can no more be gained by pure quantitative abstraction than a man can quench his thirst by measuring the cubic capacity of a tumbler.

What is true of sensory knowledge is true, for Goethe, of other forms of knowledge. This is because there exists between the *subject* (the observer) and the *object* (the observed) an inner unity. The nature of this unity, of which both man and Nature are a part, is a mystery but with our intuitive faculties and our imagination we can enter this mystery and actually know things—so to speak—from the inside. Hence, it is possible for the subject to know the object *by means of contemplating it.* "My thinking does not separate itself from objects . . . my contemplation is itself a way of thinking, my thinking a way of contemplating." As Karl Vïetor puts it, "Speculative thinking (for Goethe) can only operate positively when it contributes to the process of heightening feeling and intuition into a clear awareness, so that we are led more deeply into the phenomenon itself." Man can know Nature, not by reasoning abstractly, but by discovering himself, in contemplation, as part of her.

Goethe's approach to knowledge is cited here to illustrate the distinction between the quantitative and qualitative view of things. There is no need, of course, to adopt either view to the exclusion of the other. That there is such a thing as quantitative truth, all of mathematics and all of theoretical and applied sciences bear witness. But what led to the clash between Goethe and Newton was the former's

V

A DIRECTION FOR ADVENTURE

1

MATTER AND REALITY

It may seem that this detour into these abstruse branches of thought has been unnecessarily burdensome and has carried us far from our central theme—the world conflict over freedom. But it is important to show how profound are the underlying issues in the war of ideas. Nothing less is involved than man himself. Who is he? Where is he going? For what purposes is he on earth? On our answers to these questions our definition of man's freedom must ultimately depend.

During the exciting centuries when science was in hot pursuit of the mastery of nature, the underlying question of whether its quantitative concepts represented the truth about man and the universe could be disregarded. But today, with the hydrogen bomb hanging as by a diplomatic thread over all the great centers of civilization, no one can help asking himself whether the conquest of nature has not, in itself, gone far enough. For what are we to *do* with our mastery of nature? What goals are we to establish, what truths are we to pursue? Does the free world accept a quantitative view of nature and of man? *Can* we accept it? And if we do not accept it, what shall we put in its place? Goethe's "intuitive contemplation," Dr. Heisenberg's "immediate and living knowledge," and our own concept of a qualitative aspect of reality give us a clue to our answer. The balance of this study will be concerned with the amplification of that clue, in the hope that it may lead us out to a view of man capable of supporting the free ideals that we intuitively cherish.

It might be supposed that in depriving matter of virtually every quality that the human being can recognize as material, physics destroyed the doctrine of Materialism. And yet this is not the case. Modern Materialism is just as materialistic as the original version, even though modern physics shows matter to be, so to speak, nonmaterial. And this fact leads to a rather startling conclusion. Materialism, we are forced to admit, does not depend upon any particular view of matter. Indeed, it does not seem to be a philosophy of matter at all. It is a way of looking at the world. Even if science should succeed in showing that matter is composed of nothing hard, nothing solid, nothing material—even if matter turns out to be nothing but insubstantial and evanescent waves acting and reacting on one another—the doctrine of Materialism could still proceed along an unswerving course, to provide men with an apparently consistent philosophy of life.

This point is important. For in the first place, if valid, it demolishes at a stroke one of the most cherished Marxist assumptions. As already pointed out, the Marxists have insisted that they are building a social philosophy upon a strictly scientific basis. They were relentlessly driven to the doctrine of Materialism—so they inferred—by the discoveries of science, which showed that the evolution of the earth and of man could only be accounted for in material terms. It escaped their observation, and escaped the observation of most of their critics, that they were not really equating being to matter. They were equating being *to a hypothesis about matter*—a very different equation. They equated being to that particular view of matter—something hard and identifiable—which prevailed in the nineteenth century, but which is a view modern science has since discredited. Inasmuch as the ultimate nature of matter is wholly unknown, this is like equating being to x. In a scientific sense, then, the Marxists themselves have discovered no absolute. They have merely extended a nineteenth-century hypothesis into the twentieth century in a wholly dogmatic way.

But if Marx and Engels were not really consulting science in the development of their idea, what were they consulting? The answer is that they were indulging in a certain point of view toward reality which, as we have seen, has become dominant in our entire civilization. We can identify it by means of the fundamental distinction we have already made. It is the point of view, rooted in the outward-looking consciousness, which insists that external observation and analysis provide us with our only means of access to truth. Reality, in other words, is what we can perceive with our senses and our instruments by looking outward from ourselves while the inward-looking consciousness is entangled in endless illusions, so the argument goes. It is only by examining and analyzing things from the outside that we have any chance of reaching objective truth; it is only in the external world, indeed, that truth is to be found.

Analysis of Marxism thus reveals two important keys to an understanding of it—Materialism and Externalism. But may it not develop that the keys are identical? May it not be that the doctrine of Materialism, though deriving its name from matter, is nothing more or less than the doctrine of externalization—that reality can only be discovered by looking at things and experience from the outside? Such a definition of Materialism enables us to explain how it is that although the concept of matter has been, so to speak, dematerialized, the doctrine that takes its name from matter has not been affected. It was merely given the wrong name. Materialism is not, in fact, a doctrine of matter but is a doctrine of truth—a way of looking at things, which asserts that the human mind can only come to truth by the use of the outward-looking consciousness. Indeed we can go further. The very concept of matter which dominated nineteenth-century science, and which is still active in the thinking of the average man, is the result of this deep-seated assumption. Matter, in other words, did not create Materialism. Externalism created matter as Marx and Engels and the whole nineteenth century conceived it.

What is really in question here is what we have termed a metascience, partly anticipated no doubt by older Materialists like Democritus and Lucretius, but, as we know it, springing from the preoccupation of modern man with the scientific method of inquiry which accepts one kind of truth (the outward and quantitative) and rejects all others. And in this attitude, as we have tried to show, the free world as well as the Marxist is deeply implicated. Americans have increasingly sought to define the values of life in outward-looking terms. When the American optimist interprets the purposes of human life as being confined to earth, those purposes become inescapably oriented, just like the Marxist purposes, to the economic and the social. And as a consequence, the American optimist, when faced with the total optimism of Marxism, can no longer justify the key idea of his own revolution—the principle of individual liberty.

2

THE DIGNITY OF MAN

Almost every American will feel inclined to combat the statement that the principle of individual liberty cannot be justified. The point, however, is not whether liberty can be justified at all, but whether the philosophical optimist can justify it within the limits of his assumptions. What is there observable in life on earth, reasonably accessible to the scientific spirit of inquiry as thus far developed, that can enable American optimists to demonstrate the validity of this embattled principle?

There is only one means and all the various American optimistic schools resort to it. The point at which they all rally is the concept of the dignity of man, the dignity of the individual. This phrase has acquired the special meaning, that the human being must not be treated as a mere means to some other end (such as, for example, the state), but must be regarded as an end in himself. His self-fulfillment is an indispensable goal of human life, and that society is backward, unjust, even evil, that does not promote it. It is through this concept, we may say, that the American optimistic tradition goes into opposition against Marxism.

It would seem at first glance that the concept provides the optimist with the philosophical method of blocking the entire Marxian thesis. For if individuals are ends in themselves they cannot be treated as the mere pawns of the dialectical process of history; and as for the dictatorship of the proletariat, this can be shown, on these philosophic grounds, to be one of the greatest evils imaginable. A classless society may be a high social ideal, but it cannot be brought about by force but only through a slow process of educating individuals. The classless society would then be an organic composition of such individuals, each an end in himself, but each increasingly able to fulfill and realize himself in terms of the welfare of his fellow men—that is to say, in social terms. The principle of human dignity, in short, provides the American optimist with a way to the achievement of social goals in a free and voluntary manner —a kind of absolute which does not have absolutist results.

One additional argument the pragmatic optimist has, which almost every American has used at some time. He invokes the "evidence." Society works best, he contends, and men are happier, when the assumption is made that the human being has an inherent dignity that must not be violated. Because, it works, in short, the assumption must be a valid one.

We can say of this concept of human dignity that it is a philosophical bastion of the free world. For nearly a hundred years Dialectical Materialism has been expanding, until, here in the mid-twentieth century, it has virtually encircled us. In practice, the dignity of the human being is the single most important concept that stands between us and engulfment. It is this idea—or at any rate, what it stands for—that has given meaning to our policies, other than that of a mere struggle for power; it is this that has caused us to

lay down our lives to block the encroachments of total-
itarians like Mussolini and Hitler; and it is this that gives
us the courage and the will to call the bluffs and oppose the
maneuvers of the Kremlin. American philosophical optimists, as we have seen, have led us into many disillusionments; but we have to thank them for recognizing this
bastion of freedom, and for daring to defend it.

But it is to this bastion, the dignity of man, that we now
have to look. Do human experiences and American philosophical concepts actually support it? The American optimist's pragmatic arguments are just what the Marxists
specifically deny. The principle of individual liberty, the
Marxists contend, can never lead to a solution of the ills
and grievances of society. It can only preserve and expand
those ills and grievances. And the contention of the American optimists, therefore, that their way is best because it
works, is based, say the Marxists, not on evidence at all,
but on prejudice and self-interest. We may not agree with
the Marxist argument. But we cannot escape the fact of its
power.

Furthermore, the American optimist's position with regard to the dignity of man is philosophically untenable.
For the scientific outlook on man and his origins *betrays*
the American optimist. It leads him up to the heights of
optimism regarding man and his potential development.
But when he turns to it for support for his concept of
"human dignity"—indispensable to the progress of his own
revolutionary stream—it vanishes away like Mephistoph-

eles. The optimist is then left like Faust in his palace just
before his death, and might well exclaim, with that disillusioned old scientist of another age:

"Not yet have I my liberty made good."

For to what scientific hypothesis or discovery can the
optimist turn in order to prove the reality of human
dignity? Certainly not to the Kant-Laplace theory of the
creation of the solar system, or any of its modern cosmolog-
ical derivatives, for all purely materialistic or naturalistic
theories of creation reveal man as a mere submicroscopic
speck in a megagalactic infinitude. Certainly not to the
theory of organic evolution, which shows man to be the
descendant, via apes and saurians, of a primeval slime.
The optimist cannot validate man's dignity through physics,
where the concept of dignity is nonexistent; through bio-
chemistry, which reduces the human being to an agglomera-
tion of cells; or through zoology, in terms of which man
is just another animal; or even through modern psychology, which recognizes certain interior distinctions between man and animal, but constantly tends to reduce these
differences back again to the level of natural drives and
instincts characteristic of the animal world.[1] In virtually
every instance, indeed, the inferences to be drawn from
natural science point away from the dignity of man. They
do not support the concept of human dignity, they make it
untenable.

[1] An exception must be made here for the work of C. G. Jung and other
pioneers in what has been termed the analytical branch of psychology.

3

PEOPLE FROM A TO X

The predicament of the optimist cannot be blamed entirely upon the natural sciences. Prominent in the optimistic stream of thought are a number of human and social sciences, whose object is the study of the human being. These sciences, however, instead of approaching man in a new spirit of inquiry have adapted, or sought to imitate, the scientific spirit of inquiry as evolved by the exact sciences. It is true that the social sciences cannot be strictly mathematical, in the sense that physics is. Nevertheless, they all exhibit that leading characteristic of the scientific spirit of inquiry that we have already examined. Every year the American social sciences produce thousands of documents dealing with community affairs, public opinion, juvenile delinquency, labor, the divorce rate, crime, educational methods, etc., etc. Many of these documents contain observations and comparative analyses of great significance; yet the spirit of inquiry that animates them is essentially a *spirit of measurement* and external description. The task is never to tell us what the human being *is*, any more than it is the task of the chemist to tell us what an atom of oxygen is. The task is to find out how the human being acts and reacts under given circumstances, to trace the immediate and distant causes, and sometimes to estimate the results. Man, the individual, the mysterious "I am" at the core of every human consciousness, is left out

of these investigations. That unknown is simply denomi-
nated "X"; and the task of the social scientist then reduces
itself to ascertaining the complex relationships between
"X" and the observable phenomena around it.

The main questions that the social scientist asks are
concerned primarily with the society or community in
which an individual lives. His virtues and faults are
assayed in terms, not so much of his self-realization, as of
the *effects* that their practice may have upon others. From
an individualistic point of view, the tragedy of a kidnap-
ing such as that of Kansas City's Greenlease case, in which
$600,000 ransom was demanded and obtained after the
child had been murdered, lies in the terrifying realization
that a human soul can fall to such depths of callous de-
pravity. From a social point of view, on the other hand,
the evil is to be measured in terms of its effects and potential effects upon society, including the minds of young
people who read about it.

An increasing accent on social good as the ultimate
ethical determinant is the result of the scientific spirit of
inquiry. An investigator with a quantitative and external
orientation is always at a loss in classical ethics where
measurement can reveal nothing. The dismal attempt of
Jeremy Bentham to measure pleasure for the purpose of
defining the good speaks for itself. If one is determined to
approach man from a quantitative orientation, the only
kind of good that one can deal with is social good, because
this is the only kind that lends itself even approximately
to measurement. The social scientist can tell us a great deal

about what man's social goals should be, and even how to achieve them, but he can tell us virtually nothing of substance about what man is. Social science can help us to find out why and how a recognition of the rights of labor, a better distribution of resources, or the encouragement of alcoholic temperance among the young, can make for a better society, but it will not get us very far in accounting for the "goodness" of a saint.

Useful as the scientific spirit is to practical research, the exclusive pursuit of this view of truth and the good strikes at the key idea of the libertarian revolution, the idea of the *individual*, and inevitably minimizes it. The individual gets lost or becomes merely a part of the social whole. This is made specific by the leading philosopher of the experimental approach to social questions. Writing of the problem of the relation of the individual to the society in which he lives, John Dewey said:

> We might as well make a problem out of the relation of the letters of an alphabet to the alphabet. An alphabet *is* letters, and society is individuals in their connections with one another. The mode of combination of letters with one another is obviously a matter of importance; letters form words and sentences when combined, and have no point of sense except in some combination. I would not say that the latter statement applies literally to individuals, but it cannot be gainsaid that singular human beings exist and behave in constant and varied association with one another.[2]

And writing of the "historic claim of philosophy that it occupies itself with the ideal of wholes and the whole,"

[2] John Dewey, *The Public and Its Problems*, Chicago, Gateway Books, 1946, p. 69.

Dewey continues, "I do not say that the social as we know it *is* the whole, but I do emphatically suggest that it is the widest and richest manifestation of the whole accessible to our observation."[3]

Not all of the free world adheres to this, or to related schools of philosophy; and yet millions of persons in all countries of that world have come, if by different routes, essentially to the position outlined here. The qualitative life of the individual, which is all that the human being knows of reality at first hand, is dismissed as merely private; and in its place there is erected the social reality which, because it can be measured in quantitative and described in external terms, is accepted on all sides as the measure of the good and even of the real. So man becomes engulfed in society.

And not the least appalling aspect of this state of affairs is the similarity between the thesis of these libertarian optimists and the thesis of the Marxists. What has been happening is perfectly plain. That quantitative spirit of inquiry has seized both the totalitarian and libertarian revolution. A total capture has not yet taken place, because the libertarian tradition still runs strong and has erected emotional barriers. What has taken place, however, is a kind of rupture, a cracking of the libertarian tradition through its center. The West no longer says one thing but two things. It says that the individual has dignity and

---

[3] John Dewey, *Philosophy and Civilization*, New York, Milton Balch & Co., 1931, p. 92.

must therefore be treated as an end in himself—though the free world cannot support this assertion by any means of inquiry that it is willing to recognize. And it says, on the other hand, that the ultimate criteria of the good, and even of truth itself, are social—though it cannot follow this proposition to its logical conclusion, because the dignity of the individual stands in the way. As a result of this fundamental crack in the doctrine, American optimism can convince no one. It must ultimately give way everywhere to the absolute optimism of the Marxists, who can promise salvation on the earth in quantitative and measurable terms without reservation.

We may at this point remind ourselves of the statement of the French Catholic intellectual, François Mauriac, quoted in Part I, to the effect that it is not what separates the U.S. and the U.S.S.R. that should frighten the free world, "but what they have in common." Mauriac may have been guilty of a certain amount of glib generalization, but we can see now that he was not talking about nothing. What "those two technocracies" have in common is the doctrine of philosophical optimism, in one case absolutist and brash, in the other, relativistic and hesitant; an optimism in both cases, however, which sees man as a creature of earth, whose salvation must be expressed in terms of social goals, and can be achieved only by means of a high degree of industrial production, economic plenty, and a cooperative attitude of mind. It is perfectly true that totalitarian optimism and libertarian optimism result in two different ideas of Man: Dialectical Man and Industrial Man. The hidden embarrassment from which the course of freedom suffers, however, is that Industrial Man, while different from Dialectical Man in many dramatic respects, is not different enough. Dialectical Man is in fact the offspring of Industrial Man, as the history of Marxism shows. The son exhibits violent characteristics that the father does not possess, and has invented an absolutist philosophy to justify them. The father, who has been taught to respect certain human ideals, remains confused. But should they take arms against each other, the question arises as to what would be gained by the "victory" of either. This is a question that freedom-seekers throughout the world are asking, and the American failure to answer it goes far to explain the reluctance of the free world, during the last several critical years, to arm itself for battle.

4

IN SEARCH OF A SYNTHESIS

The analysis of the American predicament has carried us a certain distance in understanding the ideas at stake in our momentous struggle. At mid-century the outlook for Industrial Man, as he girds himself for the struggle with Dialectical Man, is not a happy one. He finds himself living in an inner darkness, confronting the most important questions of life with doubt, and faced everywhere with the possibility of catastrophe. It is a very different picture from that which presented itself to this same citizen, or to his parents, at the beginning of the century, which seemed to justify an optimistic view of man and his prospects upon the earth. The question naturally arises of what we are now to do with that optimistic view. If it has thus led us into darkness and doubt, must we not now undertake to liquidate it? The philosophical pessimists, of course, will answer this question in the affirmative. According to their view of man and the universe, the plight of the Western world at mid-century was in large part predictable. The high hopes for the salvation of man through progress were bound sooner or later to be disappointed because they were based upon illusions, not upon the realities of human life. The wonder only is, the pessimist would suggest, that those illusions of progress are still capable of working such magic. The wonder is that so many men and women who deeply share the doubts and fears of our time are still able to believe that Industrial Man—with the help, of course, of economic aid,

education, and democracy—is about to bring forth a new
age of peace and enlightenment; that technology can succeed
in providing men with all they need; that science, that great
source of truth, will not only show that no life beyond our
present life exists, but will, so to speak, render obsolete the
hope of such.

The conflict between the philosophical optimists and the
philosophical pessimists is among the most fundamental in
all of philosophy and the attempt to resolve it could lead us
into a very great debate. There is, however, no need to make
this arduous attempt, and for a very practical reason:
philosophical optimism is now so deeply embedded in the
American tradition that Americans cannot get along without it. They are steeped in philosophical optimism; it per-
meates their entire outlook and enters unobserved into all
their thinking. However conclusively we might show that
it is erroneous and self-contradictory, it could not be
liquidated out-of-hand because it is too closely bound up
with what America *is*.

Moreover, even if it were possible to liquidate this
philosophical tradition, the question would still remain
as to whether it would be desirable. If we set the optimistic
tradition in the broad perspective of history we see that it
has consistently supplied the world with a certain kind of
strength that it now very much needs. However fallible, its
assumptions have been profoundly exciting. They have
opened up an invigorating vista of man's life on earth.
Out of them the United States of America was born, from
them it received its mission, in their spell it grew to power,
and fought wars, and established victories. The optimistic

assumptions gave meaning to the technological revolution and inspired the enormous industrialization of American life; and we who have participated in their magic power have had an experience unique in the history of the world, which has led us to breed hopes for mankind higher than any people have ever had. Nor have the efforts of the optimists to fulfill these hopes been entirely in vain. Their efforts have alleviated pain, improved the health of millions, encouraged education, helped men to free themselves from the grip of fear and ignorance. Their efforts have always kept the future open for better things. In a world overshadowed by despair they have been the harbingers of hope.

And indeed, this point applies not only to America, it holds for modern man generally. It may well be true that man does not belong to the earth alone, and hence, cannot really fulfill himself in terms of earthly goals. Still he cannot abandon these goals either. The improvement of his earthly lot is important, not merely in selfish terms, but morally. It is criminal to permit poverty and suffering to dominate people's lives, if these can be prevented. The answer of the Buddhist monk cannot be the answer for most of humanity. To this fact, which is basic to the economics of our time, millions are now awakening. And to that awakening American philosophical optimism has been— and remains—indispensable.

The dilemma that these considerations suggest is the dilemma of America at mid-century. The doctrine of progress, which, in terms of man's inner life and inner requirements, leads to endless disillusionment, has nevertheless become vital to the health—indeed to the survival—of modern civilization. This fact is as apparent in the East, where the standard of living is low, as in the West, where it is almost unbelievably high. The East must adapt its thinking to the doctrine of progress in order to rescue its destitute millions from starvation and misery; the West must support it in order to prevent the collapse of what has already been won. To abandon the optimistic tradition entirely would then, in effect, be to abandon America, to abandon the *meaning* of America. In terms of human destiny we are committed to the optimistic tradition in an irreversible way; we must follow where it leads, whatever the consequences.

But what if the choice is not black-and-white? May there not be some means by which these two conflicting views of man can be reconciled? To put the question more specifically, may it not be that that inward looking view of reality which characterizes the pursuit of happiness of the Buddhist monk, and which leads to such pessimistic conclusions regarding life on earth, is in some valid way connected with the outward-looking view, which so deeply influences American life and leads to such optimistic evaluations? Is it really the case that one of these views of human life is true, and the other false, and that the human being, therefore, must choose between them? May it not be true that each represents a different aspect of the human struggle, that one supports the other, that one can be fulfilled in terms of the other? May there not be available to him who is willing to seek for it, a mighty synthesis between the great hopes that Americans have for mankind, and the old and wiser sense of tragedy that has for so many centuries filled the hearts of seers—a synthesis which, could we discover it, might provide us with the foundations for a doctrine of freedom possessing that quality which our present foundations so glaringly lack, the quality of universality?

Our analysis has at least brought us to the point where the problem can be defined in these somewhat explicit terms. What is needed is not more debate but a bold search for a new synthesis. To this end, our task is not so much that of the technical philosopher as of the adventurous explorer. We must try to look into the human spirit with a certain freedom of thought that is not always to be found in academic circles. From a purely intellectual standpoint, this may be risky business; but from the standpoint of mankind, which cannot live by intellect alone, it is necessary if we are to find a new and fruitful approach.

Such a synthesis is to be found, not in any philosophical school which merely represents our present attitude of search, but in the actual development, however gradually, of a new attitude of search. This thought suggests that a task lies ahead of America of truly overwhelming proportions: the task, namely of learning how to inquire into the nature and destiny of man in a new way, of which our current spirit of inquiry has not yet dreamed. It suggests the possibility of knowledge that we do not yet have, of vistas that we have not yet opened up. And it intimates, finally, that in this knowledge and these vistas we might find, not merely the solution to the American dilemma, but the foundations for an Idea of a Free Man.

5

THE SPIRITUAL REFERENCE

The observer of our time can hardly fail to be struck by the increasing frequency with which the word "spiritual" is appearing—or is being implied—in the speeches and writings of those who are seeking or offering solutions to our problems. Not only many political thinkers, but lecturers, convention speakers, politicians, pundits, businessmen, and commentators, tell us over and over again that the foundations of our democratic life are spiritual—and even prescribe, as the only hope of the future, a spiritual awakening or revival. Said President Eisenhower at Columbia University in 1950: "But man's spiritual side is still the dominant one . . . justice, freedom, equality [are] things of the spirit . . . that make important the satisfaction of man's creative needs." In 1949, before the American Political Science Association, John Foster Dulles spoke to the same effect. "Our future greatness and our power," he said, "lie, not in aping the methods of Soviet communism, not in trying to contain them—and us—within walls of steel, but in demonstrating, contrastingly and startlingly, the infinitely greater worth of practices that derive from a spiritual view of the nature of man." And in his little volume *War or Peace*, Mr. Dulles quotes from an article by Woodrow Wilson: "The sum of the whole matter is this, that our civilization cannot survive materially unless it be redeemed spiritually."

Businessmen make the point as frequently as statesmen. For example, Admiral Ben Moreell, President of the Jones & Laughlin Steel Company, and head of the Seabees in World War II, said: "The main precept of our philosophy of life is not democracy, but our faith in God . . . Our founding fathers . . . thought democracy to be the best system of government to fulfill the spiritual objectives and aims for which they came to America. . . . You may ask, 'Why does a representative of American industry attach such great importance to this matter of spiritual strength?' It is because I believe that it is the source of that power which is essential for our ultimate victory (against the Communists)."

These samples are quoted, not because they are unique, but on the contrary, because they are typical of hundreds of such pronouncement. What may be called the "spiritual reference" is being urgently made by secular leaders who apparently have the feeling that there is something lacking in our contemporary view of man. A peculiarity of this phenomenon is that it is not directly connected with the churches. The men just quoted happen to be devout churchmen. Yet, the attitude of many of the persons who talk about the importance of the spiritual often implies, if it does not openly state, a certain criticism of organized religion, to the effect that it has failed to provide mid-century man with adequate answers to his spiritual search, or adequate content for his spiritual aspirations. It is not our task to examine this criticism here. Millions of persons throughout the world are at home in the spiritual reference, mostly in terms of well-defined religious convictions, as formulated by various religious creeds and organizations. To these persons the problem we are raising scarcely exists: they have resolved it in accordance with the tenets of their creeds, at least for working purposes, and the man of good will searching for spiritual enlightenment can have no quarrel with them, but may rather learn a great deal from them. The fact still remains, however, that there are millions of persons, especially in America, who seem unable to gain in that way the light that they are looking for, but who nevertheless insist that that light is spiritual. These persons have awakened to the enormous importance in the affairs of mankind of what we have called the inner world, but they find themselves unable to follow either science or organized religion into that world.

Now there can be no doubt that they have something of fundamental importance in mind, but the difficulty is to tell just what it is. They are referring to some special characteristic of man, an understanding of which, they affirm, is necessary to his survival, or to his welfare, or to his freedom, or to all three. Yet one has the feeling, in almost every instance, that they would find it very difficult indeed to define this aspect of man or to give it any realistic content. A certain content, of course, is inherited from the general background of our civilization, which is a Judaeo-Christian background; and at times it even seems that Western speakers and writers who invoke the reference are using spiritual as virtually synonymous with Christian. The synonymity, of course, is unacceptable, since there are other paths to the spiritual than the specifically Christian ones; and even if we were to accept such a synonymity for working purposes, it would not get us very far, because of the confusion regarding the word "Christian" itself. The importance of Christianity to the free way of life is self-evident and has been set forth by many scholars. Yet almost insuperable difficulties arise as soon as we try to define, in terms intelligible to the mid-century, just what a Christian is. The variations run all the way from the acceptance of Jesus as a great, though somewhat impractical, teacher, to the acknowledgment of Him, or of the Christ in Him, as the veritable Son of God. Far from providing a content for the word spiritual, these variations of the Christian doctrine seem to arise from different interpretations of that word. A man's view of Christianity will be deeply influenced, if not actually defined, by his idea of what the spiritual is, or is not. To the Christian true-believer it may well seem that the term is given adequate content by the life of Jesus, as presented in the Gospels, by the great insights of St. Paul, and by what the church itself says. But this is to beg the whole question. What the mid-twentieth century seems to need is not instruction for true-believers but a content for the word spiritual for those who are outside. This cannot be derived, for those persons, from a simple reiteration of the Gospels, or of what the church says about them. We must find some other way.

Almost everyone who has recourse to the spiritual reference would agree that what he has in mind is intimately related to the concept of God. Here, again, however, the variations are so great that the concept cannot help us much. To some, God is an immediate and intimate Presence; to others, a remote abstraction that has little if any reality. Some see God in nature, others in man, others in the cosmos. For pantheists, He is the universe and expresses Himself through its forces and laws. For deists, He is an impersonal Being who exerts no influence upon men or the universe that He has created. For some He is anthropomorphic, for others formless, or formed in some way that we cannot conceive. Outside the pale of theology, there is really no telling what anyone means by God. And even within the pale, there is enough fundamental disagreement to make it imperative, if the churches are to be held together, to resort to dogma.

Many of the greatest contemporary scientists, to be sure, make the spiritual reference. They emphatically affirm the existence of God, and declare that nothing demonstrates this so conclusively as the wonders that science has revealed. But almost without exception, when scientists speak thus, they speak in their personal capacities—as men, not as scientists. They step out of the world of science in order to make the spiritual reference, and when they return to that world they eliminate the spiritual from their considerations. The result of this is the very kind of conflict that underlies all our lives. When an Einstein or a Millikan tells us of his belief in God he becomes an impressive witness to the spiritual; but if the moment he turns to the search for truth by those means of which he is an acknowledged master, he abandons the spiritual reference, as if it

had no bearing upon truth; he in effect bears witness
against his own witness. The question that the intelligent
layman cannot fail to ask is this: If the spiritual aspect of
things is of such fundamental importance, how comes it
that science can disregard that aspect of things? Must we
not choose between two irreconcilable views: the view of
science that the spiritual reference is not really important,
that it is indeed a sort of illusion that has no bearing on
things as they really are; or, on the other hand, the
spiritual view?

Our time has wholly failed to resolve this conflict, and
the failure leads us back again to that darkness that characterizes our lives. The question goes far beyond the question of any particular religion; it is a question of our
concept of man. We may even say that what is sometimes
described as the "failure" of the churches, is not a failure
in the ordinary sense of the word. In his search for truth,
mid-century man has followed the sciences, which takes no
cognizance of the spiritual, and the result is that he cannot
see in the church what the church has to offer. The word
"spiritual" has become divorced from what we conceive to
be reality. It has been ousted from the world of thought,
relegated to the world of feeling. Sometimes it seems to
denote nothing more than a rather high degree of refinement, a special sensitivity, or an advanced cultural development—as for instance, one might say that the French are
spiritual, as contrasted with the less subtle Americans. It
even has sentimental overtones. We say of a man that he
exhibits a certain spirituality, meaning that he is kind and

has regard for human intangibles. These are what might be called favorable uses of the word. On the unfavorable side it has become almost a term of denunciation; we are inclined to say that a man's view of things is merely spiritual, meaning that it is unrealistic. And finally, confusion is confounded by the use of this same word to denote that form of indulgence in the supernatural called spiritualism, which consists in the supposed invocation of departed spirits and ghosts.

It goes without saying that these are not the meanings that they who invoke the spiritual reference have in mind. But the truth is that what they have in mind has become, in a sense, nonexistent; it is an aspect of the human being for which contemporary thinking provides no real content. Those who invoke the spiritual reference know that the spiritual is something, but few of them can say what it *is*. They are in fact in the position of a man who has been born blind. This man knows that there is such a thing as sight, because people who can see tell him so. He may even, from the workings of his own imagination, obtain some dim intimation of what sight is like, and in his idea of existence learn to allow for it; it is a concept which, for him, is empty, but to which he must nevertheless concede some kind of meaning. Mid-century man has been told by ancient documents, and by all the great art and literature of the past, that there is a spiritual reality, and of it he has—like the blind man—certain intimations. But he cannot see this reality; it is something distant from him, something transcendental, alien to the nature of the world in which he lives. He can, therefore, only refer to it, as something which he knows about but cannot know. It has become, not a reality, but a reference.

He who would inquire into the inner world thus has three choices to make. He may return to the churches and seek to reanimate within himself the deep convictions and insights which they represent and through which they moulded Western civilization. If he cannot bring himself to this, he may follow the path of science into the field of psychiatry and content himself, chiefly, with the therapy that it has to offer. Or, refusing both of these, he may strive to give the word "spiritual" a content capable of revealing the realities of the inner world, to himself and to others, in living terms. Any one of these avenues of search involves dangers and requires effort. Yet he who is willing to forego all three must virtually give up searching at all, and must make the best he can of the inner uncertainties, the inner darkness, into which he has fallen.

It is my belief that twentieth-century man cannot extricate himself from this inner darkness unless he can give a content to his spiritual references, which they do not now possess. The word "spiritual" means something and he who would understand the inner world must learn what that meaning is. I would further contend that what the church has to offer, on the one hand, and what science has to offer on the other, are by no means so contradictory as a superficial examination appears to indicate when that to which so many now refer as the spiritual is rightly understood. It will be found to contain the means of reconciling, in a profound and satisfying way, these two conflicting impulses of twentieth-century life. This, no doubt, is a proposition that a single study cannot explore, for it leads into Sphinx-like questions that have troubled mankind for millennia. They are questions which, on the whole, have never been answered, and the attitude of modern man is, that since they have not been answered, they cannot be answered. Possibly so. But without claiming any special endowments for the exploration of such matters, it is permissible for the layman to take note of a certain distinction. Whenever it is a question of exploring some mystery of the outer world, twentieth-century man does not invoke the failures of the past as an excuse for his ignorance. No one in the past was able to split the atom, but this fact did not stop us from inquiring into how it might be done. It is only when we turn to the inner world, to questions pertaining to the nature of man himself—questions comprehended under the general heading of spiritual—that the failures of the past are invoked. It is only then that we say, that because man has never been able to answer the Sphinx, he never can answer the Sphinx.

VI

THE SWORD OF MICHAEL

1

THE INNER WORLD

To students of philosophy, the distinction which we have made throughout these pages between the inner and outer ways of looking at things will seem somewhat unconventional. Technical philosophy accounts for this distinction in various ways, but it has on the whole avoided the simple terminology that we have used. However, the present study is not a work in technical philosophy. It is not our task, for example, to enter into a critical analysis of Idealism, or to distinguish it in technical terms from its philosophical opposites, such as Empiricism, Positivism, Materialism, etc. Our approach to the problems of man is that of the intelligent layman who is deeply involved in the forces of his time and earnestly seeking a way to master them. Such a person must be prepared to deal with the major issues of philosophy, but he is entitled to do so in terms that have meaning for *him*. But from a nontechnical point of view the distinction we have made has the merit of easy and immediate recognizability. As we plunge into this inner world, observing with our consciousness the various phenomena that present themselves to us, we have the distinct impression of different *layers*. We encounter different degrees, so to speak, of consciousness, semiconsciousness, and unconsciousness. The whole is extremely confusing, even to the professional psychologist, and is made the more so because the phenomena of this world differ in profound ways from those of the outer world. Yet the differences are extremely difficult to put into words, because our working concepts, and hence, our language, are outward-looking. We do not have words adequate to define these inner phenomena, which have almost no regard for the laws and structures of our ordinary world; to know them we must *live* them, experience them.

The best way to do this is to consult actual situations that involve the use of the inward-looking consciousness and to try to relive those situations imaginatively. Our task, in any case, is not a thorough exploration of the inner world; what concerns us here is a certain leading characteristic of this world, a certain kind of "knowing," a recognition of which is essential to our attempt to orient ourselves to the question of truth.[1]

Let us take as a prosaic example a football game. For the average American this is an outer event in which so-and-so performs such-and-such feats resulting in such-and-such a score. A little reflection, however, will show that this view is somewhat superficial. Imagine any of the great "classics" that break out in a rash across the length and breadth of the land every fall: the fur coats, the big chrysanthemums, the pennants, the excited girls and their shouting escorts, the cheer leaders prancing along the

[1] The lay reader who is unfamiliar with this terrain will find much to enlighten him in Fritz Wittels' *Freud and His Time,* especially the chapter entitled "The Primary Function." This is a description of the workings of the Freudian "id." We do not subscribe to the Freudian thesis in its entirety, and our own term "inner world" has been chosen, in part, to escape identification with it. Nevertheless, the Freudian exploration of the inner world is an immense scientific achievement and every student of this aspect of the human being must reckon with it.

side lines, the teams running onto the field in the cold autumnal air. As the drama unfolds the stadium becomes a caldron of human excitement, and finally boils over when thousands of spectators surge onto the field to surround the victorious team or demolish the goal posts. And then imagine someone sitting in this howling stadium who has never heard of football. To make the case a perfect one, imagine him to be a representative of some civilization— let us say, that of China—where competition in the Western sense of the word is unknown. What does the football classic look like under these circumstances?

Such a person can only view this spectacle from the outside. And when thus seen the game can have neither purpose nor meaning. It makes absolutely no difference to our alien onlooker whether A wins, or B. When one or the other team makes a first down, the fate of mankind is not in the least altered. Why, then, do the spectators respond as if their very lives were at stake? The Chinese sage—if he be a sage—will have two alternatives to choose from: either these people are insane; or else the realities of this spectacle are not at all the outer realities, which he can see, but inner realities, which, as an outsider, he cannot see. He knows that the spectators are not insane. They may be dedicated to what appear to him to be false goals; they may be immature, excitable, etc., etc. But when the game is over, he knows, they will act more or less as rational beings and will resume comprehensible daily tasks. He must, therefore, choose the second alternative; he must acknowledge that the game is primarily an event whose realities are the inner experiences of the players and their sympathizers—an event of the inner world.

This inwardness of the reality is indeed characteristic of any kind of game. "Play," says Jung's collaborator, C. Kerényi, "can only be understood from the inside. Once we become conscious while playing that it is only an expression of vitality and nothing more, then the game is up. People who stand outside the game and regard it only in this light may be right in one point, but all their knowledge tells us nothing."

A golfer is making an approach shot. His care in measuring the distance, his concentration, his earnestness are all wholly inexplicable from the outside; they are quite incommensurable with the triviality of the problem. As experienced by the player himself, however, the shot is an intensely serious affair—more important, perhaps, to his happiness and sense of well-being than all of the outwardly "significant" events of the day. Seen from within, and only so, his care, concentration, and earnestness are understandable. He is of course bound into the outer world. These are his golf clubs, the ball, the caddy, his partner, his opponent, the fairway stretching invitingly toward the green. He is conscious of all those outer things. He is conscious, also, perhaps, of what the professional has told him about his golf stroke. Unfortunately the pro is not able to get inside of this stroke. The pro could only explain a stroke from the outside, and our golfer is now faced with the problem —exceedingly profound in its implications—of how to transform that outer explanation into an inner reality. For a fleeting moment he must be able to remove himself from the outer world and plunge down into the inner world; and in this plunge he must carry with him the instructions of the pro and connect them into something for which there are no words. For a moment he must live inside of everything that bears upon his stroke—inside of his own muscular system, inside of the carefully weighted club, inside of the ball; inside, indeed, of the majestic laws of mechanics themselves, which govern the course of the ball in its arc toward the green.

Let us try for a moment to get into this inwardness. We can gain a clue to it from children. "A small boy," writes Fritz Wittels,

lies in his little bed in the morning and seems to be meditating. If asked of what he is thinking, he becomes embarrassed and answers, "Nothing." Afterwards he says, still in confusion: "I am playing flowers." If now the adult with his stern logic insinuatingly says: "Yes, you are a flower; your arms and legs are the branches, your face the blossom," then the child replies: "No, no, no!" The play of the child is not logical and cannot be put into our logically directed words. The child has already learned how different his own imagination is from that of adults and rejects the comparison of his limbs with branches, his face with a flower. What the child feels is not an allegory but an actual oneness with the flower (a "tautegory"). As long as he plays flower he is not a child in human form, makes no comparison between the parts of his body and the botanical divisions of a plant. . . . The child is without any trouble that which he wishes to be. It is not a matter of likeness to an actual flower. He *is* an actual flower so long as he plays flower. . . . All the play of a child is of this character. When a child plays railroad the railroad is an actual one and not the allegory or the symbol of a locomotive. When he shoves a building block before him and plays automobile, this block as long as the child is playing is by no

means a mere symbol; in the child's conception there is no distinction between the block and the automobile.[2]

The golf player making his approach shot is much more
bound into the outer world than is the child playing flower.
If the golfer's plunge into the inner world is successful
he makes a perfect shot and has the satisfaction of seeing
the ball drop on the green close to where he wanted it.
What is the source of this satisfaction? Is it merely a kind
of sense of power, that he has been able to impose his will
on the ball? It is certainly that—and yet more than that.
The deeper satisfaction of play lies in the fact that for that
fleeting moment when he was inside of everything the player
was in contact with truth: not truth as we divine it from reason; not truth that can be weighed, measured, catalogued,
or passed along to anyone else; but truth that takes the form
of an experience of reality, to which the high arc of the ball
bears eloquent testimony. In making a perfect stroke the
golfer is like the child playing flower. He is not playing *with*
the club and ball; he *is* the club and ball, and, while he is
thus inside of them, connected with the far-flung universe.

When we talk about the inward-looking consciousness,
then, we are not talking about something strange and rare.
The athlete uses it in a dogmatic way that is easy to understand, but all of us use it every day in innumerable situations, as further examples could show.

The popularly held idea that the inner world is merely
subjective (that is, pertains merely to the observer or sub-

[2] Fritz Wittels, *Freud and His Time*, New York, Liveright, 1941, pp.
143-44.

ject) cannot be right; for if it were so, how could faculties
of the inner world reveal in a truthful way situations and
states of being outside of that world? The fact is that when
we plunge deeply enough into our own inner world we come
up—*in an outer world*. We possess within us faculties that
are capable of grasping, in their different ways, situations
that are outside of us, beyond us. Though they are subjective
in action and origin they have a validity wholly comparable
to what is ordinarily denoted by the word objective. The
distinction between subjective and objective certainly exists,
but the modern evaluation of it is wrong.

A certain word arises to confront him who inquires into
the relation between the inner and outer world, a word
that he may hitherto have taken for granted, or even
resented. It is the word MYSTERY. There exists today a
strong animus against anything mystical and this almost
universal skepticism has much to recommend it. But we do
not have to be mystics in order to recognize the mystery in
the universe. The great scientists do not seek to escape it. At
the end of every trail, whether it be blazed by the outward-
looking or the inward-looking consciousness, mystery confronts us. To deny this is to deny the most certain fact ever
discovered by human knowledge.

Yet the meaning of mystery is very different, depending
on whether one comes to it outwardly or inwardly. To the
outward-looking consciousness, mystery is negative: it sur-
rounds the human world like a darkness, which, so far as
any evidence goes, is impenetrable. The positivistic scientist
faces mystery in this sense wherever he turns. He pushes
his knowledge of matter outward and reaches the atom,

beyond which is darkness. He pushes farther and reaches the electron: and darkness still lies beyond him. In genetics he finds the chromosome, which apparently controls heredity; eventually, knowledge sheds enough light upon the chromosome to reveal that it comprises smaller units called genes. What lies beyond the genes? The answer is, darkness. The advance of knowledge by the use of the outward-looking consciousness is an endless process. At the end of every step darkness remains. The knowledge is always finite, the darkness infinite. There can therefore be no end to the search.

But when we face mystery with the inward-looking consciousness, this is not necessarily the case. The mystery that confronts the inward-looking consciousness is also a darkness; but it is not a void. We cannot say of the inward-looking consciousness that what lies beyond the known is necessarily unknown. For when we look inwardly, that which is unknown *can* be known. In the inner world a given mystery may be wholly metamorphosed: that is to say, it may suddenly be converted from darkness into light; it may suddenly ignite and flash forth, revealing some truth that leads us far beyond whatever data we had assembled. In the inner world, mystery is not something that passively awaits the end of a given line of investigation. It is something that comes to meet us, bearing with it the potentiality of revelation.

The failure of the modern mind to accept the inward-looking consciousness as a phenomenon equally real and quite as valid as the outward-looking consciousness is a giant stumbling block to the contemporary search for truth. It is the fervid conviction of the enthusiastic followers of modern psychology, psychiatry, and psychoanalysis that through a scientific approach, man can learn how to master his inner life in such a way as to achieve an adjustment to the complexities of the twentieth century and thus open the way to an intelligent and consistent pursuit of happiness. And yet there is a serious question in the minds of millions of persons as to whether all this scientific probing of the inner life is dealing with the realities of the inner life at all. These people, indeed, question the whole thesis that the leading problem of the inner life is that of adjustment. Certainly, adjustment to one's society and one's environment is a highly desirable achievement. For the pursuit of everyday happiness and success, it may even be described as necessary. But—these persons ask—can it adequately define the purposes of man's life on earth? Are there not values and insights which refuse to be adjusted—which, indeed, when subjected to a process of adjustment, are weakened or lost?

The well-adjusted soldier can live under fire and do his duties in a creditable way. There are always a few individuals, however, who, because of inner evaluations peculiar to themselves, go far beyond this—and they are the ones to whom we give the medals. When we decorate a soldier we are not commending his adjustment, but his refusal to adjust, his willingness to hurl himself *against* a set of outer circumstances in a nonadaptive manner. And what is true of courage is true of almost every quality that we admire. The heroes of the world are the men and women who have combatted their environment and their society on behalf of inner convictions, the validity of which was believed by them, and by almost no one else. Whether it really is a virtue and not a maladjustment—whether, indeed, there really is such a thing as virtue at all—are questions into which the psychiatrists do not feel called upon to enter. Indeed, to do so would endanger the theory that they have to offer. They must proceed by begging all such questions as the question of what virtue is, let alone the question of what man is. That is why those millions of persons who, consciously or unconsciously, are seeking enlightenment regarding the realities of the inner life, find themselves thwarted and disappointed by the scientific approach, as at present practiced. They must turn else-where if they are to seek a deeper truth, to give body, to give *qualitative meaning* to their own deep recognition of the dignity, indeed the sanctity, of the human individual.

The failure of American philosophy to provide what these millions are seeking underlies our failure in the struggle against communism. That the task is an easy one, no one would claim. It will mean the awakening of a whole new spirit of inquiry not yet born. But first it is necessary to understand that the new spirit of inquiry, whatever it may be, cannot be derived from the naïve and fragmentary propositions of the American optimistic tradition. So long as that tradition dominates our thinking, to the exclusion of any other way of thinking, our arguments can no more overcome the idea of Dialectical Man than the twitter of a sparrow can drown out the roaring of Niagara Falls.

2

THRESHOLD OF FREEDOM

In recognizing the two basic aspects of human consciousness, and of the relationship between them, we at least obtain a glimpse of the real nature of the search for truth. So long as we confine that search to either the outer or the inner aspect of consciousness, it is bound to lead us into error: for the outer aspect, as we have seen, can concern itself only with the world of outer appearances, a world of shadows, the inner substance of which must remain forever unknown. And it goes without saying that the inner aspect by itself leads to confusion and contradiction which can only be resolved by outward testing. So the way to truth must lie in a combination of the two.

If it is really so, that these faculties of our inner world can see into the world around us, from the inside of that world, our view of the human being is radically altered. The old nineteenth-century concept of man as a being living in a three-dimensional world, dominated by Newtonian mechanics and limited by the horizon of his waking consciousness, is shattered. And more than this, the conventional materialistic view of man is shattered. If faculties of the individual's inner world can grasp situations in the outer world without first passing through consciousness, we must assume that some kind of links exist between that inner world and the outer world. We cannot inquire here too deeply into the nature of these links, but we can scarcely refrain from noting the absurdity of trying to imagine them as material or physiological. We may, if we like, call them "psychic," though we would be hard-pressed to define just what that word means. We are not aware of them, for they are not accessible to our normal consciousness. But our unawareness gives us no rational grounds for denying their existence. But what we cannot do, as seekers of truth, is overlook the certainty that such links exist.

The search for these links, then, becomes inescapably part of the search for truth. We do not attempt to answer the question of what truth *is*, which is perhaps the most abstruse question in all of philosophy; we do say, however, that to be free, man must *relate* himself to truth. We have reached, by a quite different route, the same position as that which is stated in the Gospel of St. John: "Ye shall know the truth and the truth shall make you free." Any modern study of freedom which is not to lose itself in the mazes of mere political theorizing must somehow come to grips with that pronouncement. Only when it has done so—at least in a preliminary way—can it proceed to an examination of the more practical questions that the study of freedom involves. Anyone who will meditate on this proposition in an open-minded way will begin to have a certain inner experience regarding the contemporary world. He will begin to understand contemporary issues in a new way, and to formulate new purposes for himself and his society.

Let him imagine, for example, or call to mind some instance, perhaps from his personal life, involving some kind of conflict. Two partners, let us say, disagree about

the conduct of a business. So long as the disagreement
exists the business is impaired, perhaps endangered. Moreover, the freedom of each is curtailed—both are frustrated.
How then do they cure this conflict? By searching out the
truth about the business. They may not be able to find it,
but the mere *search* has the power to change the whole
situation. For by the very act of searching they acknowledge
that there does exist such a thing as truth—truth, in this
instance, about their joint enterprise—truth which transcends their merely personal views and which ought, therefore, to prevail. In this acknowledgment, the bitterness, the
threats, the dark passions that formerly caused the partners
to thwart each other, are everywhere exposed to the simple
question of what is the *right* thing to do for the welfare of
their enterprise. And this question has the power to dissolve
the merely personal questions, and to bring into the enterprise a kind of light, which could not exist before the
existence of truth was acknowledged.

It is a trivial example, yet the principle that it embodies
can be extended as far as one likes. From the genuine
search for truth, which in itself implies the acknowledgment that such a thing as truth exists, light is always born.
And it is only in such light that we can intelligently speak
of freedom. In the dark recesses of the purely personal
world, dominated by the passions and appetites, freedom
is not to be found. It exists there as a mere illusion. In the
instance just cited, before the partners begin to search for
the truth about their business they were free only to destroy
it and themselves. The possibility of real freedom exists,

we can say, only where men enter upon a relationship to the universe around them. This relationship is not the result of academic philosophizing; it is brought about through the search for truth. The moment men begin to search for the truth about any situation or problem or circumstance, they create a relationship, however microscopic, between themselves and the surrounding world; and it is in this relationship that freedom becomes *possible*.

The truth is that when we speak of human freedom we have in mind something absolutely unique. What we mean by human freedom cannot be found in the outer world of nature. There is a sense in which the phenomena of nature may be said to be free, but not in *this* sense.

When we examine what we mean by human freedom we see that the external use of the word cannot really explain it. We say that air is free, but this is just a way of speaking; we know that it is only apparently free, that it is harnessed to causes. We say that deer are free. In an outer sense they seem to be. But we know that they are creatures of natural laws. Rousseau's theory that man is free in a state of nature is the exact opposite of the truth. This is precisely where man is *not* free, but is bound to laws he cannot disobey and which determine his existence. The concept of freedom can emerge only insofar as man emancipates himself from nature and the material world.

We will find a further hint of the nature of human freedom in considering the basic meaning of the word "free." In our materialistic world, where we look outward so much, we have completely lost touch with the original meaning of this word. "Free" comes down to us from the old Aryan word *priyo* and the Sanskrit word *priyá*—the root being *prî*, which means to delight, to endear. In old English this word became *fréon*, meaning to love. Free thus has the same root as "friend." In this ancient form it was applied to all those members of the household who were connected by ties of blood to the head of the house, to whom they were consequently "dear," and it thus distinguished them from slaves and outsiders. When we consider this old Aryan and Gothic use of the word "free," to designate one who is especially dear, a certain relationship between human beings emerges, which, if it could be experienced by humanity, would bring about an entirely different kind of society than any we have hitherto known. One is reminded in this use of the word of another passage in the Gospel of St. John. Toward the end of his three years' ministry, just before his capture, Jesus said to his disciples: "Henceforth I call you not servants, for the servant knoweth not what his lord doeth: but I have called you friends." They are no longer servants, they are friends —that is to say, in the Old Aryan sense, they are free men. And why are they free men? Jesus himself explains: "For all things that I have heard of my Father I have made known unto you." The disciples have been initiated, in short, into the fundamental truths about man. And this initiation has freed them from servitude. They have become *free*.

3

THE PLACE OF BROTHERHOOD

This study began with the assertion by a Russian officer that the goals of the Red Army in World War II were freedom and brotherhood. As our inquiry progressed we have found that we are engaged, not just in a military and diplomatic conflict, but in a great war of ideas in which the very life of freedom is at stake. Yet we cannot, without inviting total disaster, fight that war in a narrow sectarian sense. That which is at stake is the spirit itself in which men inquire into truth. The historical task that faces the mid-twentieth century is to kindle new light for freedom-seekers everywhere. If our Idea of Man embodies a belief in the existence of truth, the question then becomes, not whether our Idea or that of the Communists is the more powerful, but which Idea is true. And the resolution of this question will be found, not in armaments, but in the minds and hearts of men.

It just so happens that Sidney Hook, the American naturalist philosopher and social democrat, writing in 1940 in *Reason, Social Myth and Democracy*, provides us with the clue to the Russian officer's statement. Mr. Hook, who uses words carefully, tells us that Marx set out to give abstract terms, such as "humanity," "justice," and "brotherhood," a material content. This is in strict conformance with Marxism, which supposes that the content of anything real must be material. And yet the absurdity

272

of such a statement is obvious. Consider "brotherhood," for example—not the abstraction but the concrete reality. What is it? What material content has it? What makes one man some other man's brother? The Marxists are surely not talking about common parentage, or the ties of blood—assuming that even such ties can be explained and accounted for in purely material terms. The brotherhood they refer to is social brotherhood, an ideal to which we are supposed to give content. As soon as we try to do so, however, we find there is absolutely nothing in the material world that can give it content. Brotherhood is not wealth, for example; nor is it the distribution of wealth, nor is it the common ownership of the means of production. Particular arrangements with regard to wealth and production might encourage the birth and growth of social brotherhood. But it is obvious that such arrangements, in themselves, do not constitute brotherhood, do not give it any content whatever. What is true of economic arrangements is equally true of political arrangements. One cannot *legislate* brotherhood with laws any more than one can *manufacture* it with a lathe.

It is certainly true that if we are to speak of social brotherhood in a meaningful way we must bring it down out of the misty realm of what Mr. Hook elsewhere calls "unanalyzable abstractions"—that is to say, in his terms, we must give it content. But what we cannot do is to give it *material* content, because brotherhood is a quality of human experience which cannot be defined in terms of matter—indeed it is a concept which cannot be derived from matter or the laws of matter, even by analogy. Matter knows nothing of brotherhood and we simply do not say of material phenomena that they are brotherly. Brotherhood is a phenomenon that must be inwardly known and experienced. It is a phenomenon of the inner world, the content of which can only be understood in spiritual terms. Spiritual knowledge is direct and intuitive. It cannot be demonstrated like a theorem. But all who have experienced it will testify that it is just as real as any phenomenon of the material world. And this is equally true of freedom. It is the spiritual reality—the spiritual fact of the inner world—that opens the way to the understanding of freedom.

Below the conventional surface of modern life there exists a vast spiritual unrest. The terrible pressures of our time are causing men more and more to search themselves inwardly. And what do they find in that inner world? They find *other men and other women*. Of course, each of us is selfish and seeks to satisfy his own needs first. But what we are discovering is that the selfish, self-centered being is only a partial reality. Lying behind him is a being—a truly spiritual being—whose reality is intimately linked with that of other men and other women. Try as we will to deny this universal being, this real "I" within us, we cannot escape it and at the same time be honest with ourselves.

The effects of this inner discovery are gradual, diffident, and uncertain. Most of us dare not even admit it: the counterthrust of the outer world is too powerful. Yet the keen observer of our time can scarcely fail to note certain outer changes that are being brought about, nevertheless. This is not to say that we have outgrown selfish motivations. But new, social motivations are growing up in all of us; each of us is increasingly aware that, if he would serve himself, he must serve others. And because this is a fundamental truth about man, it is a fundamental truth about freedom.

In short, the equation that freedom equals brotherhood is one which because of the nature of his philosophy cannot belong to Dialectical Man. It belongs to Free Man and through it we shall find the synthesis to our antinomy between the individual and the social good by developing what might be called the *social* or *socialized individual*. Let us set up this concept in contrast to the social or socialized state. Men have come to the socialized state by working outwardly farther than man has ever gone before. We shall reach the socialized individual by working inwardly to the depths of the spirit within each of us. There we shall find that a man, the individual, the "I," recognizes himself in all the other "I's" inhabiting the earth, and in this recognition of a spiritual brotherhood we shall discover the meaning and purpose of freedom.

4

BEYOND THE FOOTHILLS

We have said of Western man in general, and of Americans in particular, that they have developed to a very high degree the technique of thinking about things. They have developed very little, and philosophically have neglected almost entirely, the technique of thinking about living entities. The characteristic of thinking about things is that the observer always stays outside of the object of his observation. The characteristic of thinking about living entities is that the observer actually enters into the object in an intuitive way; he lives it, he becomes it; he obtains an understanding of it from the inside, so to speak, where the living truth about it is to be found. It is the thesis of this book that an understanding of this way of thinking is indispensable to the comprehension of freedom.

It is only through life that man has access to the divine. If God exists he is a *living* being. We can therefore no more comprehend Him by thinking in terms of things than we can comprehend a gasoline engine in terms of love and hate. Nor ought we to be surprised at the dictum of those who are oriented to thinking about things, that there is no such "thing" as God. Of course there is not!— because God is not a thing. As Jesus said to the woman of Samaria, God is spirit; and spirit, if the word has any meaning at all, is *alive*. Those who know and use only the techniques of thinking about things are, therefore, honestly forced to the conclusion that there is no God. Their reasoning is faultless. And so long as one accepts their basic (although entirely hidden) assumption that their techniques of thinking about things are the only valid and creditable ones, there is no way of refuting them. The analytical, quantitative approach of modern science has barred man from the perception and recognition of the spiritual. For the spiritual is always qualitative—never quantitative.

This, in very loose terms, is the problem that Western philosophy now faces. Philosophy cannot fail to face this problem, because it is being pushed into it by the scientific revolution, which has carried the techniques of thinking about things beyond the intelligible horizons of the very things it is thinking about. Abstraction has abstracted away all reality. It is possible to guess that in the interstices of the atom, as well as in the majestic infinitudes of intergalactic space, the physical sciences have come face to face with the spiritual without knowing what it is or how to think about it at all. It vanishes before them into high abstractions, because the only kind of thinking they know is a kind that cannot grasp the spiritual. The problem this raises is not a problem for the natural sciences to solve; it is a problem for philosophy. Nevertheless, one of the dramatic facts of our time is that the scientists are much more keenly aware of this problem than the philosophers themselves. They are pushing the philosophers for new concepts and new thinking; they are demanding a philosophical revolution, to support and fulfill the scientific revolution. And this is a demand that philosophy will not be able to escape.

These observations and reflections bring us to the very

heart of our inquiry. Our position may be summed up in the statement, that so long as the concept of the spiritual remains a vacuum, darkness will prevail in the Western world. What has happened, in effect, is that this concept has been eliminated from the search for truth. We search for truth in matter, we search in mathematics, we search in history, geology, paleontology, archeology, astronomy, and all the other sciences relative to our existence on earth. But we do not search in the spiritual—in fact, it cannot even be said in any scientific sense that we search *for* the spiritual.

The great mysteries of the inner world rise like a snow-capped Himalayan range before him who dares to approach them. It is certainly not our present assignment to attempt to scale those lofty mountains. Yet mountaineers who are faced with such challenges do not rush in to overcome them. From observations in the foothills they can learn a great deal about the glaciers and cols, the chimneys and the passages that might lead some future explorer up to the summit. Moreover, the fact that the mountain has never been climbed does not stop them from climbing; they work on the assumption that the mountain can be climbed, and someday will be. With regard to the mysteries of man's inner life, it is the assumption of the present study that they can be known and someday will be known. And however radical this view may seem, we would contend that without it the entire course of freedom, as the Western world has hitherto interpreted it, and hopes to interpret it, might as well be abandoned.

If we are to extricate ourselves from this predicament we

must begin to exercise, in a bold and new way, the prerogative of free men. We must come to grips with the realities of the world of thought. If we knew freedom as well as we think we do, we would not be so frustrated; for in a world that seeks freedom so universally, it is inconceivable that, if Americans had the real answers, they should find it impossible to share them, let alone to express them.

We have said that modern man has foreclosed the search of the great mysteries of life. Do we mean that modern man should be able to *think* his way to answers to these mysteries? This is indeed what we mean. But it must be noted that thinking is not ordinarily used by Western writers to denote a probing of such profound and mysterious questions. These questions, many feel, are the province of religion, in connection with which they speak of faith, vision, mystical experience, revelation, and so forth. We do not deny that they are. But is religion, then, without thought? No great religious teacher has ever succeeded in showing it to be so. Certain Protestant Christians have come closest to rejecting thought as a means to religious understanding, but they have never been able to overcome the argument that Luther and Calvin, the leading proponents of this rejection, were themselves great thinkers and reached their radical positions by thinking. There is certainly a distinction between faith and thinking, but we do not concede that they are mutually exclusive. Christian theology places a special emphasis upon faith, without which, it contends, it is impossible to arrive at the Christian life. But the Thomist doctrine, that Reason is the handmaiden of

Faith, has never really been overthrown; and as for older religions, such as Buddhism, thinking is accepted by them as a means to religious enlightenment almost as a matter of course. The idea that religious faith can exist in a kind of vacuum, almost unrelated to thought, is a theological innovation, corresponding roughly to the dawn of empirical science, and related in an inevitable way to the inner darkness of modern man. Not only is it permissible to approach the great mysteries of life through thinking, but no way has yet been discovered, even by the greatest mystics, of dispensing with it.

Our trouble today is that we too closely identify thinking with the organ of the brain, and when we try to describe it we do so in terms of the merely logical processes by which it appears to work. These associations or descriptions are not inaccurate in themselves, but they result in a very inadequate idea of what thought really is. To identify thinking with the brain is like identifying a man with his body, and to describe it in terms of its logical processes is like describing a man in terms of his skeleton only. Thinking is more than a brain, more than logic. It has a content which transcends the brain and clothes logic. If we contemplate the majestic structures that the thought of man has produced, not just in our time but in all times, we can begin to understand how limited and restricted our modern conventional view of thinking is. It is, in fact, a highly specialized view, developed for the better achievement of our scientific, technological, and industrial purposes.

We can get a better comprehension of what is involved here if we turn to the word "wisdom." Tennyson wrote: "But she (Knowledge) is earthly of the mind, but Wisdom heavenly of the soul." In Corinthians we find the divine nature of Christ referred to as "Wisdom," and one of Christ's historic titles is "The Wisdom of the Father." The second meaning of wisdom in the Oxford Dictionary is: "knowledge (especially of a high or abstruse kind); enlightenment"; and it is pointed out that in early usage the word was connected with philosophy and ancient science. These deeper meanings of wisdom, which reach far beyond the idea of mere intellect, help us to define our concept of thinking. Wisdom, we would say, is a state that men can reach only through thinking. It is the result of thinking. And it is in *this* sense that we wish our concept of thinking to be understood.

If the reader will meditate upon the proposition to which we have referred earlier, the proposition contained in the Gospel of St. John: "Ye shall know the truth, and the truth shall make you free," he will more and more come to see that here lies the central problem of our time (and the key to the understanding of freedom)—the problem of truth. That is why we cannot escape it, however difficult its examination may be. In our struggle with the Soviets, in our negotiations with our allies, in our efforts to formulate new policies for our own domestic affairs— everywhere we turn, we are confronted with the question of truth. There stretches out around us a dark world of prejudice and emotional symbolism, pressure groups and propaganda, power-seeking and nationalism. Nowhere is it possible to achieve freedom in such a world, where pressure must be met with counterpressure, prejudice by prejudice, power by power, nation by nation. Only if we succeed in shedding light into this world can we dissolve the dreadful specters and illusions that are constantly born of it. This light can only be the light of truth.

One of the ancient symbols for thinking was a sword. The sword of Michael was the sword of thought, which had the power to cut through error and thus to overcome evil. The image is a priceless one for our time, but we must be sure that we understand it. How was it possible for this sword to slay the dragon of evil? Only because it was wielded in the cause of truth. In any other cause, thinking —the sword—leads to dispute and conflict, to strife and warfare. But in the hands of Michael the sword represents the thinking of God, thinking that has in it the power of truth which is the power of the divine; for Michael grasps it with the grip of the truth-seeker. Mid-century man is in possession of a sword, but he has not yet learned the difficult grip. This is what he must seek.

FRAGMENTS

A NOTE:

Mr. Jessup has outlined in his biographical sketch how the direction of the present volume changed from a book on political economy to an analysis which probes questions that have concerned men for millennia. In searching back through these fundamentals to try and clarify our current dilemma Russell Davenport wrote, "We are like people on the second floor of a house with the foundations and the first floor still to be constructed." This book represents his effort to begin the construction of those foundations.

What follows under the heading of "Fragments" are unrevised notes and thoughts that were not developed to a point where we felt they could be included in the main body of the work. "The American Task" is made up of notes from the author's files for a future book; it indicates in practical ways how a new political and economic structure could be built to carry forward the continuing adventure of American life.

N. P. D.

FREEDOM AND FREE WILL

We assume the validity of the concept of freedom, although, to be sure, systematic philosophy has never been able to demonstrate in a conclusive way that freedom even exists. Brilliant arguments have purported to accomplish this; they are, nevertheless, countered by arguments, seemingly just as brilliant, proving that freedom is an illusion. The battle has raged around the specific issue of the freedom of the will, and the net result of the long debate is a profound skepticism, which characterizes most modern thinking on this subject. Indeed, "skepticism" is too mild a word. If one can speak of a prevailing opinion in such a controversial field, one must say that among contemporary scientists and philosophers the opinion prevails that the human will is not free.

In the light of the present world struggle this is a somewhat extraordinary fact. For what sense does it make to talk as we do about a "free world," and to spend our fortunes and our lives defending it, if there is no such thing as freedom for the individual, after all? Perhaps someone will reply that freedom, as implied in the phrase "free world," is a *social* freedom and has no relation to the philosophical question of free will. And yet, what meaning can social freedom have unless it is to give individuals freedom to act (within whatever necessary limits) *according* to their will? And if this will is not free, is incapable of freedom, how can we regard social freedom as anything more than a seductive verbalism, unfounded in reality? On the contrary, once we grant that there is no such thing as individual free will, the whole nature of the world struggle must be viewed quite differently. We can then speak of a free world only in a figurative sense, as a world embodying certain institutions which we call free, but which cannot lead to real freedom, since real freedom is nonexistent. We can only conclude from such premises that the world struggle is not *really* a struggle for freedom, but a struggle for power; that the only question at stake is, not whether men are to be free, but whether unfree men are to be governed our way or the Marxist way.

The two concepts—free will and social freedom—must stand or fall together. The schizophrenic attitude of the twentieth century, whereby the concept of free will is accorded little, if any, scientific value while we continue to make freedom our battle cry, appears to us wholly untenable. On the contrary, we believe that freedom is, or can be, a reality which manifests itself at the individual level as free will. We recognize, however, that relative to the thinking of our time, this position is a radical one; it is perhaps necessary, therefore, to indicate the grounds on which we have founded it.

Essentially our thesis is simple. Metaphysics, we would contend, has been unable to demonstrate the reality of free will, because metaphysics rests on logic, whereas freedom does not. By this we do not mean, of course, that

freedom is inherently *il*logical; we say only that an understanding of it cannot be achieved by logical argument
alone. The point may be a somewhat difficult one for those
who have not previously thought about it in these terms.
If an understanding of freedom is inaccessible to logic,
by what means can we attain to it?

We hold that there are different ways of approaching
reality, of which the logical processes of ratiocination
represent only one. It is also possible to speak of a mathematical (symbolical) approach to reality, which is related
to the logical approach, but in certain ways transcends it.
Less fundamental, perhaps, but distinct nevertheless, is the
mechanical approach, which combines both logic and
mathematics with the laws of matter. Modern scientists
employ also a statistical approach—which has become,
indeed, a kind of ultimate criterion in modern physics. We
hold, however, that when reality is approached in any of
these ways, freedom cannot be observed with certainty:
logic cannot lead us to it, nor mechanics, nor mathematics,
nor statistics. For the observation and understanding of
freedom we must approach reality in quite a different way,
and for this our term is the word *living*. Freedom has
reality only in terms of life. Accordingly, to understand
it, we must learn to think in living terms.

Since contemporary science does not think in such terms,
or even recognize such terms, this statement, thus dog-
matically expressed, may be somewhat puzzling. Let us try
to clarify it with a simple example.

Choose at random any paragraph, and choose from the

midst of this paragraph, any sentence. Between the sentence and the paragraph a peculiar relationship may be noted. The paragraph, we may say, is the mother of the sentence; it embodies a system of causes from which the sentence springs, and these causes mold the sentence and to a considerable extent predetermine it. However, they do not wholly predetermine it. The sentence emerges as something in its own right, an organic unity with its own beginning, middle, and end. Its content cannot be predicted with any definiteness from a consideration of the material preceding it. We can say that the sentence flows logically from the preceding sentences, but we cannot, by logic, predict exactly what the new sentence will say. The words chosen may conform to certain characteristics statistically observable in all the work of the author; yet these statistics are as powerless to predict the sentence as logic is. With regard to the paragraph, in short, the sentence exhibits a strangely paradoxical relationship: it is both dependent on it and independent of it. That this relationship has reality, all of literature attests; yet it is basically different from a logical relationship, or a mechanical one, or a mathematical one. In our terminology we call it a *living* relationship, because investigation shows it to be everywhere characteristic of life and living forms. This peculiar combination of dependence and independence, which neither logic, nor mechanics, nor mathematics, nor statistics can explain, is one of the prominent characteristics of anything that lives.

It is only in such terms, we suggest, that freedom can be understood. The unfree act, it is clear, is embedded in a system of causes and never emerges as anything but the predetermined result of them. It never stands on its own feet, never acquires a separate life of its own; and if one were sufficiently familiar with the causes and their necessary or probable effects, one could predict it in great detail. We shall contend, however, that this kind of action does not exhaust the potentialities of the human will; that there is such a thing as a free act, which is of course also embedded in causes, but which is characterized by the fact that it does emerge as in some degree independent of them. The free act bears the same paradoxical relationship to its causes as the sentence bears to the paragraph; it is an organic entity growing out of them, but possessing its own beginning, middle, and end. It is a creative act, exhibiting the characteristics, not of mechanics, but of life itself. It can be understood only if we are able to approach reality in living terms. And it leads to a concept of man as something more than mind and matter—as, in fact, a spiritual entity possessing creative power.

We are far from contending that all of man's actions achieve this status. On the contrary, relatively few do, relatively few are significantly free. The genuinely free act is an effort, for it is literally an act of creation; it is only on occasions—perhaps one might say, only in crises —that ordinary men attain to it. Nevertheless, the fact that it is possible is the all-important fact; for the intimations to be derived from this mere possibility give meaning to the entire cause of freedom and to the existence of that whole world that we call the free world.

Yet, as indicated in the text, this possibility can be main-

tained on one condition only: it is necessary to explore and
to master *a new approach to reality*. For the word "new"
we might substitute the word "forgotten," because this
approach that we have described as living was indeed
known and practiced in ancient times. But for us of the
twentieth century it is *new*. Our ideas of reality are predominantly logical and mechanical, and this is the case
not only in the sciences but in philosophy, and even to
some extent in religion. The result has been great progress
in material things; but in human terms the price has been
high and the time has come for an assessment. If we are
right in our contention, that a valid concept of freedom
cannot be achieved on merely logical or mechanical
grounds, then we must either break through to new grounds,
or else abandon as a delusion our belief that we are or
can be, free.

BLUE HAZE OF FEAR

A kind of thick blue haze lies over the landscape in
which twentieth-century man has become lost. Through
the haze he cannot see the stars or the heavens, cannot
determine his course.

We find that the haze is compounded of fear, which
pervades the entire earth in our time and is just as powerful in the East as in the West. Not a nation—scarcely
even an individual—escapes it. And this fear itself con-

stitutes a constant danger to all, because nothing is so unpredictable as the decision of a man who is afraid.

What is it that we fear, here in the middle of the twentieth century? Many things. Yet it is very easy to be mistaken about the real nature of our fear. There is the fear of the U.S.S.R., most prominent in America, which is far removed from the U.S.S.R. Those who know the international scene are constantly struck with a peculiar paradox, that, the closer one gets to the U.S.S.R., the less one finds this particular fear to be. In the U.S.A. it is greatest. In Britain, it is considerably less. In France, still less. In Finland, which lives almost at the sufferance of Russia, it is least of all. The Finns do not share the American fear of Russia—at least, they do not share it in the same way. As for the French, who live between the two great power centers of the present world, they are apt to tell you that they are just as much afraid of the U.S.A. as of the U.S.S.R.

This universal fear may manifest itself as fear of aggression, but its origin is really much more profound. Men have always been exposed to aggression—in our time, perhaps, even less than a thousand years ago. But today men are in possession of something that was much less in evidence a thousand years ago. The best word for it, perhaps, is a sense of *self*. There has been an enormous increase in our time of what we call individualism—the segregation of the individual from his social context—his emergence as a being in his own right. Obviously, one can only speak of such a development in relative terms. Individualism is more evident in the U.S. than in India, which is still dominated by a caste system. It is more obvious in the West generally than in the U.S.S.R., where the individual is the tool of the party and mass murder can still be countenanced. But even the Russian peasant of today is more of a person than the Russian serfs of old; and under the placid traditions of the Far East one finds everywhere explosive forces that have their origin in the self-awakening of individuals.

However it may have come about, one fact concerning this phenomenon is clear: it is a fearsome experience. In a deep psychological sense it is analogous to physical birth, when the child is ejected from the nourishment and protection of the mother's womb. As we glance back over history, we can see why this is so. Unindividualized man (speaking always in relative terms) is securely embedded in his institutions, which provide him with economic and political protection, and with intellectual and spiritual nourishment. However poverty-stricken such institutions may be, they provide him with a known and relatively predictable means of livelihood. They shelter him politically against strangers and enemies from without. In large measure, they do his thinking for him. And what is more important, they tell him what to believe. But the more a man becomes individualized, the less he finds himself able to rely on these womblike social organisms. He must find his beliefs within himself. He must increasingly do his own thinking. His political environment, increasingly affected by other individuals, becomes increasingly turbulent; his means of livelihood, though perhaps much more abundant, increasingly insecure.

Many psychologists and psychoanalysts have noted how these experiences and challenges beget fear. It does not necessarily manifest itself at the conscious level in connection with the phenomena that cause it. A man may be quite satisfied, consciously, of his political convictions: but underneath his consciousness there may exist a kind of *malaise*, a doubt as to whether he is really right. But who knows whether he is really right? As a highly individualized human being he cannot fail to mistrust the opinions of all highly individualized human beings—including his own. For who among these individuals really has authority, in the sense that the Church has authority, or the paternalistic state? So fear is there—the fear of error—the fear of not being clever enough—the fear of the darkness into which he has been plunged. It is a substratum of the modern soul.

The fact that it is so largely subconscious—that he who experiences the fear does not always know what he is afraid of—leads to immeasurable delusions and the creation of personal or social apparitions that have little reality at all. Individuals who are supposed to think for themselves, but are afraid to do so, will accept almost any kind of a symbol as a substitute for thinking. Propaganda wields enormous power among modern men just for the reason that, in their fear of thinking for themselves, they eagerly catch some symbol that crystallizes their inner fear and make it a common experience with that of thousands—or millions—of others. We know that all we have to do, in order to test the validity of a given fear, is to *think*. Yet the fact remains that the danger of mass symbols, in lieu of thinking, is in our time overwhelmingly great, whether in the U.S. or anywhere else; because we have become individuals, and thinking for oneself is a fearsome task.

THE CONFUSION OF THE FREE WORLD

The free world treats the human being *as if* he were a spiritual entity; but when it comes to explaining what this means, or what a spiritual entity is or could be, the free world is confused and inarticulate.

In answering the question of why the Communists have been so successful, therefore, we must on the one hand take into account the clarity and consistency of Marxism, and on the other, the confusion and ambiguity of the doctrines of the free world.

THE CHALLENGE OF AN OPEN MIND

American techniques of thought have been phenomenally successful with "things." But a stubborn attempt to apply such methods to the problems of "life" can only end in disaster. If the East has taught us anything, it is that the fundamental questions of life, which lead into the fundamental questions of man, are wholly different from the fundamental questions of things, of matter. These problems of life do not have to be approached in the identical manner in which the East approached them; but what is certain is that they cannot be approached with the same techniques as the problems of things.

But if Americans are at least open to the possibility that the problems of man require different techniques and methods, then all we have to ask is an *open mind*. The American task at mid-century is to muster the courage *to enter the depths*. It is not easy to abandon ways of thinking that have led to one breath-taking achievement after another. These ways, moreover, are embedded in an enormous background of scientific and professional learning. That they have led us to no profound knowledge of man, makes no difference, we think.

But as Arthur Eddington wrote, "I have little excuse for extending my survey beyond the limits indicated by the term 'knowledge.' But I would not like to leave an impression that the description of the human spirit as 'something which knows' can be accepted as the whole truth about its nature. . . . Consciousness has other functions besides those of a rather inefficient measuring machine."

Unless Americans can muster the courage to plunge into the mysteries of man, no possibility remains of escaping the atomic holocaust that everyone feels in his bones. If it is a question of wishful thinking, no thinking can be more wishful than that which pretends that by proceeding as we are the conflict can be avoided. There may, of course, be a possibility that the American people could survive such a conflict, in a literal physical sense. But that their civilization could survive it, all history denies. History, indeed, is a witness to the fact that there come times in the struggles between peoples when victory *cannot* be won; that the effort required on the part of the victor to beat off and overcome the vanquished is so great that the victor himself is destroyed. Arnold Toynbee has documented the point. He who fails to see that it is just that kind of a struggle that is now brewing in the Western world has failed to read or to understand his time.

The American who sees this urgency and decides to respond to it in the way we have indicated stands in a relationship to the world very different from that of a man acting purely out of instinct. When an American undertakes to enter into those questions that were formerly answered by the East, he does not by any means have to follow the methods of the East. He does not have to spend his days, for example, like a Buddhist seer meditating on the nature of things; nor even like a Hebrew prophet living in the desert on locust and honey. The methods developed by the East for the acquisition of wisdom were adapted, naturally, to the temperament of the East. The East has many things to teach us about the search for wisdom, but it has no monopoly upon the techniques for searching it. In short, if Americans were to take over some portion of what we have here called the obligation of the East, there would be nothing to prevent them from developing techniques of their own. Indeed, they would be required to do so.

But if the task is not to imitate the techniques of the East, then what is it? It is this willingness to enter into questions pertaining to man, rather than questions pertaining to "things," with our *own* techniques.

The *kind* of evaluation that Western civilization is unable to make is of man and his relation to the cosmos, his relation to the divine. And it is just this *kind* of evaluation that America must begin to make. But for one thing, a great many Americans, including their intellectual leaders, are in doubt as to the very existence of anything that could be called divine. And for another (even if this difficulty can be overcome), the techniques of thinking about things do not carry us very far in the direction of discovering anything about the divine. The challenge to hold an open mind toward any different way of thinking is not easily met. One is exposed to murderous cross fire from the academic world, deeply entrenched in the very way of thinking that has led civilization into darkness and disaster. One is even exposed to ridicule.

The achievement of a truly open mind in our time requires courage, and whether enough people in America possess this kind of courage is a question. Americans have courage; as a people they have always responded to challenges. One of their deep troubles today is that, for all the obvious danger of their predicament, they do not quite know what the challenge is. The challenge of an open mind may be a different kind of challenge from what they have been expecting.

A DOCTRINE

The carrying into effect of a doctrine: this is the need of the world today.

The doctrine is that of Jesus Christ. But, to be carried out, it must be rediscovered.

THE AMERICAN TASK

1. THE AMERICAN PREDICAMENT

We shall find as we approach problems of politics and economics, or to use the old-fashioned term "political economy," that a philosophical discussion is necessary to a fundamental understanding of the practical problems of our time. For political economy is really no more than the science of man's management of himself and is bound, therefore, to be an extension, or reflection of his idea of himself. It is impossible to frame a political-economic system without making certain assumptions concerning the nature and purposes of the creature whom that system is designed to serve.

It is axiomatic for Americans that human beings are possessed of certain rights. In what are these rights grounded? Whence are they derived? The eighteenth-century American founders were careful to answer this question before proceeding to the practical task of establishing a nation. In the American Declaration of Independence the flat statement is made that men are "endowed by their Creator" with the rights upon which their freedom is based. This phrase has not been a popular one among contemporary political scientists. It has not supported, but has, rather, contradicted the political theories of current pragmatic schools. The interesting thing, however, is that it has not often been subjected to direct attack. Either it has been accepted on faith (an attitude rather more characteristic of the nineteenth century than the twentieth) or merely disregarded. And yet this is precisely the kind of question to which Americans must now address themselves if they are to fulfill the responsibilities of leadership. It is important, and of the very first importance, to know whether man was endowed by his Creator with certain rights, whether this is true or false, and, if true, what it means.

If we believe that only through seeking truth can we find freedom, and if there is any truth or validity in the phenomena of the inner world of our consciousness, then we must include the criteria of this inner world in our concept of freedom. In practice, this is precisely what we do. The basic principles of a free society could not have been derived from a pragmatic study of the outer world. The pragmatist will defend equality on the grounds that that society works best which grants it to all. But where did the idea of equality come from? Not from looking outward. When we look outward into Nature we find nothing to suggest that all men are equal, other than their physical needs represented by the doctrine of the French revolutionary, Babeuf, that men are equal because each has only one stomach. But when we have acknowledged this equality—which we share with the whole animal kingdom—we see elsewhere in Nature nothing demonstrated but *in*equality among men. One man can think fast, another run fast; one man makes money easily, another cannot make it at all. One man is truthful, another is a liar. The idea of equality comes, somehow, from the inner world; from a looking inward at the self; from a realization, half subconscious perhaps, that in a way that eludes pragmatic analysis each self is of the same value as any other.

When men have reached such an inward truth as this, then they have found a law quite different from any which a state, a mere government, can pass. They have found what we call a *right*. It is of course true that a majority, by sheer power, can take such a right away. But we say that it *ought* not to do so; we say that, in matters involving basic rights, we must have freedom *from* law—that is to say, freedom from man-made or state law. Such is the very essence of our constitutional system. To deny this higher law, this freedom from man-made law, is to deny those very truths that we discerned when we looked inward. And since these truths are self-evidently truths of our own being, to deny them is to deny freedom.

Thus even the questions of political freedom are characteristically philosophical. They are questions that have to do, not just with laws and institutions, but with *man himself*, his origin, his nature and his purpose. In this country we take political freedom for granted much of the time, but we should never forget that we are able to do this only because generations of our forefathers struggled and died to reach the basic truths upon which our political institutions are constructed. Where new problems of freedom face us no lasting solutions are possible except by again searching for the basic truths with regard to man which we must seek to understand if we are to preserve and extend our freedom.

2. THE MIDDLE WAY

In exploring a new approach to a free way of life in industrial society we have given it the name, "The Middle Way." This approach must in no sense be confused with Sweden's socialistic "middle way," or with the usual concept, "middle-of-the-road." The middle-of-the-road approach is simply a compromise, combining policies derived from the right and the left. Our interpretation of the Middle Way is not to be understood as a halfway course between left and right. It embodies, literally, a new approach to political economy. It is our thesis that the categories left and right, liberal and conservative, as currently and conventionally defined, are actually obsolete. This immediately becomes evident to anyone who tries seriously to characterize in these terms current political policies or personalities. One cannot escape the conclusion that these categories have ceased to be useful, and the reason for this is that their content has become hopelessly confused. For example, traditionally, conservatives have stood for the disciplining of individual liberty to keep it within the limits of established customs and institutions, and historically conservatives have been on the side of strong government. But in the last two decades we have come to describe as conservative those persons and policies favoring individualism and opposing the trend toward increased government power. This gives the word "conservative" a new meaning which reverses its historic meaning. The same is true of the current use of the word "liberal" as signifying those who favor increased centralization of government, high taxes, and almost any kind of action by the state in the field of social welfare. On each of these issues the stand of the modern liberal is the direct opposite of the eighteenth-century followers of Thomas Jefferson and John Taylor of Caroline, or the nineteenth-century disciples of Spencer and Sumner.

This observation is not original with us. Various attempts have been made to rationalize the transformation of these traditional political categories into their opposite, or to force new definitions of the old terms. The theory here advanced, however, is that the old classifications, left and right, conservative and liberal, have lost all meaningful content. It becomes increasingly difficult to escape the impression that the free world is living under the spell of political notions and formulae that have very little bearing upon the human realities of the present.

Individualism has played an enormously creative role in our political and economic life. The belief in the right and duty of the individual to pursue his own interest in his own way enabled us in a comparatively short time to settle the continent and to create the mightiest industrial and economic structure the world has ever seen. But in this very process extreme individualism in the economic and social field was rendered obsolete. It can no longer meet today's needs. And it can no longer really lead to freedom because in the vast complexity of modern industry the average man is unable to fend for himself. In order to provide security for himself and his family every man is involved with countless others in complicated relationships. Thus, we can no longer think of real freedom in terms of the isolated individual. In modern society interdependence has replaced independence.

This fact has given powerful support to those who think in terms of society and the pre-eminence of social goals. And they have developed an overwhelming practical case against the individualist. For in practice, they point out, human beings do not act like ends in themselves. Of their own will they form combinations, and they voluntarily endow these combinations with powers that extend beyond the individual. Modern man identifies himself with social groups—corporations, labor groups, communities, clubs and associations, pressure groups, and so forth. And in practical terms, it is really these groups with which we have to deal.

But the rights of such groups rest upon a quite different basis than the rights of individuals. There is no inherent value in a group or corporate entity; we do not speak of the "dignity" of such an organization or assume that it derives its rights from some divine or metaphysical source. These concepts are replaced, in the case of groups, by pragmatic concepts. We give the corporation certain rights, not because of any presumed divine origin, but simply because it is useful and expedient to do so. Yet if the individual has now been taken over by group forms, and if we cannot properly speak of these forms as the end of society, what are we to do with the idea that society should have an end other than itself? The welfare of society, not of any individual or any group, becomes the only proper end of society.

According to those who adopt this view, this principle alone and only this, is capable of giving freedom to the modern individual. It is through the principle of functionalism, of group action for functional ends, that the individual is able to participate in collective goals that would otherwise lie beyond his grasp. In a world that depends for its survival upon collective actions, the individual who is deprived of collective goals has no goals at all; his supposed pursuit of individual freedom leads him into one illusion after another. The normal and healthy person finds ends other than himself, or other than his own ends, through which he fulfills himself; and individuals who fail to do this, who remain wholly centered upon themselves, are in some sense pathological. Far from taking the individual as an end, this school holds that society embodies ends to which the individual must subordinate himself if he is to find freedom in any meaningful sense of the word. We must seek the freedom of the individual in terms of society. And in practical terms this inevitably means through government, the only organization large enough, and powerful enough, to balance the interests and control the actions of groups and individuals.

Yet, plausible as it is, the American people profoundly mistrust this view of things. They have found through experience that the older individualism won't work. But they also see that exclusive emphasis on the social leads to loss of freedom. They have before them the examples of many European countries, where the practice of increasing government responsibility for every kind of economic and social problem has led to disaster and the curtailment of free choice and initiative. The individual has an inherent value that must not be violated, even by society itself, and where it is violated freedom is destroyed.

But it is just as true that the individual finds his real self-fulfillment, not just in himself, but in terms that are in some sense social, and that modern industrial society has greatly accentuated this truth.

In seeking to convert the present unstable equilibrium into a stable equilibrium, therefore, we cannot proceed by the highhanded method of liquidating either pole of the antinomy. Our search for a solution must begin with the realization that the tension between these poles is of the essence of that state of being that we call freedom: that freedom *is* a tension. The freedom of the human being is not a negative state that leaves him at the mercy of outer or inner forces working upon him, but a tensional state of being—a state of *will*. Freedom is a creative act exhibiting the characteristics of life itself. And it leads to the concept of man as a spiritual entity possessing *creative power*.

In seeking a new structure of freedom, therefore, we must take account of the truths on both sides of the debate. We must seek, not compromise, but a living and dynamic synthesis which will not dissolve the tension we have defined but maintain it. For this tension is the very condition of the responsible freedom of the individual. We must keep our deep sense of the inherent value of each human being, and we must likewise keep, and even extend, his creative freedom to act in his own interest and that of his fellow man. But such freedom must operate in a framework which will fully accord with the social realities of our time. The social goals are of the utmost importance, but the individual must remain the agent of his own destiny.

The domestic challenges of our time have indeed been predominantly social in their nature. Out of them certain objectives have arisen that are deeply desired by the people. Such objectives include a reasonable security in old age; insurance against unemployment, accident, and ill health; year-round work; equality of opportunity for all irrespective of race, color, or creed; better education; better housing; protection of the rights of labor; aid to agriculture—to mention only some of the most conspicuous. The implementation of such goals has become necessary to that basic security without which a free society cannot long endure.

Now with the exception of a few reactionary individuals in both political parties, there is very little disagreement as to the desirability of these goals. This is as it should be. It is the very essence of the American political system that both parties should agree on the fundamental rights and needs of its citizens. The basic rights of Life, Liberty, and the Pursuit of Happiness, the concept of private property, the principle of constitutional government, and many other fundamentals of our way of life have always been accepted by both. It is nothing new or strange that both parties should accept social goals that have become essential to our well-being.

But in a free democracy the question of *means* is always of the first importance. Freedom is measured, not merely by what we do, but by how we do it. That a goal is desirable does not mean that there is not more than one road to its achievement, and if the means that most readily suggest themselves constitute a threat or danger to larger and more permanent goals, then it is only reasonable to seek other methods toward the desired end. The superstition has grown up in modern times that measures needed to accomplish social ends must come, and can only come through government. For the last twenty years, our dominant political thinking has sought to meet each social problem by setting up new bureaus, instituting new administrative controls, and increasingly concentrating power in the federal government. In this we have followed a pattern which has prevailed throughout the world. If we continue along this road, we shall have set up all manner of institutions that, insofar as they accomplish the goals at all, will have done so at the price of freedom. In the agricultural program we have had an unhappy example of how such administrative and bureaucratic solutions not only threaten freedom, but aggravate, in the long run, the very problem they were designed to solve.

Those who have seen the dangers of this road have been at fault in that they have failed to clarify where the real issue lay. Too often, they have seemed to oppose the *goal*, rather than the *means*. They have failed to think through to sounder methods by which the objectives generally agreed upon could be obtained. And they have failed to develop a consistent theory as a guide to practice in the light of which proposals for action could be measured and judged. All of these steps are imperative if a new structure of freedom is to be built.

The general line of development by which the Middle Way seeks to find such a structure is through *the expansion of private initiative for social goals*. Essentially, this approach consists in exploring and defining ways by which private parties, acting on their own initiative, and in their own deepest interests, can carry out responsibilities that, everywhere else in the world, are being turned over to the state. The interests of private individuals and groups, according to this view, are often not in conflict with those of society, but on the contrary, often in accord with them, or supplementary to them.

The mistake in the past has been that the powerful, motivating force of private initiative has been confined, in most political theorizing, to the economic field and to selfish ends. But those who have opposed the evils of untrammelled and irresponsible individualism have attacked the problem at the wrong place. They have proposed to liquidate private initiative rather than to redirect its ends. If the motivations of men are indeed solely economic and selfish, the social problem can never be solved. But we observe all about us the desire of Americans of all classes and walks of life to be good neighbors, to co-operate with their fellow citizens, to improve their communities—in short, to act and think in a socially responsible manner. The Middle Way has as its fundamental premise the assumption that Americans are in fact a socially responsible people.

The Middle Way contemplates the development of private initiative as the dominant social force in a free society— that is to say, we must first recognize that there is such a thing as *social* initiative by private parties, individual and group, as well as economic initiative. The development of such initiative as a dominant force necessitates a change in some of our postulates as to man's nature, a change involving a new kind of social outlook.

This may seem a very large and somewhat Utopian order unless we begin with the realization that such socially oriented private initiative does, in fact, already exist and that it plays a very great role at present in American society. American practice in this regard has outstripped theory. The result is that other free peoples in the world, and even we ourselves, have little idea what a large part socially motivated activity plays in American daily life. At present it works, so to speak, "unofficially" because conventional political economy does not recognize it or understand its enormous potentialities. Conventional political economy is still caught in the old and outworn argument as to how far the powers of the state should be expanded in order to achieve necessary social goals. The reply of the Middle Way is that this approaches the problem in the wrong way. If you start with an entity called government and work downward, there is no real way to limit power, because nobody has more power. True limitation of government power can come only by working from the people upward. This is perhaps the most basic concept of American politics, and we shall overlook it at our peril.

The doctrine of the Middle Way does not preclude government assistance. It is wholly desirable for federal or state government to provide funds for social projects beyond the reach of private capital. The government should also provide other things: enabling legislation, for example; comprehensive plans that give meaning and purpose to the social efforts of individuals or groups; inducements of one kind or another that make it easier to act socially than antisocially. But our thinking on any problem should start by exploring, in a creative and imaginative way, whether such a problem cannot, in fact, be handled by private initiative. And the role of the government should not be that of dictator of funds, laws, plans, and inducements. Its task is literally to help the individual, not to make decisions for him. Government should, as American political theory has always asserted, be literally the servant not the master of the people.

Those who oppose this approach base their argument, in the final analysis, on the assumption that private parties are socially irresponsible. But there is plenty of real proof that this assumption is not correct, and that private parties are capable of responsible social thought and action.

In 1947 a national survey by Gallup revealed that there were more than 50 million people in the United States who would be willing to serve without pay on committees of private citizens to study community problems such as housing, health, juvenile delinquency, strikes, employment, education, and so forth. No less than seven out of ten of the leading men of the nation, this survey pointed out, would be willing to take time to help solve such problems. Nor can this be shrugged off as merely a pious statement of intentions. In every town and city in the land leading citizens are giving money and, what in many cases is even more valuable, personal time to social projects of one kind or another. A local Chamber of Commerce, for example, will be interested in the development of wider streets, or of parks, or of smoke prevention, or of water purification. Businessmen's clubs promote higher moral standards, labor unions undertake projects in housing and community health, matrons support day nurseries, fraternal organizations maintain insurance funds, and so forth and so on. In any sizable American community the complex skein of social activity, carried on by private parties in voluntary association with one another would take volumes of research to unravel. In a town of, say, fifty thousand persons there will be literally scores of such organizations working in all fields, from the cultural to the economic, for the betterment of some aspect of community life.

Commenting on this phenomenon the editors of *Fortune* magazine wrote in 1951:

> This prodigious army of volunteer citizens, who take time from their jobs and pleasure to work more or less unselfishly for the betterment of the community, is unique in the world. It is, in a way, the mainspring as well as the safeguard of democ-

racy. . . . A modern society has a heavy social load to bear. Things are always getting out of adjustment, people are always in trouble, reforms are always needed, new ideas and new causes are always begging for attention. What proportion of the total social load of America is borne by voluntary activities . . . is, of course, impossible to know. But those who know America best know that it is enormous; that with all the billions spent by government on social problems and public welfare, the government share of the total, measured in terms of human energy and perseverance, is only a tiny fraction. Americans are a self-governing people, not just politically but also socially.[1]

In this fact we have the beginning, if we wish, of what *Fortune* calls "a new kind of social management," and of what we here have called the Middle Way. This kind of self-imposed, voluntary social responsibility is already vast in extent. At the same time, it is often less developed than it might be, partly because it is almost never fully conscious of its own potentialities. There are inevitable failures too, and at times, a good deal of wasted effort. Like all human conduct, it derives from mixed motives. Yet even at this elementary stage it sheds new light upon the contention that freedom for the individual and the achievement of social goals can be mutually compatible. It proves that the agent for co-operation between human beings need not be government, and that privately organized social responsibility is not a Utopian dream. In it we see already in existence an alternative to unmitigated individualism on the one hand, and to dependence on government on the other. Americans have found, in effect, a vital formula for implementing human rights and achieving social goals. But owing to lack of any theoretical

[1] *The Permanent Revolution, op. cit.,* pp. 132, 146.

groundwork, we cannot explain, either to ourselves or to others, the significance of what we are doing.

By way of beginning we offer the proposition of the Middle Way: that no solution to any problem of the free way of life should be provided by calling upon the state to undertake tasks which under proper circumstances of education and encouragement the citizens themselves can do. For turning to the state can only further compromise the status of the individual, who is already half-lost amid forces and organizations that are too big for him. The solution is to be found, not through a growth in government, but through a growth in the stature of the individual. The crucial American question has always been: is the individual big enough for the responsibilities of freedom? The founders of this country guessed "yes"—not without misgivings. The whole American experiment has been built upon the proposition that a free society could not work unless human beings were fit to meet and discharge the responsibilities of freedom. But no scheme, no mere blueprint is going to rescue the free world and overcome communism. The problem is a developmental one. We do not have the solution to it now, we must *make* the solution. We must get from here to there and it will take time.

3. THE THREEFOLD DIVISION OF SOCIETY

In seeking a theoretical foundation for the Middle Way we are brought face to face with a truth which in an earlier

day was one of the genuine contributions of American
political thought to a free way of life. Our political
ancestors grasped very clearly the need for a separation of
political and economic power, and for the independence
of the spiritual and cultural life from both.

This concept of a threefold division of society is fundamental to the development of the Middle Way. Briefly, it
consists in the recognition that society is composed of three
semi-autonomous areas, or fields of activity, which are
organically linked together, but which must be distinguished
from each other, and to a considerable extent kept separate,
if freedom is to be a reality.

These three areas are the *economic*, which has to do with
the production and consumption of commodities and goods;
the *political*, which has to do with human rights; and the
cultural or spiritual, which has to do with values, insights,
and beliefs. These three components should not be thought
of as ordinary, administrative divisions, but as interrelated
activities, indispensable to the life of the social organism,
just as (for example) the nervous system, the circulatory
system, and the metabolic system work together to support
the life of the human body.

A study of these three areas in connection with the question of freedom discloses an important principle: for freedom to flourish, each area must enjoy a kind of autonomy.
It must be to a very large extent self-governing and independent of the other two. The reason for this is that in
each area different criteria apply. For example, an
important criterion in the political sphere is *equality*. But

equality is not a criterion proper to the economic sphere, where the attempt to impose it leads to excessive taxation and government interference; or to the cultural sphere, where the *in*equality of individuals (e.g., mentally, emotionally, ethically, etc.) is a cultural *fact*. In the economic sphere an important criterion (among many others) is *efficiency*; but efficiency makes no sense when applied to cultural matters, and if it is too rigidly applied in the political sphere it can endanger human rights. (Dictatorship, for example, claims to be, and often can be, more efficient than democracy.) By the same token, the criteria of the cultural sphere (e.g., complete independence of individual judgment) would be damaging to free political life, and would create chaos in many economic situations, say, in the modern factory.

The principle in question was implicitly recognized by the American founders. They were careful to separate church (cultural) and state (political) and their concept of the property right required a high degree of separation between the state and the economic life of the citizen. The significant point is that wherever the attempt is made to apply criteria proper to one of the spheres, to some other sphere tyranny is the inevitable result. An analysis of communism shows this very clearly; so does the history of colonial mercantilism against which our forefathers revolted; and—in the third, or spiritual, area—so do certain epochs in the history of the church, whether the pre-

Reformation Roman Church, Calvin's Geneva, or seventeenth-century theocratic Massachusetts and Connecticut.

It is important that we understand this because in our time the tendency has grown to merge the components into a monolithic whole, rather than to separate them and grant them self-determination. In communism and fascism a monopolitical structure is actually achieved. In the so-called free world the autonomy of cultural life has been fairly well respected; but almost everywhere the economic life has been overrun and captured by the political life. This has been done in the name of human rights. Action in the economic field to protect the individual has indeed been necessary. But no real solution to any problem of the free way of life can be provided in the long run by calling upon the state to step in beyond its proper sphere.

All those dedicated to the preservation and development of the free way of life in our time must: (1) redefine these areas in simple terms; (2) encourage the development of each of them on a semi-autonomous basis; and (3) learn how to harness them together into a dynamic and interdependent whole. Such a program will lead, neither to the left nor to the right, but to the middle way.

4. VOLUNTARY ASSOCIATION

We have touched upon another principle which is essential to the functioning of the Middle Way and to the successful separation of the three areas within society; it is the organization of private groups for social purposes. Public policy must find ways to encourage such association wherever they are needed, and, especially wherever they appear spontaneously. We must learn to think in terms of social initiative and social rewards.

Brief mention has been made in an earlier section of the many forms which voluntary association for social purposes has already taken in this country. Many more examples might be cited. Take for instance the regional and local organizations which have been developed in recent years such as the Committee for Kentucky, or the Allegheny Conference in Pittsburgh. In both cases voluntary organizations of public-spirited citizens set themselves the task of meeting pressing social and economic problems and carried through their objectives with impressive success. These two examples are particularly striking in proving the possibility of fruitful co-operation between public and private agencies. Although the initiative came from private parties, in both cases the co-operation of local and state bodies was enlisted to pass needful legislation and perform other functions which only government could do. But, it should be noted, the legislative measures were only the foundation which enabled the local committees to go ahead with their own problems.

These are large and well-known examples, yet they scarcely begin to tell the tale. For every big effort there are dozens if not hundreds of lesser ones. This fact has been documented by the Extension Division of the University of Virginia where Jean and Jess Ogden have collected the record of over one hundred communities that have developed noteworthy projects in answer to community needs. Or take the co-operative self-help housing project in Philadelphia, sponsored by the Quakers, where a slum area is being made over and the work done partly by the people who will live in the hundred modern apartments that will replace a block of run-down nineteenth-century houses.

Delinquency and other city slum problems are being met on the South Side of Chicago through the now famous "Back-of-the-Yards" Council. Here, under the brilliant leadership of a young sociologist, Saul Alinksy, a thrilling and successful experiment has tested the ability of the most underprivileged section of a large industrial community to solve its own problems.

At the other end of the social scale, we find a totally different type of voluntary association devoted to social ends. Businessmen, so long the prime target of those who scoff at the idea of relying upon individuals for socially responsible behavior, have banded together and sought to discover, through research and discussion, solutions to community and economic problems, national and international. Such organizations are the Committee for Economic Development, originally headed by Paul Hoffman, or the National Planning Association whose chairman is H. Christian Sonne. These two organizations have conducted studies into almost every phase of the American economy with the twin objectives of educating both the business community and the country at large on important issues; and of seeking democratic and workable solutions. The National Planning Association, whose membership includes not only businessmen but labor leaders and educators, is an example of a private, voluntary agency operating in a field—planning—where reformers of the thirties and forties felt government alone could function. NPA has sponsored studies in world trade, business reserves and investment, tax law, transportation, foreign relief (this just after the war), farm problems, population problems (here and abroad), aviation policies, urban redevelopment, business expansion, etc. Two special committees in recent years have worked on a series of studies, one on the South (special problems of that area, such as the impact of federal policies and new industry), and the other the now famous series known as the "Causes of Industrial Peace Under Collective Bargaining."

In a different category from any of the above examples, and yet perhaps more fundamental to the idea of the Middle Way than any of them, is the development in industrial relations known as the Scanlon Plan. This plan has now been applied in several dozen companies and provides for the complete participation of the workers in a given enterprise.

There has always been a defect in the capitalist system which has been of great aid to the Marxists in giving their theories emotional appeal. This defect has to do with the status of labor. Although in our time labor has greatly increased in political and economic power, the enterprise system by and large has excluded the worker from the process of enterprising. He has been a hired hand who was not supposed to concern himself with such matters as productivity and costs. His brains have not been wanted, and his love of competition has usually been recognized only in an effort to pit him against his fellows in a purely selfish manner. His need for incentives other than monetary have been ignored, and he has been, on the whole, treated as an outsider whose vote and loyalty were desired, but whose participation in the enterprise was not.

This defect has led to what the Marxists term the class struggle. Even in the United States, where that struggle has been less extreme than in most capitalist countries, it has led to a very deep cleavage between worker and management and to a system of collective bargaining which, even today, retains many of the primitive and lawless features which we have managed to eliminate in other departments of our national life.

Nearly twenty years ago, in the gloomy Depression year of 1936, a few men under the leadership and inspiration of Clinton S. Golden, then vice-president of the steel workers' union, worked out a plan to save a marginal steel company in which they were employed from going on the rocks. The motives were simple. Management wanted to save the company, the men wanted to save their jobs. The means were simple too. Everyone in the company, down to the man who swept out the plant, agreed to pool their ideas and their knowledge of the job and the industry, with the idea of cutting costs and raising productivity. In return, all were to share in any increase of profits thus arrived at.

In the plant was a steel worker and charter member of the union named Joe Scanlon. He had been a key figure in persuading both management and men to go to Mr. Golden for help and advice. He had formerly been a cost accountant and he now worked closely with Mr. Golden and the president of the company on the mechanics of the plan and on developing a formula for profit sharing. The plan was successful beyond the highest hopes of those who had launched it. Mr. Scanlon was called into the national office of the union to assist other companies who wanted to try participation. Today, Mr. Scanlon is at M.I.T. where he teaches industrial relations and also spends a great deal of his time helping companies to start the Scanlon Plan. Such plans have worked as well in times of prosperity as when companies were in dire economic straits. They have proved successful in large plants and small ones and in almost every conceivable kind of industry from steel, where they started, to the latest kind of plastics.

The plans are very flexible—no two are alike. Individual suggestions are discussed at joint labor-management meetings. Sometimes lengthy (and even heated) argument is involved, together with considerable research. Inasmuch as the profit that will accrue from any productivity suggestion will be distributed throughout the entire plant, everyone becomes interested in a proposal, and the worker who makes the suggestion and all who take part in the discussion feel an immediate sense of real participation in the enterprise. It is no longer, as Mr. Scanlon puts it, "we" (the workers) and "they" (management), it is "*us*." A real sense of mutuality and joint responsibility for the business gradually grows up on the part of everyone. Work ceases to be mere drudgery. Everyone cares whether or not the company is making money, how it is doing in comparison with competitors, whether or not orders are coming in and getting out on time. Men find opportunities to satisfy motives other than purely personal gain. They experience the satisfaction of really working together for the mutual benefit of all. And little by little, a kind of community is created, in which democracy is a living force, rather than just something to talk about. These M.I.T. experiments, indeed, demonstrate the reality of a Middle Way through voluntary association.

In every country in the world the need for social improvement has brought enormous power to governments. This tendency in the United States has been substantially checked by the existence of the kind of private activities discussed here. If there were no such private activities the power and size of our government would have to be increased many times over. Furthermore, such questions as problems of labor-management relations can never be solved by governments. Attempts to do so can lead only to tyranny. We have here an outstanding illustration of the need to keep the economic area out of politics, yet it in no way follows that the individual should not be protected, nor that new and creative ways should not be found to solve the problems and contradictions which have haunted this area since the birth of industrialism. Co-operation in this field must be based on self-interest if it is to have reality, but it must also be based on the truth that man needs something more than a money incentive if his working life is to be satisfying and meaningful. Freedom stands or falls on our faith that in every man there is a desire to give as well as take, and that, properly encouraged, the individual American will co-operate in a responsible manner with his fellows.

Let us, therefore, mold our policies to support our faith. At the *total* level the Communists will beat us every time, because they can totalize ruthlessly and process man to the pattern they desire. But at the person-to-person level we shall always beat them, because at that level we have something to give that they cannot match.

We have the fundamental proposition of our Revolution to give: that man is the child of Nature's God; that he carries within him a spark that links him with the universe and differentiates him from the animals. A man is endowed, we say, with certain rights, not just because he is alive, but because that spark is in him.

By practicing person-to-person democracy we can teach the world to see in every individual that individual spark which gives to the principles of freedom a godlike validity. For that spark can only be seen, as God sees it, on a person-to-person basis. He does not lump us all together. He does not totalize us. Each of us is, for Him, an individual.

No human being, of course, can account for every individual on earth, or even every individual in his community. But that is just what democracy is for.

Democracy is a method of accounting for everyone,

through the little work of many hands, the little loves of many hearts, the little lights of many minds. It accounts for everyone through the little applications of universal principles—in the home, in the back yard, in the office, in the factory, in the little world in which *each* of us can act. That is the challenge. The country that accepts it will change the history of the world.

SPECIAL INFLUENCES

We claim no real originality for our work; it grew out of the accumulated knowledge and wisdom of mankind; its basic ideas have all been uttered before, in one way or another, by prophets, religious teachers, poets, scientists, and men of learning, the guides and teachers of the world. Our primary role has been to integrate these teachings in contemporary terms, to bring them to bear upon the problems of the present day. Since many of the teachings referred to have been misplaced or forgotten, our hope is that, thus united, they will be able to shed light upon a generation that has lost its way in the dark wilderness of our time.

The well-informed reader will recognize such influences as he reads; the relatively uninformed, we have felt, would be hopelessly distracted by the constant interruptions that would be necessary if our debts were to be fully and specifically acknowledged at every point. However, certain minds have had such a predominant influence upon our work that we would want to acknowledge their contributions. These minds are diverse, and in the mere naming of them we can perhaps best indicate what we mean when we say that our task has been primarily that of integrating the teachings of great men.

With regard to our specifically American indebtednesses the reader will find certain references to the ideas of Tom Paine. This is not because Tom Paine is any special hero of

ours—on the contrary, our thesis comes near to contradict-
ing his: it is only because this altogether extraordinary
individual made certain pronouncements about America
which have ever since inspired what might be called "the
American impulse." It is impossible we think, to reassess
American values for the twentieth century without reference
to these elementary ideas, for they are deeply imbedded in
our *Weltanschauung*, our outlook on the world, our philosophy of life.

As for more intellectual influences, the reader will find
that we are indebted about equally to John Adams and
Thomas Jefferson. It would be going too far to call these
thinkers polar opposites, and yet, in the development of
American political philosophy, they do occupy polar positions. With regard to human nature Adams was a philosophical pessimist, Jefferson a philosophical optimist; and
this polarity profoundly affects their influences upon American history. Of the two, we would have to concede that
Adams is the better philosopher (though Jefferson spent
more time philosophizing), but that Jefferson was the better
politician. Nor do we use this latter word in a derogatory
sense. Though we ourselves cannot be classified as belong-
ing to the philosophical optimists, nevertheless, it seems
to us probable that the cause of political freedom cannot
survive on pessimism alone. If free institutions are not to
atrophy they must constantly be revitalized, and to this end
the Jeffersonian thesis of the *improvability* (we do not say,
the "perfectibility") of men is indispensable. Our own
view of man is a profoundly evolutionary one; and while

Jefferson does not state such a view in so many words, he encourages it.

Our other chief American indebtedness is to Ralph Waldo Emerson. Where the sage of Concord retreats into a kind of Kantian transcendentalism, we do not follow. But where he gives free play to his own intuitive faculties he achieves what we have already called a *living* approach to reality—

> Line in Nature is not found.
> Unit and universe are round . . .

—and for this we are indebted to him.

The two greatest philosophers of the ancient world were Plato and Aristotle. While we would not go so far as Anton Pegis, who asserts that they "represent the two basically different approaches that are philosophically possible," we agree that the argument between them is fundamental and underlies virtually the entire history of philosophy. Our own position with relation to this argument is fundamentally Aristotelian. As Pegis says—and here we wholly agree with him: "The great virtue of Aristotle as a philosopher (granting his errors) was that he did not allow the human intellect to impose itself upon the world. In this fact lay the strength and significance of his anti-Platonism. *The Aristotelian man has always lived in a genuine world of things;* the Platonic man has always been, as a philosopher, the victim of his own intellect. So, at least, St. Thomas leads us to think."[2]

[2] *Basic Writings of St. Thomas Aquinas,* Anton C. Pegis, ed., New York, Random House, 1944, Introduction, p. xlii.

This brings us to St. Thomas himself. It is difficult to assay the influence upon twentieth-century minds of a teacher who addressed himself to an age which had no concept of empirical science and whose culture was dominated by theology and the Church. We ourselves are not Thomists in any literal sense of the word; though we have the impression that the leading Thomists of our time—such as Jacques Maritain, for example—have been able to bring to the problems that beset us a far more penetrating power of analysis than those philosophers—let us say, Bertrand Russell—who are more representative of twentieth-century ways of thinking. If he is to speak to the intelligent layman of our time, St. Thomas has to be translated, not just from Latin into English, but from an intellectual environment founded upon deductive logic to an environment that is founded upon the inductive.

This we do not propose to attempt. But we owe a specific acknowledgment to St. Thomas by reason of his fundamental position with regard to the three great enigmas of human life—Nature, Man, and God. Man, this teacher holds, has two means of dealing with these enigmas: Reason and Faith. And it is of the essence of Thomist doctrine that these means are not mutually contradictory but mutually consonant. "Natural reason should minister to Faith. . . . Hence it is that sacred doctrine makes use also of the authority of philosophers in those questions in which they were able to know the truth by natural reason."[3] By a combination of Reason *and* Faith, man can know all that he needs to know. This position, we conceive, is one

[3] *Summa Theologica:* Question 1, Eighth Article, Reply to Objection 2.

of the great milestones of human thought. On the one hand, it re-established philosophy, which had become lost in the mazes of theology, as a science in its own right; on the other hand, it opened the way for the rise of empirical science, which was to dominate the next five centuries of human evolution. It thus rescued Reason from mere mysticism and dogma; but at the same time it escaped the blind agnosticism into which a purely rationalistic view of the world is certain to fall.

In our time, except within the churches, the Thomist meaning of the word "Faith" has been lost; man has been left with natural reason alone, and as a result, Western civilization has been overtaken by agnosticism, not to say nihilism. For natural reason, as it has been developed through empirical science, cannot penetrate the mysteries of life, and since we believe in nothing else, we must either disregard those mysteries, or deny their existence. The result, as many students have observed, has been a kind of cultural and moral disintegration; and the thesis has been put forward—sometimes competently, but often as a kind of sentimental wish—that the only way to combat this is through a revival of Faith. We are in agreement with this thesis in the sense that *if* Faith could be re-established among men the apparent disintegration of Western civilization could be arrested. But this "if" raises some fundamental questions. It raises the question, in the first place, of *why* men have lost Faith; and, secondly, assuming that this question could be answered, of the means by which such Faith might be re-established.

This second question leads us, finally, to the acknowledgment of the influence of two teachers, so closely bound together in their thinking that they can virtually be viewed as one. The first is Johann Wolfgang von Goethe (1749-1832) and the second is his extraordinary interpreter, Rudolf Steiner (1861-1925). The selection of these two for special acknowledgment may occasion a certain surprise, for Goethe is known chiefly as a poet and novelist, and Steiner as a mystic whose works seem unintelligible and hopelessly out of step with his time. Anyone familiar with the writings of these men, however, will understand our special indebtedness to them.

To begin with, Goethe was not "just" a poet. He was also a scientist, and according to Karl Viëtor[4] he regarded "the scientific part of his intellectual existence as not less important than his artistic one." Modern science would disagree with many of Goethe's factual conclusions. But what it cannot escape is his *approach* to science, his instinctive and stubbornly held view of what science really is. We have shown (in Part IV) the contribution Goethe made to our thinking with his emphasis on intuition and contemplation. Goethe was the first empirical scientist to adopt what we have called a *living approach to reality*. For him, Nature—that is to say, the world and the universe—is not an inanimate void containing inanimate matter, but is alive, and can be understood by the scientist only if he is able and willing to adapt his processes of thought to that supreme fact. Goethe's fundamental position with regard to truth, in other words, is what we have already outlined with regard to free-

[4] *Goethe, The Thinker*, Cambridge, Harvard University Press, 1950.

dom. Truth escapes those approaches to reality comprehended under logic, mechanics, mathematics, and statistics.
To apprehend it, a different approach must be developed.
And Goethe's irreplaceable contribution to mankind was
that he took the first empirical, experimental steps in that
direction.

The man who made all this clear, and carried it farther,
was Rudolf Steiner. Trained in the natural sciences
in Vienna, Steiner edited Goethe's scientific writings, in the
Berlin Stuttgart edition (1882-1897). He also participated
in the editing of the Weimar edition, which still stands as
definitive. He then proceeded to apply and develop the
Goethian philosophy of science in numerous fields of learning—in physics, chemistry, medicine, zoology, botany, history, philology, religion. Christology, scriptural interpretation, and so forth. He demonstrated by his enormous works
that the Goethian scientific thesis is true: that whenever we
can win our way, in a scientific spirit, to processes of living
thought, it is possible then to enter into and understand
mysteries that the natural sciences, as hitherto practiced,
cannot reach. Steiner's life and works constitute a refuta-
tion of modern agnosticism. Man's knowledge may not be
"absolute": but it has no observable limits.

That the academic world has managed to dismiss
Steiner's works as inconsequential and irrelevant, is one of
the intellectual wonders of the twentieth century. Anyone
who is willing to study those vast works with an open mind
(let us say, a hundred of his titles) will find himself faced
with one of the greatest thinkers of all time, whose grasp

of the modern sciences is equaled only by his profound
learning in the ancient ones. Steiner was no more of a
mystic than Albert Einstein; he was a scientist, rather—but
a scientist who dared to enter into the mysteries of life. If
one wishes to disregard the mysteries of life, one can disregard Steiner. It is wholly illegitimate, however, for those
who have resolutely shunned the examination of such
mysteries to declare that his findings are unbelievable. This
is precisely the same as if we were to say—not wishing to
study the matter—that Planck's theory of quanta (which
shows that electrons can be in one place or another place,
but never in between) is unbelievable. Steiner's findings
are indeed *unfamiliar,* and for that reason one may feel
impelled to reject them. Yet this would be philosophically
permissible only if our familiar concepts and modes of
thinking had been proven to be absolutely true. And such
proof has never been offered—indeed, the very contrary is
indicated. Those who are in search of truth, therefore,
rather than merely dedicated to the defense of the familiar,
must put aside the question of whether Steiner's findings
are "believable" or "unbelievable," and address themselves to the more rewarding task of finding out, through
a sincere study of his works, whether they are true.

The Goethe-Steiner combination brings us back to St.
Thomas and the question raised by our remarks on him—
namely, by what means can Faith be re-established in the
twentieth century? Rudolf Steiner's answer is that Faith can
be re-established *only through an advance in knowledge.*

The Thomist proposition, that man can know all that he needs to know, still holds; but he needs to know much more than he presently does. Men have lost Faith, not because there was anything wrong with the Faith, but *because they have failed to develop the full potentialities of Reason.* The way to Faith cannot be found by modern man in the simple reiteration of articles of belief handed down by "authority." It is to be found only through the *further* development of Reason, as a living rather than as a merely logical process. Logic is implicit in living thought, and helps to guide it. But the logic without the life makes us blind.

It almost goes without saying, that Faith, when achieved in these terms, is something quite different from the thirteenth-century version that St. Thomas had in mind. But modern man is different from thirteenth-century man— in ways that history, were it a *living* science, could more readily recognize. Those who have learned to think in living terms see clearly enough that nothing ever literally repeats itself; that to ask twentieth-century man to breed a thirteenth-century Faith is precisely the same as asking a mature man to reanimate the convictions of his youth. This might not be an impossible thing to do, but it could scarcely be accomplished by forgetting what, as a man, he has learned. It could be brought about only by bringing to bear upon those lost convictions, more knowledge than he had when he held them—to transform them, by a kind of creative process, into their more advanced equivalents. So it is with the question of Faith. We cannot sweep aside, in

The Dignity of Man

order to re-establish it, what we have learned in the course of six tumultuous centuries. But the new attitude toward science that was pioneered by Goethe and Steiner shows us how we can develop its twentieth-century equivalent, *an acknowledgment and understanding of the divine*—in which all questions pertaining to man are rooted; which is constantly at work in human affairs, and which is, in fact, accessible to a science that employs living processes of thought.